BERLIN ⊙

GERMANY

BELGIUM
⊙ BRUSSELS

HOLLAND

LUXEMBOURG

Rhine

Nancy

ALSACE-LORRAINE

CZECHOSLOVAKIA

WARTIME
EUROPE

Stuttgart
Danube

SEE INSET
BELOW

Dachau
Munich

Kempten

Garmisch
Partenkirchen

Innsbruck

AUSTRIA

HUNGARY

SWITZERLAND

Lake Geneva

A   L   P   S

Geneva

Saone

Aix-les-Bains

Lyon

ZONE

Rhone

Nîmes

Nice

Marseilles

ITALY

YUGOSLAVIA

⊙ ROME

SEA

0   150 Km
0   150 Miles

Saulgau

Tuttlingen

Wald

Altshausen

Blitzenreute

Heimertingen
Memmingen

GERMANY

Kempten

0   20 Km
0   20 Miles

SWITZERLAND

AUSTRIA

Turncoat

Brendan Murphy

TURNCOAT

The Strange Case of
British Sergeant Harold Cole,
"The Worst Traitor
of the War"

Harcourt Brace Jovanovich, Publishers

San Diego   New York   London

Library of Congress Cataloging-in-Publication Data
Murphy, Brendan.
    Turncoat.
    Bibliography: p.
    Includes index.
    1. Cole, Harold, 1906–1946.   2. Spies—Great
Britain—Biography.   3. World War, 1939–1945—Secret
service—Great Britain.   I. Title.
D810.S8C565   1987   940.54'86'41   86-27140
ISBN 0-15-191410-9

Designed by G. B. D. Smith

Printed in the United States of America

First Edition

A B C D E

This book is for
Marielza de Almeida Augelli

"Though those that are betray'd
Do feel the treason sharply, yet the traitor
Stands in worse case of woe."

—SHAKESPEARE, *Cymbeline,*
Act iii, sc. 4, 11.83-85.

Contents

Author's Note   *xi*

1   "He Spoke Atrocious French"   *1*

2   "Was That Your Game in Civvy Street?"   *9*

3   "His Scheme Never Failed"   *20*

4   "Collect the English and Send Them Home!"   *30*

5   "This Man Isn't Simple at All"   *38*

6   "He Was Smarter Than That"   *45*

7   "A Great Devil of a Scotsman"   *55*

8   "The Antithesis of the Scarlet Pimpernel"   *64*

9   "Rumor, Suspicion, and Intrigue"   *73*

10   "We Thought He Had a Mission"   *78*

11   "Escapers Don't Win Wars"   *88*

12   "This Chap Was Running a Racket"   *96*

13   "He Just Didn't Give a Damn"   *105*

14   "He Was Being Closely Watched"   *116*

15   "I Decided Cole Needed Killing"   *127*

Contents

16   *"Everyone Seemed to Look Up to Him"*   *135*

17   *"He Is Terribly Dangerous"*   *141*

18   *"A Monster of Cowardice and Weakness"*   *149*

19   *"Meet My New Boss"*   *159*

20   *"Who Are You, Really?"*   *166*

21   *"I Swear I'll Cure Him!"*   *172*

22   *"His True Identity Was Established"*   *180*

23   *"He Was Backing a Losing Cause"*   *191*

24   *"The Widest Latitude to Operate"*   *203*

25   *"The March of Prisoners Began"*   *214*

26   *"I Decided to Bump Him Off"*   *224*

27   *"You're Cole, Aren't You?"*   *234*

28   *"The King's Enemies"*   *243*

29   *"A Fantastic Chain of Events"*   *254*

    Acknowledgments   *266*

    Notes   *269*

    Selective Bibliography   *289*

    Index   *293*

Author's Note

The name Harold Cole first drew my attention in a Paris archive in the spring of 1983. While researching a book on Klaus Barbie, the wartime Gestapo commander of Lyon, I referred to a 1944 French report on the German police services in Lyon and their local collaborators. A dozen pages of this semiofficial report consisted of notes from the interrogation of Cole and his associates. There was no apparent link with Barbie, who had not yet arrived in Lyon when Cole was arrested there in June 1942 by the Vichy secret police. But this sketchy account, hinting at something very unusual, intrigued me. I photocopied the pages and resolved to come back to them later. There was material for a good screenplay, if nothing more.

By early 1984, my interest in the Cole material was shared by William Sargent, a screenwriter whom I had met in Dublin some years before, now based in London. After hearing the story in a nutshell—an Englishman named Cole had deserted from the British Expeditionary Force in 1940, worked with British Intelligence in occupied France, turned traitor, and finished the war as a Gestapo agent—he expressed his own interest. We began elaborating a screen treatment.

It soon became apparent that we just didn't know enough about Cole. Had a person by that name actually existed? What had led him down the path of treason? That March I took a train out to the Paris suburb of Malakoff and, in a dusty church vestry, found the record of Cole's 1942 marriage to Suzanne Warenghem, the French woman he later betrayed. Cole started to take on reality. His story assumed further dimensions as William scoured the library of the Imperial War Museum for references to Cole, who figured briefly in many accounts of British secret activities in occupied France. So began our collaborative effort, which over the next three years unearthed substantial material on Cole. The more we learned, the greater was our astonishment at the outrageous luck and ingenuity of this strangely appealing scoundrel.

In all of this, William Sargent was not only an indefatigable research associate, but an invaluable partner in the task of sorting out the vexed questions attached to Cole's tale. This book, and I too, would be the poorer were it not for his contribution. Similarly, I must acknowledge the resourceful assistance of Nigel Willmott of London, who spent long hours poring over birth, death, and many other public records in order to reconstruct Cole's early life.

Furthermore, realizing this book would never have been possible without the encouragement of Carol Mann, my agent; the enthusiasm and advice of my editor, Marie Arana-Ward; and the patient support of my wife, Marielza. Last but not least, a belated word of thanks to Sam Abt of the *International Herald Tribune*, who in a way set me on the path that led to Cole's story.

Paris, October 1, 1986

Turncoat

1

"He Spoke Atrocious French"

THE WESTERN WORLD was trembling on the brink of war in mid-September 1938 as another summer season drew to an end in Aix-les-Bains, high in the French Savoy. Many a well-heeled British émigré was taking the cure of the spa town's thermal waters before migrating south to winter on the Riviera. But the tranquility of seasons past was absent. A darkening cloud of uncertainty hung over this Continental outpost of the English leisure class.

The international crisis over German claims to the Sudetenland was deepening. In London, Paris, and other European capitals, there were anguished deliberations. Within days, British prime minister Neville Chamberlain was to fly off to his September 15 conference with Adolph Hitler in Berchtesgaden. At a second summit meeting later that month at Bad Godesberg, outside Munich, Chamberlain and French premier Édouard Daladier would submit docilely to Hitler to secure what they hoped might be peace in their time. Not for another twelve months would Europe be plunged into the caldron of total warfare.

These distant rumblings caused consternation even at the remove of Aix. Many of the British subjects there were "worried about future developments and seeking advice" from H.M. vice-consul Philip E. Laughton-Bramley. The thirty-eight-year-old envoy was busy evacuating two thousand British tourists on the two daily trains to Paris, amid a "general exodus" from the town. He was also occupied with the visit of the former British prime minister Stanley Baldwin, who had spent his summer holidays in Aix since 1922. Local officials wanted to make Lord Baldwin, seventy-one, an honorary citizen. Early on Tuesday, September 12, Laughton-Bramley went to the Hotel Bernascon to make the necessary arrangements with the statesman. It was late in the morning by the time the vice-consul arrived at his offices on the place de l'Établissement Thermal.

Awaiting Laughton-Bramley was an Englishman in his early thirties, who had shown up a quarter of an hour before to request an interview. The vice-consul found little initial cause for concern. The visitor was tall and slender, with ginger-colored hair and a toothbrush mustache, and wrapped in a gray-green, military-style trenchcoat. But his manner, as he introduced himself, struck Laughton-Bramley as particularly brash.

"Wing Commander Wain," said the stranger as they shook hands. "Royal Air Force."

Wain then took on a confidential manner, informing Laughton-Bramley that he was on a "hush-hush" mission to Egypt. But his aircraft had developed mechanical difficulties, obliging him to force-land northwest of Aix. He required the loan of fifty pounds—no paltry sum in those days—to have his plane repaired at the nearest French airfield.

Laughton-Bramley was immediately skeptical. "When I asked him for his passport," the envoy noted, "he replied that he had left it in the aircraft." Wain (or was it Wayne?) lacked the polish one expected of an RAF wing commander in that age when an officer obligatorily was a gentleman as well. Noted Laughton-Bramley: "He spoke atrocious French with, it would appear, a Cockney accent."

Wain told Laughton-Bramley he had borrowed twenty-five pounds from another British resident, a certain Captain Milburn. But this only put the vice-consul more on his guard. Milburn, secretary of the Aix-les-Bains Golf Club, was related by marriage to Lord Derby, the former ambassador to France. The captain was unlikely to have lent money to a perfect stranger on the basis of some far-fetched tale about a secret mission to the Middle East. Laughton-Bramley concluded that this Wain was purely and simply a bounder. He advised the man to go see the manager of the local Barclay's Bank, whom he "felt sure would give him some advice."

When Wain had left empty-handed, Laughton-Bramley picked up the telephone and called the banker to warn him. But the transient aviator never appeared at the Barclay's branch and was not seen again in the district.

Wing Commander Wain, it seemed, was a man who could take a hint.

◆ ◆ ◆

WAIN'S CHANCE of obtaining a loan had been slight from the first. Even before the impecunious airman turned up, Laughton-Bramley had been warned by his superior in Lyon that an Englishman was circulating through the region running various frauds under several false identities. The name Wain did not correspond with any of these. But that merely attested to the swindler's powers of invention.

Not until a month later did Laughton-Bramley hear more of Wain. Traveling to Great Britain on his annual leave, the diplomat called on a colleague in the English Channel port of Boulogne-sur-Mer. At the Gare Maritime, they encountered the local head of the Sûreté nationale, the French internal security service. The two British diplomats accepted his invitation to a drink and adjourned to his dockside office.

As Laughton-Bramley sipped his Dubonnet and chatted with the official, his attention drifted to the collection of wanted posters tacked to the wall. Out of this rogues' gallery loomed the familiar visage of Wain.

Swindlers are an unavoidable feature of any age. In ordinary times Wain might have disappeared into the annals of petty crime, the dusty charge books of the Bow Street Court and the beribboned dossiers of the Paris Préfecture de police. But these were not ordinary times, nor was Harold Cole, alias Wing Commander Wain, any run-of-the-mill criminal. He was not the most successful of felons: Scotland Yard and the Metropolitan Police already maintained files on Cole, then thirty-two. But this Cockney scapegrace would exceed even the expectations of the Yard's hardbitten inspectors as he wandered on an erratic course through the most tumultuous period in modern history.

The lives of men, like history, are often rich in ironies. The laughable episode in Aix-les-Bains later would seem to have strangely prefigured the wartime career of this singularly enterprising confidence man. Cole's penchant for impersonation would lead him into His Majesty's service as an authentic British secret agent escorting downed RAF flyers and stranded Allied soldiers out of a France gripped by Nazi tyranny. But his proclivities for larceny and imposture, combined with a streak of cowardice, were to lead him far astray.

By the time the war had ended, he would betray scores of Allied agents, don the uniform of the Gestapo, and earn the epithet assigned him by an eminent Scotland Yard investigator: "The worst traitor of the war."

◆　◆　◆

YET THE CASE of Cole was not that simple, any more than the Cockney ne'er-do-well was a plain scoundrel such as flocked by the thousands to the brutal banner of Fascism. Of the abundant crop of villains produced by the Second World War, few were of as complex and contradictory a character as Cole. Stumbling headlong into disgrace, Cole was a moral chameleon, a blank page on which was written whatever the age could inspire—at times the best, but most often the worst.

His own essential emptiness enabled him to take on any guise, serve any cause to fulfill his own petty ambitions. Yet Cole also possessed remarkable powers of persuasion, which he brought to bear on friend and foe alike.

A deserter, a thief and a liar, this swindler and imposter obtained the trust of men and the love of women—then betrayed them without the least hesitation. Yet for a time he was regarded as a hero, a resourceful and valued British agent in the perilous business of guiding Allied servicemen along the hidden pathways out of occupied France.

He caused more damage and human suffering than any other British traitor of World War II. He delivered at least fifty and, by some authoritative accounts, as many as 150 Allied agents and civilian helpers into German hands. Many of these disappeared into the night and fog of the Hitlerian gulag. Later Cole served German counterintelligence at a high level in France—apparently the only instance of this in the entire war where a British subject was concerned.

On the run from the British Army before Dunkirk, hiding from the Germans after the fall of France, Cole became the principal organizer of an escape organization based around Lille, in French Flanders. According to one of the many RAF pilots Cole returned to the war in the air, he exerted "a great hold over the Frenchmen who knew him, owing to his fearlessness and the splendid work he was doing."

Thus handed the opportunity to distinguish himself, Cole lacked the capacity for greatness. His greed for money and appetite for women first led him to embezzle large sums from the British escape organization employing him, then brought about his downfall by leading the German police to his door. Once he was caught in the toils of German counterintelligence, Cole descended from petty theft and minor peccadillos to high treason and cold-blooded murder. But to the very end he retained the personal magnetism that had proven the downfall of so many around him. Even the British Security Service agent who interrogated him after his arrest in 1945 could describe the Cockney as "at once an engaging rascal and a totally selfish monster."

His career spanned an entire era, beginning in 1939 with the British Expeditionary Force in Flanders and ending in 1946 in liberated Paris. In between, Cole moved with astonishing ease along the dark ways of the struggle for the soul of Europe, losing his own in the process. Marked for execution by the French Resistance and British Intelligence, condemned to die before a Vichy firing squad, Cole repeatedly cheated death by his wits and an abundant supply of luck.

He exploited the British, the French, the Germans, and finally the Americans, continually shifting his loyalties as opportunity dictated. Hunted by the Allied powers at the war's end, Cole pulled off his most remarkable confidence trick of all and entered the ranks of the very security apparatus that sought to track him down. Wearing the American uniform, living in a commandeered villa and traveling in a chauffeur-driven Mercedes Benz, Cole played the gracious host to Allied officers whose ranks on one occasion included a British major general.

Eventually he was run to ground, arrested, returned to Paris, and imprisoned. But Cole, whose ingenuity and resourcefulness seemed limitless, contrived to escape yet one more time and disappeared into postwar Paris for a last desperate fugue.

◆ ◆ ◆

TREASON, wrote Rebecca West in her 1946 work on the subject, "has always been the crime most abhorred by the English." One modern British jurist concluded that the betrayal of Crown and country "ranks before murder in the calendar of heinous crime." Yet the dark thread of treason runs through English history from Guy Fawkes to Anthony Blunt.

British treason in World War II has been associated most closely with William Joyce, the Irish-American fascist and, fatally for him, holder of a British passport, whose radio broadcasts from Berlin earned him the sobriquet "Lord Haw Haw" and a rope's end after the war.

But despite what West described as their "hideous novelty," the broadcasts of Joyce and other radiophonic traitors were more of an annoyance than a threat to Britain's wartime security. So was the handful of men who joined the British Free Corps, the "Legion of the Damned," which recruited disenchanted British prisoners of war into the service of German propaganda. Harold Cole, however, aided the enemy in a very direct way.

This Royal Engineers sergeant was "at once the most interesting and dangerous of our particular opponents," concluded Airey Neave, a top officer in MI9, the escape-and-evasion branch of British Intelligence that Cole betrayed. "Deputy Commander Reginald Spooner of Scotland Yard regarded him as the worst traitor of the war."

Despite the enormity of his crimes, Cole's strange case remained a mere footnote in the literature of British clandestine activities inside Fortress Europe. The official version of his compelling, if appalling, story was sealed away in the hermetic archives of the British intelligence establishment.

There were several reasons for this. For one thing, Cole was that worst of all traitors—a secret service agent who betrayed his own. He not only divulged the names of his Allied coworkers—most of them French—but actively worked for German security. "British intelligence is not very proud of that," comments Roland Lepers, a Frenchman who knew Cole before he shifted his loyalties. "They have every reason to keep it quiet."

But it went deeper than that. The standard version of the Cole story describes an open-and-shut case of a secret agent with limited responsibilities and knowledge who, out of greed and cowardice, threw in his lot with the Nazis. But evidence strongly suggests that Cole had greater intelligence responsibilities than ever has been acknowledged. Officially an escape line organizer for MI9, Cole was also gathering intelligence for the Secret Intelligence Service, or MI6. He was given significant responsibility and the lives of French agents were placed in his hands—even though his London superiors knew he was a convicted felon and a deserter.

Some go even further, suggesting that Cole's treason, real as it was, served the arcane purposes of MI6 and so would not bear close inspection when the war was done. By this account, British Intelligence was obliged to remove Cole from the scene in 1946 to prevent his story from being disclosed in an English courtroom. Whether or not this was the case, Cole's story was an embarrassment to those emerging from the war at the head of a potent intelligence empire already undermined by Kim Philby and others working for Moscow since the 1930s. Philby and his ilk could not be filed away; Cole could.

Unparalleled in the extensive literature of World War II, his story is all the more intriguing for having remained in the shadows so long. Britain's espionage files still hold the answers to some questions about Cole. What circumstances allowed a known criminal to hold a sensitive intelligence post in occupied territory? Why were British officials so reluctant to believe reports from inside France that Harold Cole had turned traitor? Some of these questions cannot be answered with certainty until the veil of Britain's Official Secrets Act is lifted and the dust blown off files long left undisturbed. Official revelations appear unlikely for the moment. But enough now is known to give an essentially complete account of the strange case of Sergeant Harold Cole, British turncoat.

2

"Was That Your Game in Civvy Street?"

PRIVATE MARTIN MORAN could have told them the fellow was a troublemaker from the very day he showed up at the recruiting station outside Colchester. It was in the first week of September 1939. Summer was almost over and the peace had just expired. Great Britain and France had declared war on Germany after Hitler trampled on the last hopes of the Munich talks by sending his Panzers and Stukas into Poland. Able-bodied Englishmen were elbowing their way into the packed recruiting offices.

On September 4, one day after war broke out, Moran, twenty-three, a former miner from Yorkshire, drove northeast of London to help muster the Eighteenth Field Park Company, Royal Engineers. Near Colchester, on the gently rolling farmland of East Anglia, Moran and his mates raised a collection of tents. Moran, in the Engineers for nearly two years, installed himself under canvas and started signing up reservists and civilian volunteers.

Engrossed in his work, Moran was startled when a recruit stepped forward and, without prompting, sang out the necessary particulars. Harold Cole, a Londoner who claimed to be an electrician by trade, had watched those before him in line and memorized Moran's questions. This sort of thing was not expected of a humble enlistee in the British Army.

Irritated by this impertinence, Moran scowled at the new arrival. Cole stood at nearly six feet tall, with a slender build and a prominent Adam's apple over the precise Windsor knot in his tie. His reddish-blond hair was oiled and parted to the right in a careful wave, the thin mustache neatly trimmed like those of Moran's superior officers. Altogether, Cole bore himself as though Moran were his subordinate, not the other way around. Part of it was the man's studied accent, which did not quite conceal a Cockney inflection. But it was more the look in his close-set, blue-gray eyes, which seemed slightly crossed. Some might have called it presence; Moran called it impudence. When Cole volunteered the information that his previous military service had included a long stint with the King's African Rifles, Moran didn't hide his skepticism. "You've never been fifteen years in the King's African Rifles," he told Cole.

One sergeant who overheard this exchange was even more blunt. He reckoned to all within earshot that it was more likely Private Cole, who received serial number 1877989 RE after taking the King's shilling, was fresh out of one of His Majesty's penal institutions. The NCO was an astute observer of his fellow man, having pegged Cole on first glance with a remarkable degree of accuracy. By the age of thirty-three, Cole had accumulated a long criminal record that included convictions for larceny, fraud, housebreaking and passing bad checks. As much as he sought to conceal his roots, he was very much a product of the East End of London, a Cockney enclave where petty crime often was viewed as just another form of gainful employment.

◆ ◆ ◆

HAROLD COLE was born on January 24, 1906 at Queen Charlotte's Lying-in Hospital in Marylebone, near Paddington Station in central London. His parents, Alice Ann Godfrey and Albert Cole, had married only a month before. Albert Cole's family background remains obscure. But the Godfreys had deep roots in the Hoxton district of Shoreditch borough, from which, in 1904, Alice Ann's parents had moved to the Clapton district of Hackney borough, three miles to the northeast. Alice Ann probably met Albert Cole while working as a servant in Hackney. Explained Thomas Sansom, one of Harold Cole's many cousins, "There wasn't work for girls in those days, so when they got to fourteen or fifteen, they shipped out for service. It was a few quid coming in and they hadn't got to be looked after." By the time Harold Cole was born, however, Alice Ann's family had moved back to Hoxton. The Coles resided there for the next twelve years.

Hoxton was desperately poor. In 1908 one observer noted the "ruinous broken pavements and many dilapidated houses" of Hoxton Square. It was an area of tenements and factories laid out along the Hackney Regent's Canal. The Coles lived at five different addresses near the canal in the decade after Harold's birth; in this time a daughter and three more boys were born. Meanwhile Albert Cole moved from one unskilled job to another. Over the years he worked as a stoker, a bottlewasher, a cooper or barrelmaker, and a longshoreman on the canal docks: Timber Wharf, Stone Wharf, Brick Wharf, Manure Wharf.

It was one of the roughest sections of Cockney London. The southern part of the district, called The Jago, had been a stronghold of the criminal underworld at the turn of the century. Popular wisdom had it that "if you put a net around Hoxton you'd have half the criminals in the world." Even in British history the name of Hoxton bore sinister connotations. The 1605 Gunpowder Plot, in which Guy Fawkes and others schemed to detonate twenty barrels of gunpowder beneath the Houses of Parliament, was uncovered there. One Lord Monteagle, who resided in a Hoxton manor house, received a letter of warning from one of the conspirators. Fawkes was arrested and tortured on the rack, then drawn and quartered. Out of the incident came a bit of doggerel verse that Cole no doubt recited in his early school days, and may have reflected upon later: "Remember, remember, the fifth of November; Gunpowder, treason and plot."

On the outbreak of the First World War, Albert Cole enlisted in the British Army. After he died in 1916, perhaps one of the 400,000 Tommies fed to the machine guns on the Somme, his widow remarried a carman named Robert Thomas Mason. Cole was eleven at the time of their 1917 wedding. In 1918 his first half-brother, also named Robert Thomas Mason, was born. Later would come another half-brother and three half-sisters. In 1919 the family moved north to Clapton, where Alice Ann had lived briefly before her marriage. They settled by another commercial waterway, the River Lea.

The Masons' fortunes were then on the decline. Their home on Ivy Terrace, recalled Sansom, was one in "a row of slum hovels that was taken over by the Salvation Army to house homeless people or to house people who would foster children—that's what Alice and Bob Mason did to earn their living." The Mason-Cole family remained there for nearly ten years. It is uncertain what effect this makeshift existence had upon the young Cole—but it was during this period that he began his criminal career. He left school at the age of fourteen, a common practice in his social milieu. Within three years, in 1923, he was beginning his first prison sentence.

◆ ◆ ◆

QUICK OF INTELLIGENCE and adept at social camouflage, Cole decided early on that he was "going to get the best he could out of the world." The young Cockney was moved by a desire to escape from his hole-and-corner life in the East End. Cole found easy advancement in the confidence game. He worked up a series of disguises and suppressed his Cockney accent, passing himself off as a member of the British middle class in order to bilk those who actually did belong.

Sansom recalled that Cole, who had acquired the nickname Sonny Boy, was always "a bit fly," or "Jack-the-lad." In 1928, when Cole went to prison for a second term, the Mason family moved from Clapton to Dalston, just north of Shoreditch. There they shared a four-room house with the Sansom family. Thomas Mason and his brood occupied the two upstairs rooms while the ten Sansoms squeezed into the small ground-floor apartment. But Cole spent little time in the Mason home after his release from prison. He would show up once or twice over a month or two, then disappear for years at a time.

"You never knew when he was in the nick or away somewhere else," said Sansom. When he did appear, Cole showed an aversion to honest labor and disdain for his humble origins. "To us he was a toff—he didn't speak like us. He was a six-footer, slim-built, and always well dressed, the type of person that can walk into clubs, attractive to gullible women."

A lone wolf, Cole moved on the fringes of the big East End gangs, looking for the easy score. He once even worked a swindle on his half-brother Robert, making off with the youth's earnings as a milkman. Strictly small-time, Cole was always ready to strike a bargain with the police to save his own skin—a trait he would show later to far more serious effect. He had a considerable talent for manipulating those in authority. Cole gained release from prison in 1935, according to Sansom, by convincing the warden that he was consumptive—all the while playing the trombone and the trumpet in the prison band. "He was that good at conning," said Sansom. "He could con his way out of the nick."

Cole stayed out of trouble—or at least out of reach of the law—for most of the late 1930s. By his own account, he spent some of that period kicking around the Far East, in and out of military service. But by late 1938, authorities in Great Britain and France were after his hide. The British caught up with Cole at the beginning of 1939, a few months after his Continental escapades. Among the few available documents from this period of his life is a set of the full-frontal and profile mug shots normally taken during police bookings on criminal charges. They are dated February 13, 1939. Dapper but threadbare, Cole faced the prison sentence he then was contemplating with a dignified expression of resignation.

Just seven months later Cole appeared before Moran in the Engineers bivouac outside Colchester. So it was probable, as the NCO had suggested, that Cole was then in the first flush of his regained liberty.

◆ ◆ ◆

THIS JAILBIRD PAST did not hinder his new career with the Royal Engineers. Cole knew that in this credulous world, appearances count more than reality. One contemporary noted that he affected the neat mustache of the English officer class and "constantly used such expressions as 'old man' and 'old boy' to ingratiate himself." The Cockney applied these techniques to his superior officers and proved a quick study in drill and small arms instruction. He was promoted from private to lance corporal inside of a week.

Moran watched this with dismay. Cole had let the Yorkshireman know he wouldn't forget the scene in the recruiting tent. Cole was given ever greater responsibilities and within a short time, Moran recalled woefully, "everyone had the lash of his tongue."

By then the Eighteenth was ready to embark for France. On September 24 the unit left Colchester for the port of Bristol Avonmouth, on the southwest English coast. Cole and a few others were assigned to an advance party lining up accommodations near Saint Nazaire, France. But Cole wriggled out of this detail, probably fearing the French port authorities might recognize and detain him for further inquiries.

Instead he served as dispatch rider during the move from Colchester to Bristol, overseeing the orderly movement of vehicles and men along the convoy route. During the trip, Moran and his companions stopped for refreshment at a pub. Cole pulled up just as Moran was reinflating the tire he had flattened to have a ready alibi. He dismissed

Moran's explanation that the vehicle had struck a raised drain cover. Before roaring off again, the Cockney promised to bring charges against Moran when they reached France.

"That's up to you," countered the private. "If you get there, the way you're driving that bike."

It was true that Cole had not fully mastered the 500 cc. BSA. A short time later Moran saw Cole seated jauntily astride his motorcycle at a traffic circle near the pub, one foot on the pavement, as he waved the convoy through. But at that very moment he toppled over and was pinned under the bike. Moran would as soon have left him where he was. But a sergeant riding with the private insisted they stop to lift the heavy machine off Cole.

An hour and a half later Moran came across a scene that gave him even greater pleasure. "In a country lane and on a left-hand bend, Corporal Cole was found to have gone through a hedge." The men who had witnessed the accident said Cole went into the curve too fast to negotiate it. He was fetched out of the underbrush and the convoy continued to Bristol.

◆ ◆ ◆

THE FEUD between Cole and Moran continued. In Bristol, loading could not begin until the following morning. The troops slept wherever they could find space to lay out their bedding. Moran hunted out an agreeable spot on the hillside above the port, but after nightfall the air turned damp. He went back to his truck and took off the hood to use as a makeshift shelter. Cole loomed out of the mist and accused him of taking it to sell.

"Was that your game in Civvy Street?" Moran inquired. Cole offered no rejoinder, and Moran sensed he had hit home. But Cole would not forget it.

At daybreak they boarded ship in a scene repeated up and down the Channel coast in those days of urgent mobilization for the expected fight on the Continent. The men chewed on bully beef and hardtack as their ship cast off its lines and slipped away from the dock, blacked out except for a blue light at the masthead, and steamed for France. After many hours of evasive zigzagging, the Engineers rolled onto the docks at Saint Nazaire, regrouping inland at a farm.

Moran's truck carried kitchen equipment, so it fell to him to distribute breakfast. In the hayloft accommodating the company's NCOs, he again crossed swords with Cole. The Londoner complained loudly that there was salt in his tea. Moran pointed out that it came from the common pot, suggesting that Cole had not rinsed his mess tin of the previous evening's bully beef.

Their exchange drew roars of laughter from the other NCOs. But Moran left the hayloft with the premonition that he "would suffer when we settled down at our first station."

◆ ◆ ◆

COLE AND THE OTHER MEN of the Eighteenth Field Park Company were among 394,165 British troops sent to France between late 1939 and early 1940 with the British Expeditionary Force. BEF activity in those first months of the war centered on Lille, an industrial city of 200,000 inhabitants located squarely astride France's northern marches.

In early times control of Lille was disputed by Flemish and French feudal lords. Briefly ruled by the Habsbourgs and the Spaniards, it fell into French hands in 1667 after a brief siege by the forces of Louis XIV. In modern times it became known as "an agreeable city whose people ceaselessly pursue their fortune" in textiles. But Lille never lost its strategic value. Such was its importance in the cycle of Franco-German warfare that began with the Franco-Prussian War of 1870 that historians described it as "the key to France's treasure house."

The British Tommies arriving in the north of France were received warmly. The French, facing renewed German expansionism, had not forgotten the carnage of World War I or Britain's role in that conflict.

German forces had occupied Lille from October 1914 to October 1918, when it was freed by the British Second Army. So in the north, at least, the French unconditionally favored this renewal of the Entente Cordiale.

"Twenty years later, they're back," announced an article published that fall by the *Grand Echo du Nord de la France,* a daily newspaper in Lille. The story described a café encounter with a group of Royal Air Force officers. Seized by Allied fervor, a Frenchman installed himself at the piano to bang out the chords of "It's a Long Way to Tipperary." The song was closely associated in French minds with the First World War predecessors of these English servicemen. The tune was taken up by the entire assembly as, "very dignified, the officers stood up and . . . loudly toasted France and [French President Albert] Lebrun."

The *Echo* reported that such demonstrations of Franco-Britannic solidarity were common. But the often rowdy English soldiers sorely tested French hospitality. BEF troops released by the thousands on weekend leave scandalized the French with their public drunkenness, brawling and skirt-chasing. French enlisted men envied the far higher pay of their English counterparts. They were further galled to see the Tommies monopolize the attentions of local females.

German propagandists tried to exploit the Anglophobia that fermented below the surface in France and was freely vented in the scurrilous right-wing Parisian press. But this often lacked effect, as the British Major General Sir Edward Spears liked to point out with a humorous anecdote that circulated after the BEF's arrival in France. A German unit holding one sector of the front had hoisted a banner warning the French troops opposite them of British perfidy. "Soldiers of the northern provinces, beware of the English," it stated. "They are destroying your properties, eating your food, sleeping with your wives, raping your daughters."

The *poilus* reflected on this momentarily. "Who cares?" they responded. "We're from the south!"

◆　◆　◆

COLE'S UNIT was stationed in Loison-sous-Lens, a mining village and railhead twenty miles south of Lille. The Eighteenth Field Park Company had taken over a lumberyard and there maintained a depot of vehicles and materiel for the construction of fortifications. It rained constantly that fall, and the troops were often soaked. But cups of hot coffee spiked with rations of rum each morning took the edge off the hardship.

A martinet to those under him, the Cockney was well liked by the other NCOs. He traded tales of the Far East with a sergeant named Holmes, who had been stationed for many years in Hong Kong. Cole talked with apparent familiarity of the Hong Kong Defence Force, in which he claimed to have served.

Off duty, Cole befriended the Belgian-born proprietress of the railroad station café, Madeleine Marie Deram, thirty-three, an outgoing, petite brunette whose husband was off in the French Army. Dazzled by the Englishmen crowding her *estaminet,* she was particularly impressed by the tall corporal with reddish-blond hair.

From behind her zinc counter, Deram could see that Cole was of a different cut from the enlisted men who drank, quarreled over endless games of vingt-et-un, and carved their names in her wooden tables. He was more like the officers who came by on Sundays for a drink after services in the church hall. She saw him as a sensitive man. This impression was reinforced by his seemingly deep grief on receiving word that his grandmother, Annie Godfrey, had died in September. Cole wore the black armband of mourning for days thereafter. Deram saw that Cole was free with his money and carried favors for local children.

But the Londoner was less solicitous about Moran and the other men under his command. He continued his vendetta against the Yorkshireman through that harsh winter, which the Eighteenth Field Park Company spent constructing pillboxes on the Franco-Belgian frontier.

This was the Phoney War, in which the Allies waited and Germany gathered itself for a spring offensive. Endurance and patience were required more than valor and enterprise. Record cold, snow, and ice were the BEF's most present enemies. The rare periods of thaw brought deep clinging mire, the particular bane of the Royal Engineers. Even General Sir Edmund Ironside, whose looming stature and hard-bitten character perfectly matched his name, remarked that he had "never seen such mud."

After Christmas, the Eighteenth Field Park Company moved to La Madeleine-les-Lille, a town just north of Lille. The subzero temperatures were mitigated by the better quarters to which the men were assigned: hotels for the officers, billets in private homes and converted warehouses for lower ranks. The cafés, brasseries, cinemas, and dance halls of Lille were only a streetcar ride away. Even La Madeleine offered more amenities than Loison.

Cole, promoted to lance sergeant, continued to harass Moran. On one of the coldest days that February, he ordered the private to take a six-ton truck out of the company compound. This went against a standing order. Because of the extremely low temperatures, vehicles were not to be used except when absolutely necessary. Before Moran had gone a hundred yards, he went into a bad skid and narrowly escaped a serious accident. Formal charges were avoided only through the intervention of a friendly officer he had known in England. But he lost the two weeks' leave in "Blighty" that he had been looking forward to for months.

Worse, Cole came through the episode unscathed and, by the beginning of March, was Moran's direct superior. As company guard commander, Cole supervised the sentries around the Eighteenth's compound in La Madeleine. The Cockney made sure Moran received more than his share of night watches—but in doing so helped assure his own undoing.

3

"His Scheme Never Failed"

HAROLD COLE's appealing personality and sharp wits enabled him to rise quickly through the ranks of the Eighteenth Field Park Company. But he had also been helped by his earlier experience in the British armed forces. When he told Moran that he had served with the King's African Rifles, he may have been spinning another of his fanciful stories. But as always when Cole manufactured a new past for himself, he sowed a grain or two of truth along with the required bushel of falsehoods.

All evidence is that Cole did serve in the British Army at some point preceding his enlistment in the Royal Engineers. An official veil of obscurity remains drawn over the exact details of this service. But it appears that Cole's criminal record obliged him to sign up with a colonial regiment under the assumed name of Richard Godfrey, one of his earliest aliases. Richard was the first name of his paternal grandfather; Godfrey his mother's maiden name.

Cole was initially successful in this army career—until he broke the traces, stole a colonel's uniform and automobile, and launched on the spree that ended in his being cashiered. The commanding officer of the Eighteenth Field Park Company, remarked Sergeant Holmes, "seemed to have great faith in his abilities." But the wild streak in Cole was about to assert itself.

The worst weather northern France could offer had settled over La Madeleine on a Friday night in March when Moran and three other unfortunates drew sentinel duty under Cole. Bundled up in heavy storm coats, they reluctantly walked the perimeter on two-hour shifts between 6:00 P.M. and 6:00 A.M. On their tours, they also had to run vehicle engines for ten minutes every hour to keep them from freezing up.

Even a seasoned trooper like Holmes felt relief that he hadn't drawn this assignment. In full battle dress, loaded down with fifty rounds of ammunition, marching over an irregular terrain coated with ice, the sentries "had a choice of standing at their post and freezing to death, or attempting to march to the adjoining post and breaking their necks," he recalled.

On this evening, Moran and a private named Penny had found a spot out of the elements behind a garage. During their watch they took refuge there, trading complaints "about Sergeant Cole and what kind of a bastard he was and other items." When the watch was over, they happily returned to the guardroom, from which Cole was absent, and settled in for a rest and a cup of tea.

When Cole showed up at about 10:15 P.M., Moran asked for permission to go to the latrine. The sergeant gave his approval, but admonished Moran to go all the way to the toilets instead of relieving himself in the first convenient spot. But Moran ducked between two stacks of lumber as soon as he had left the guardroom and set about relieving himself. Glancing off to his left, Moran was startled to see a lone figure clambering through the transom over the door to the company headquarters. When the Yorkshireman had a better look at the burglar, he was dumbfounded. It was none other than Sergeant Cole.

◆ ◆ ◆

MORAN SAID NOTHING to the other guards of what he had seen, preferring to mull over this turn of events until his next tour of duty at 2:00 A.M. Cole came back at 4:00 A.M., but immediately went out again with one of the company drivers. Moran saw no more of the sergeant for the rest of the night.

In the morning Moran was called before the company sergeant major and informed that the noncommissioned officers' mess funds had disappeared. He now understood Cole's strange behavior and told the officer what he had seen. Instructed to say nothing to anyone, Moran spent the morning directing traffic in and out of the compound. At 10:00 A.M. he was ordered to the barracks for a general inspection.

Moran felt uneasy about the situation, given Cole's grudge against him. Suspecting he might be victimized in the search to come, he decided to shift his belongings from where he had been sleeping. The Yorkshireman had acted wisely. In the search that followed, Cole discovered a roll of one hundred-franc notes in the magazine of a rifle belonging to the soldier who had changed places with Moran. The man was handcuffed and led away by the military police.

The enlisted man was held under guard that Saturday afternoon in March as the company mounted a search for the rest of the loot. Wads of money were found behind the toilet cisterns in two local cafés. But the bulk of the stolen currency could not be found, and the suspect eventually was released.

Despite Moran's statement, no action had been taken against Cole by the commanding officer. Instead, the Cockney was assigned full-time to recovering the stolen money and identifying the thief. He was given a car and a driver by the name of Rose. One of the first spots to which Cole directed Rose was the Lille racetrack, in the neighboring town of Marcq-en-Baroeul, where some of the Eighteenth's troops were quartered.

In some tall grass by the sheds in which the troops were billeted,

Cole and Rose discovered the strongbox removed from the company headquarters. It had been broken open and emptied of its contents. Before they made their report to headquarters, Cole took Rose aside. So as not to make the company look bad, they would say the safe had been found on racetrack property.

But after this version had been given to the company commander, Rose went back and told the truth. The officer, perhaps reluctant to believe Moran's testimony, now was obliged to look further into the activities of Lance Sergeant Cole. The Cockney was put under surveillance by the military police. He was followed to a Lille apartment where the bulk of the loot was found, along with two easy women whom Cole had set up in the love-nest.

Cole was placed under arrest. His promising career as a noncommissioned officer had sustained a major setback that promised to land him in yet another correctional institution—this time of the most harsh, military variety.

♦ ♦ ♦

MORAN WAS DELIGHTED to see his antagonist marched away by the MPs. But this feeling gave way to consternation when he heard the next morning that while Cole's guards were eating dinner, the prisoner had picked a lock and strolled out of the stable serving as a brig. Cole then went to the quartermaster store where he demanded a revolver and ammunition from the soldier in charge. Cole assured the clerk that he had now been cleared of all charges, but "was refused and then cleared off."

Armed search parties were formed. Knowing Cole's penchant for dalliances, they resolved to inspect a café whose owner was friendly with the Londoner. Confronted by armed soldiers, the proprietress admitted Cole was lurking in the back room. They called on him to surrender, which he sensibly did.

The MPs now locked up Cole on the second floor of the stable. But two weeks later he again was loose. He had wriggled through a small hole in the floor of his makeshift cell and shinnied down a blanket into the stable. Then he stole the uniform of the company sergeant major and fled La Madeleine. A fortnight later he was picked up in a different uniform stolen from an officer in the Royal Army Service Corps. He had also taken the officer's checkbook and covered the region with bad paper bearing the unfortunate man's name.

This time the military police took no further chances. They flung Cole into the stony fastness of Lille's Citadelle, a star-shaped fortress constructed in the seventeenth century for Louis XIV by the military engineer Vauban. He was locked behind steel bars on the top floor of the prison, under twenty-four-hour guard provided by his comrades in the Eighteenth Field Park Company.

No stranger to confinement, Cole exhibited the skills of a proven escape artist. At the end of each watch, the guard detail handcuffed the Cockney in his jail cell and marched off down the stairs for a changing drill in the courtyard where, by then, lay the manacles Cole had slipped off and tossed out his cell window. This greatly swelled his reputation among the troops, while his guards found him an amiable enough prisoner.

Holmes on one occasion served as guard commander for the errant Cockney, who was the only prisoner in the entire stronghold. His duties included accompanying the prisoner on his daily walk up and down the courtyard. As they strolled, Holmes noticed that Cole was wearing an officer's battle dress, but with the badges of rank removed. When he asked about it, Cole described his two weeks of freedom.

"His story was amazing," Holmes stated. "He told me he had escaped from the MPs by the simple method of asking to go to the latrine, and that as his escort stood outside the door he had crawled out of the window."

Cole then had gone on an inspection tour of neighboring units, supposedly to see that barracks were up to army standards. If they failed to satisfy his criteria an Engineers building party would come behind him to improve them, Cole told his military hosts, who fed and housed him.

"He told me his scheme never failed," recalled Holmes. Cole continued this masquerade for a fortnight until he was captured in a hotel in Lens, to the south of Lille. The Cockney had encountered a friendly RAF pilot, who invited him to dine in the hotel restaurant. During their meal, Cole said he was due for leave. The airman very kindly offered to take him along on a scheduled flight to England the next day. Cole jumped at this proposal—but never had a chance to fly back over the channel. "Just when things were going well and he was finishing his meal," recorded Holmes, "he found himself confronted by an RE sergeant and two sappers."

The two combat engineers were from another unit of the Fourth Division. They knew of Cole because of his rapid rise through the ranks. Neither they nor the sergeant had heard of his arrest for theft, but when the NCO heard the two sappers marveling at Cole's promotion to captain he realized something was wrong. He and the two armed sappers hurried to the hotel and arrested the imposter.

The Londoner took this setback in stride. But his equanimity did not extend to superior ranks. After Cole had finished this account, a junior officer arrived in the fortress courtyard to see if Cole had any complaints.

"Sod off," he told the subaltern. "I don't want you here."

◆　◆　◆

COLE'S MISADVENTURES had relieved boredom that spring. But after May 10, Phoney War ennui was no longer a problem. On that day the German armies violated territory of the Netherlands, Belgium, and Luxembourg and raced for the borders of France, the old enemy.

Belgian neutrality earlier had prevented the BEF from assuming forward defense positions there. But the German attack enabled it to shift to a more advanced bulwark along the Dyle River east of Brussels. The Eighteenth Field Park Company stood in reserve in Brussels itself. Cole's company took him along under guard when the Fourth Division left La Madeleine on the evening of May 13.

On May 14 the main BEF force repelled an assault by the German Sixth Army. But the overall battle turned rapidly against the Allies.

German tank divisions surged toward the French coast in a sickle movement intended to cut the BEF off from its escape ports. The Allies reeled back in disorder. By the end of May, the Royal Engineers were back in the Lille area demolishing bridges.

That week Cole was also back in La Madeleine. He had thrown off his police guard in a chaotic Brussels train station as the rest of his unit headed for the channel port of Boulogne. He then traveled south for a final confrontation with Moran.

◆ ◆ ◆

WHILE THE WORLD turned upside down, the Yorkshireman had been guarding an equipment depot at the Lille racetrack and befriending an Alsatian dog named Bette, given to him by a French child about to be evacuated. The German shepherd became devoted to the young private, sleeping under his bed at the racetrack and snarling at anyone who approached him.

On May 31, while Moran was eating at a La Madeleine café, military policemen rolled up and informed him that Cole was again on the loose. Moran grew more apprehensive when he called at a local shop the next morning and heard that "the tall sergeant had been seen in the area."

Cole was telling everyone that the Eighteenth Field Park Company had been destroyed in a bombing raid near Brussels. Only he and two other soldiers were spared. Now distraught with fear, Moran retired to the local café where Cole had first been recaptured. Seeing his haggard condition, the English proprietress invited him to rest in the back room. Moran slept with a loaded rifle at hand.

Whether in search of food, drink, or revenge, Cole did show up that morning. Awakened by a fearsome racket in the café's main salon, Moran grabbed his rifle and rushed out to find Cole at bay on the ground, the faithful Bette at his throat. At that moment the MPs arrived and hauled Cole away. It was the last Moran ever saw of the Cockney sergeant.

◆ ◆ ◆

THE GERMANS now were approaching, and Moran left for Dunkirk. On the beach, he found pandemonium as thousands of Allied troops attempted to escape capture by the oncoming enemy forces. He had his first real taste of war when a German plane strafed the mass of soldiers and killed many of the men around him.

On the aircraft's third pass, Moran leaped into an antiaircraft emplacement. When the attack ended, he was looking down the revolver of a British officer determined to maintain discipline. Moran and others, surrendering their rifles, were brought to a "reception camp" inland. The former vacation colony was crammed with French, Belgian, and British soldiers "laying around expecting the worst."

Among this cheerless crowd, Moran found two friends from the Eighteenth Field Park Company, the same pair of sappers from whom Cole had escaped in Brussels. The Eighteenth had embarked for England ten days before. But these two had missed the boat, "having been out drinking and sightseeing." Moran, who owed his close shave in La Madeleine to their lack of vigilance, "had different thoughts about that." But this was not the time for recriminations. At dawn the three slipped out of the pen, which looked more and more like a prisoner-of-war camp. They walked back to the water's edge.

"All three of us remarked how quiet it was—no gunfire, no planes." Coming upon some English soldiers trying to rig up pontoon bridges to reach a trawler offshore, the three Engineers volunteered their expertise. When all 250 men had loaded onto the Dutch fishing smack, Moran and his friends followed and reached Margate, England, in safety.

◆ ◆ ◆

WHILE MANY SUCH small miracles were happening at Dunkirk, Cole had once again recovered his liberty. He had been put back behind bars at the Citadelle. But with the approach of the Germans his guard detail had decided one Cockney prisoner was not worth sticking around for.

Holmes, who located his unit in Somerset, England a month after Dunkirk, had the story from a sergeant named Buck. "When Jerry came tearing into Lille," Buck told him, "I opened Cole's cell door and said, 'I don't care a bugger what you do, we're off.'"

Amid the chaos of defeat and the fog of war, Cole dropped entirely out of sight. His movements and intentions in those desperate days remain obscure. Did he try to reach Dunkirk and find passage to England? Was he captured by the Germans, as he would later tell French officials, and held for three weeks until he again escaped? Or was he simply roaming the devastated landscape of Flanders with no other plan than avoiding capture until something better turned up?

We do not know. But at the end of June, Cole showed up at Deram's *estaminet* in Loison looking for shelter. He and another British soldier stayed above Deram's café for a night and two days; then the second man left to seek shelter with a family he knew in Belgium. Deram told Cole he too would have to find another hiding place. Loison was too small a town for his presence to go unnoticed for very long. She was a married woman. People would talk.

They took the train up to Lille and sought new lodgings for Cole. But this first attempt produced no immediate results. For the next few weeks Cole remained in hiding at Deram's place.

He was in the café one day in July when a group of Germans arrived. Cole dashed into the toilet off the hallway and huddled there as Deram met the enemy. She had experienced the German occupation of Belgium during the previous war and knew what they wanted.

The military officials said the café and her home were being requisitioned for the administrators and guard detail of the Loison train station. She could keep the kitchen for her personal needs. Deram protested. Her husband was already a prisoner of the Third Reich;

deprived of his company and support, was she now to be stripped of her livelihood?

Not at all, responded the German officer. "You can count on us," he said. "You'll be well paid and well fed."

But Deram did not care to live at close quarters with a dozen German soldiers. Nor was this particularly advisable as long as Cole was around. When the Germans left, she and the Englishman hastily conferred, packed up her household affairs, and, with her son Marcel, left for La Madeleine-les-Lille.

There Cole picked up the thread of his wartime career.

4

"Collect the English and Send Them Home!"

THE DUNKIRK EVACUATION already had passed into history and legend when the Battle of France ended on June 21, 1940, with the signing of a Franco-German armistice in the clearing at Rethondes. But several thousand British and Commonwealth soldiers were still roaming northern France, looking for a way home and doing their best to stay out of German prisoner-of-war camps.

These prodigal sons of the devastated BEF made for the only havens they knew: French homes around Lille where they were billeted in 1939 and 1940. Some had taken refuge while the battle still raged. In full retreat from the Low Countries, they sought food and shelter in abandoned homes. Unaware how rapidly the front was advancing, they succumbed to fatigue and awakened to find themselves in towns like La Madeleine, Marquette-lez-Lille, Tourcoing, Roubaix, and Wattrelos that were in enemy hands.

When the fighting was over, many of the inhabitants of these towns were sorely discomfited to find themselves with British soldiers on their hands. They were sympathetic with the plight of their former lodgers and allies. But the experience of the last war had shown that harboring English soldiers was an offense not smiled upon by the German occupier.

The people of Lille could call to mind the "Case of the Four" of 1915, during the first year of the city's First World War occupation. Eugene Jacquet, a wholesale wine merchant, had undertaken to shelter Allied troops and aviators caught behind enemy lines. In March 1915, a British aircraft was shot down in Lille after attacking a German telephone exchange. Jacquet hid its pilot, and the merchant's daughter Geneviève led the flier through German lines to the British sector in Belgium.

Elated at his escape, the pilot unwisely flew back over Lille to drop the inflammatory message: "Lieutenant Mapplebeck sends his compliments to the Kommandant of the German forces in Lille, and regrets that he was unable to make his acquaintance during his recent pleasant stay in the neighborhood."

This set off a hue and cry among the Germans, who posted notices threatening the death penalty for anyone hiding members of the enemy forces. Meanwhile a double agent approached Jacquet in the guise of a French prisoner of war and asked the merchant to conceal him. Denounced, Jacquet and three associates were tried, sentenced to death, and executed by firing squad in the grassy Citadelle moat.

Similarly, the British soldiers of 1940 knew the story of Miss Edith Cavell, the English country vicar's daughter who helped six hundred British soldiers escape from occupied Belgium during the First World War. Cavell, a forbidding forty-eight-year-old spinster when the Great War broke out, was matron of a nursing school attached to a prominent Brussels clinic. Her escape work began in November 1914, when her institution took in two wounded British soldiers. Thereafter she concealed a stream of Allied troops in the wards and cellars of her medical establishment, arranging passage to friendly territory.

This did not escape the notice of the Geheime Politische Polizei, the German secret police. She eventually was betrayed by a French turncoat named Georges Gaston Quien, known as "Lamp Post" for his six foot, five inch stature. Quien showed up at the clinic posing as a French officer wounded at the Battle of Charleroi and gathered evidence against Cavell.

By August 1915, the German authorities had fully developed their case against the nurse and raided the hospital. Cavell was tried that October with thirty-five others and admitted her involvement in the escape of two hundred British soldiers and officers. Convicted and sentenced to death, that October she was tied to an execution post outside Brussels and shot by an eight-man firing squad.

Cavell's death was seized upon by English propagandists, who deplored this new barbarism by the Hun. Postcards circulated, depicting the slain nurse at the feet of a pistol-toting Prussian, urging: "Remember!"

◆ ◆ ◆

THE CROWD OF GERMANS arriving in 1940, imbued with the Teutonic discipline of their forefathers and a potent dose of Nazi ideology as well, were no more tolerant of the population's wish to aid and succor the battered Tommies huddled in their attics, basements, and barns.

The French provincial governor of the north soon would report that the occupation policies of the German general Niehoff "bordered on terror." The glacial *Kommandant* showed a "predilection for imperious formulations, haughty refusals of any objections, distant and contemptuous politeness, warnings mixed with threats against the least hint of independence."

Even more dangerous were the German secret police services. Most active at this stage of the occupation was the Abwehr, the intelligence and counterintelligence arm of the German High Command. Its commander in Lille was *Hauptsturmführer* Karl Hegener, a seasoned officer wounded as a young artillery lieutenant at the Chemin des Dames during the First World War. A fervent Nazi, he had worked as a lawyer and notary in the grimy industrial Rhine port of Duisburg between the wars. Hegener installed his service in the rue de l'Arc and began setting out the lines he knew would pull in conspirators against the Reich.

His star agent was a former Dutch sailor and private eye named Cornelius Johannes Antonius Verloop, who had deserted from the French Foreign Legion in 1940. This cunning and energetic soldier of fortune became a *Vertrauensmann* or *V-Mann*, a trusted German secret agent. Throughout the war, Verloop would relentlessly penetrate French networks that were aiding British troops, aviators, and secret agents. He was a dangerous opponent.

Hegener's more visible arm was the Geheime Feldpolizei, or GFP, headquartered in central Lille in the rue de Tanremonde. It carried out searches and arrests based on leads provided by operatives like Verloop and other informants.

Captured British escapers or agents were in most cases imprisoned after interrogation, which might very well involve torture. But many of their French helpers, as they were described in the studiously homespun jargon of British Intelligence, "could expect no mercy and received little. They would be tried by a military court; acquittals were unknown." Deportation to Germany or execution were the most common sentences.

♦ ♦ ♦

YET THE PROBLEM remained: what were the French to do with all those British soldiers? It was resolved spontaneously by northerners who had not forgotten the rules set a generation before. Writes Natalis Dumez, founder of an underground newspaper and Resistance movement called *La Voix du Nord* (Voice of the North): "Our duty was simple, clear, distinct; its execution natural!"

The Widow Samiez, who had lived through the First World War in Lille, spread the word: "We must collect the English and send them home!" Day after day, Dumez and others saw her on the way to the Lille train station leading three or four Allied soldiers barely disguised in civilian clothing. "She made the travel arrangements, and our friends left for Paris."

Others rode with them in the trains as interpreters and guides. One *convoyeur*, named Antoine Hegedos, explains that the soldiers and aviators left in groups of about ten, escorted by two guides. "They couldn't travel in third class; talkative passengers would have wanted to enter into conversation with them and the situation could have become difficult." So the British evaders traveled in second class with a *convoyeur* posted on lookout duty in the corridor.

Young women were particularly sought as guides. They could "easily simulate a gallant adventure with one of the aviators to deflect the suspicions of the Germans." When female helpers lacked, British escapers and evaders constituted soccer teams on their way to games.

The general confusion of the first months of occupation worked in their favor. June and July 1940, for one expert in evasion, were "romantic months in the history of escape." Some BEF stragglers settled down with families in the north and waited out the war. Others, more enterprising and dutiful, hiked or bicycled southwards to the Unoccupied Zone. There seemed little threat from the Germans, who were otherwise occupied. Weeks after France had fallen, "bewildered figures in khaki battle dress could still be seen on the streets of Paris."

There were inevitably misunderstandings, as when three British privates found they were virtual prisoners of the French peasant who had offered them shelter. The deluded farmer was acting in "the confident belief that the British secret service would one day pay a large ransom for them."

Despite such cultural and linguistic barriers, the British and the French shared deeply held myths concerning the ways and means of outwitting a common and long-time foe. The northerners tapped a wealth of lore handed down during the single generation that had passed since the Great War.

The British boasted an equally rich heritage. Escape and evasion gripped the imagination of the British public after World War I. This was the first conflict in which capture by the enemy was no longer regarded as a personal disgrace, so much had the nature of warfare changed. Escape provided an often symbolic but at times real extension of the battlefield and had all the makings of a new upper-class sport.

One signal British publishing success between the wars was *The Escaping Club*, about an RAF officer's breakout from a German POW fortress. More escape classics followed, with titles like *The Road to En-Dor*, *An Escaper's Log*, and *The Escapes of Captain O'Brien*. Many an English schoolboy who cut his teeth on these would know what to do when he found himself in the same situation in 1940. Indeed, when British Intelligence formed its MI9 escape-evasion branch in 1939, the British Museum was asked to comb second-hand bookstores for these same sagas. They were then distilled into guidelines for a new generation of escapers.

◆   ◆   ◆

IN THE LILLE-AREA town of Wattrelos, it became known in July 1940 that if one was burdened with a British soldier or two the person to see about it was the local midwife Jeanne Huyge. Most town officials had taken to their heels during the invasion. Few returned during that first summer of occupation. Lacking any other authority to turn to, the women of Wattrelos appealed to the only remaining figure of trust.

An enterprising woman of thirty who was already running the local hospital, Huyge began to receive British escapers in her consultation every evening. She learned that with a forged demobilization document from the French Army, these soldiers could obtain a one-time payment of eight hundred francs from an obliging local town hall. This was just about enough to purchase a ticket to the Mediterranean port of Marseilles in the Unoccupied Zone, that third of France left under the nominal control of a puppet government in the southern spa town of Vichy.

Moving these Britons out of the north was another matter. After the armistice, the Germans hived off the Nord and Pas de Calais provinces, placing them under the German occupation authority for

Belgium and northern France, based in Brussels. A sensitive area of operations against England, the Nord-Pas de Calais was declared the Forbidden Zone. Travel and communications were restricted. Months were required to obtain a pass for a journey to Paris, in the Occupied Zone of France. It was as if the north had become another country.

This presented a major obstacle for people like Huyge who were dispatching British troops to the south of France, complicating what was already a very hazardous business. The Tommies, mostly young men who had seldom ventured out of Great Britain before the war, had been confined in French homes for weeks. Oblivious to the danger courted by their guides, they often showed excessive high spirits in what seemed a grand adventure on the road home.

While changing trains at Bethune, thirty miles southwest of Lille, some of the British soldiers in Huyge's charge recognized it as their post in 1939 and 1940. They "rushed off to the ticket window of the station shouting, 'Jules! Henri!'" The station emptied, and everyone was off to the local bistro while Huyge waited impatiently at the track. The Englishmen, fortified with drink, arrived minutes before the train and further dismayed her by taking up the Nazi goose-step behind some German officers on the platform.

They were, Huyge concluded, "dangerous merchandise."

◆ ◆ ◆

THIS WAS CONFIRMED by the experience of her coworker, Maurice Van de Kerckhove, recruited into her tiny network in the normal way: he was a friend of a friend of her brother from Boy Scout days. One day that summer, Van de Kerckhove traveled into the countryside of the Pas de Calais to pick up an English soldier. The man was lodged with a family in the village of Cauchy-à-la-Tour, the birthplace of Marshal Philippe Pétain, the Hero of Verdun and lately the figurehead of Vichy collaboration with the Germans.

When he arrived, he found the villagers in a state of anxiety. The Englishman was in the midst of a game of darts with a German soldier. "Each was as drunk as the other, while everyone in the café knew that one was English and the other was German." Van de Kerckhove eased the British sportsman out the door and sped him on his way. The incident provided a measure of the political attitudes of the northerners. Even in the home village of Pétain, then leading France down the "path of collaboration," a British escaper was safe from denunciation.

The grandfatherly *Maréchal* and his Calaban-like second, Pierre Laval, urged France to quaff the bitter dregs of defeat as a palliative for prewar moral decline. But their formula of *"Travail, Famille, Patrie"* was for popular consumption. Privately, Pétain engaged in more cynical calculations. "The reality is that we have sustained the most frightful and complete defeat possible," he wrote to the president of the Lille Chamber of Commerce.

After a display of the Anglophobia that quickly became a hallmark of his government, Pétain continued, "A good number of things will fall into place in the event of an English victory. It is therefore in the prospect of a German victory that we must maneuver. This is what the French government is doing."

But most northerners had little use for this craven strategy. Subjected daily to German humiliation, spectators of the battle overhead between the Luftwaffe and the RAF, they knew their only hope lay with the resisting British. Local feeling against the German occupation took the form of a mass demonstration in Lille in August 1940 at the grave of an English officer.

Less publicly, stranded soldiers and downed aviators were spirited to safety and helped to return to England. At this early stage there were no organized groups to speak of, writes Voix du Nord Resistance leader Jean Catrice. "People simply reached agreement among friends." But more structured escape networks soon began to take shape. Eventually they came under the direction of a shadowy British agent based in La Madeleine variously identified as Captain Colson, Captain Paul Delobel, and Captain Paul Cole.

He was, word had it in the north, no less than the special emissary of Britain's Secret Intelligence Service.

5

"This Man Isn't Simple at All"

ON THE RUN and destitute in July 1940, Cole by the end of that turbulent summer had acquired a home, a bicycle, and a few more aliases. More important, he now was a man with a mission. One hot Saturday afternoon in early September, the deserter could be found on his new bicycle riding north along the main highway out of Lille, cycling toward La Madeleine, Marcq-en-Baroeul, Tourcoing, and the Belgian frontier. Farther along the rue de Lille, on the corner of a narrow street lined with red-brick row houses, a French businessman named Henri Duprez anxiously surveyed the avenue as it led away south.

Duprez, thirty-eight, the owner of sixteen textile factories in the wool center of Roubaix, was a self-made man who had gone into business at the age of seventeen. When the German Army stormed through the north, Duprez took his family to the coast ahead of the fray. Along the way he retrieved a bundle of documents from a ditch, finding them to have been abandoned by the Deuxième Bureau, staff intelligence of the French High Command. A good citizen, Duprez delivered these in late June to the Bureau's headquarters at Toulouse, in Vichy France.

The officers there first debated whether he should be locked up for handling secret materials. Then they asked him to work as an agent for them in the north. Some time later, he was contacted by people in his region who had organized themselves into the first cells of the French Resistance. But for the moment, Duprez and his new associates were simply moved by an unexamined patriotism and an ingrained dislike for German military government.

So it was that Duprez was asked to go to a hairdressing salon on the rue de Turenne in La Madeleine to meet with a British intelligence officer named Delobel. By nature cautious, Duprez arrived well ahead of time. He stationed himself on the corner near the beauty salon, keeping watch in readiness for this important meeting. After some minutes, a lone figure astride a bicycle appeared in the distance.

As soon as the man on the two-wheeler came into sight, Duprez was "absolutely certain that he was an Englishman." Even before the Frenchman could make out his features, he remarked the tall, lanky frame propped over the handlebars, pedaling in such a way as to all but shout his British origins. Duprez wondered what *l*'Intelligence Service had been thinking when it dispatched Delobel to Lille.

◆ ◆ ◆

DUPREZ WATCHED the supposed agent dismount his bicycle, lean it against the wall outside the shop, and disappear inside. After a moment's hesitation, he followed. A hairdresser motioned him up the hallway stairs to the second floor, where Duprez came face to face with Captain Paul Delobel of British Intelligence.

He examined the man with curiosity and not a little admiration. Like most northerners, he was at heart an Anglophile—and Delobel was "the prototype of an Englishman": five feet, eleven and a quarter inches tall, thin of build, with blue eyes, reddish-blond hair, and a long, pale face.

Cole got down to business, explaining that he was setting up networks to assist stranded soldiers and downed aviators on their way back to England. Duprez was already involved in sheltering, clothing, feeding, and financing British escapers. Cole said his assignment was to bring the French networks into one coordinated organization in the north.

Duprez was eager to cooperate. But as Cole talked, the Frenchman's enthusiasm was tempered by a more equivocal sensation verging on distrust. Cole's first question was whether he and his associates could finance the network until official funds came along from London. Put off by Cole's indelicate approach, Duprez may have caught a glimpse of the petty swindler behind the English spy. But he dismissed these unworthy thoughts and agreed to come up with the money.

Next, Cole offered Duprez some advice that seemed very professional, though of limited practicality. "Our one great enemy," Cole declared, "is the police dog." He no doubt had in mind the beast which had bested him in La Madeleine some weeks before. "If you are attacked by a dog, don't lose your head. Just give it a good kick under the jaw and that will take care of it." Duprez took note.

Then Cole explained how to get off a train in motion. This was something British secret agents obviously had to do quite often. At that time trains had a foot-plate below each external compartment door. Cole explained that first one should wrap oneself in a coat, then lie down on this plate with feet positioned in the direction the train was traveling. Then one simply had to roll off to absorb the forward motion in a slide.

There was no guarantee against injuries. But this was, Cole assured Duprez, the approved method of parting company with an express between stations.

Duprez was altogether impressed with this Captain Delobel. He had "the strong feeling that this was someone out of the ordinary," mingled with "the wonder of being in front of someone from the British secret service."

Cole was playing his part with the same gusto he once had brought to the role of Wing Commander Wain. It was second nature to him by now. He had been polishing this character for years. Besides, his French interlocutors were predisposed to trust someone who seemed to embody the British virtues that for them represented national salvation.

But now the Cockney swindler was playing on a larger, more hazardous stage, with his own life and those of others in the balance. The price of being unmasked would far exceed the accustomed stretch of prison in Broadmoor, Brixton, or Wormwood Scrubs.

The question remains as to why Cole embarked on this perilous course. There were easier ways to survive living underground in France. His actions ran counter to the self-serving pattern of behavior he had established to this point. Perhaps he realized that meritorious conduct would go a long way to redeeming his sorry past if British officialdom ever laid hands on him again. Then, too, there were promising opportunities for profit at the expense of wealthy patriots like Henri Duprez. Cole knew a good thing when he saw it.

But there was something else drawing the Cockney into the role of British secret agent: it gave free expression to the inmost Cole, who had always yearned for rank, respectability, and the admiration of others.

Here in northern France, Cole could remake himself in the image of all that was beyond his reach in England. In London Cole had been a petty criminal and ex-convict; here he could cryptically allude to prewar service as a Scotland Yard inspector. In the Royal Engineers he had been a lance sergeant about to be broken down to private; now he was a captain, however spurious, in His Majesty's Secret Service.

♦ ♦ ♦

COLE'S TRANSFORMATION had begun modestly enough. When he and Deram arrived in La Madeleine in July 1940, they presented themselves at the town hall as refugees whose home had been commandeered by the Germans. Cole was going by the name of Joseph Deram, borrowed from Madeleine's husband, who had been taken prisoner by the Germans in the battle of May and June. They secured the use of a small brick row house in the rue de la Gare, up the street from the small La Madeleine train station. There they settled with Deram's son Marcel, then eleven or twelve years old.

Cole likely felt at home in La Madeleine, where he had been stationed for five months in early 1940. The red brick homes were in a Flemish-influenced architecture closer to that of Britain's cities than to the styles seen in the rest of France. On the street corners stood numerous *estaminets*, public houses operating in a tradition not so different from that of a London pub.

The couple owed their good fortune to François Duprez, thirty-two, the La Madeleine city administrator in charge of housing and relief. (He was unrelated to Henri Duprez; the name was common in the north.) When the BEF was in La Madeleine, Duprez had handled the assignment of billets to the Allied troops. When the Germans took over he remained in the same job. The situation provided a convenient cover and allowed him to collect useful information on the disposition of German troops in the region.

Tall, lanky, and blond-haired, François Duprez had lost his right leg in an industrial accident three years before the war, when he and his brother-in-law were operating a tannery. One day in September 1936 Duprez's hand slipped as he was cutting a hide. The short but viciously sharp knife slashed through his heavy leather apron and opened up his femoral artery just below the hip. His life was saved by a worker who sat on him to stanch the flow of blood. But infection subsequently developed and the leg had to be removed.

The loss of his limb did not unduly affect Duprez's peacetime life. He still walked long distances and bicycled. But when war came he was greatly disappointed to be declared unfit for duty in the major test of his generation. He traveled each weekend to visit his brother, an infantry sergeant stationed in a nearby province. Duprez worked for a grocery concern in La Madeleine until his knowledge of English and reputation for reliability secured him the job of liaison with the British.

Like many of its neighbors, the Duprez family evacuated La Madeleine as the Wehrmacht approached in May 1940. Not only was the population horrified at the speed of the German advance and the disarray of the retreating Allied armies, but there was also the conditioning experience of the First World War. Lille had been shelled heavily by the Germans in October 1914. By the time the French garrison surrendered, eighty civilians had been killed and much of the downtown was flattened.

Duprez took his wife and three children to the Normandy coast, then returned to Lille while the battle for the city was still in progress. Seven German infantry divisions and an armored division led by General Erwin Rommel were held off for three days by 40 thousand French colonial troops. When the dust had settled, Duprez returned to his municipal duties. Conquerors, not allies, the officers of the Wehrmacht were less gracious about requisitioning billets than the British had been. One of the few town officials remaining, Duprez was kept busy meeting German demands and sorting out the enormous confusion left after the battle.

To complicate matters, several members of the BEF were hiding in Duprez's own home. On his return, he found in his mailbox the front-door key and a note of thanks from the British officers he had lodged during the Phoney War. They had taken the key off to war with them and stopped briefly during their retreat. When they left, others replaced them in the house. Duprez allowed them to stay and started helping others like them to survive and move south toward home.

◆ ◆ ◆

COLE AND DUPREZ had not known each other when the BEF was still established in La Madeleine. But within a short time of the Cockney's return they were working closely together. Cole had every interest in cultivating this friendship. As one of the few city-hall employees still at his post, Duprez had ready access to the official forms and stamps needed to produce reliable false identity papers. Duprez established the identity of Paul Delobel—complete with birth certificate, national identity card, and ration book—into which Cole stepped with ease.

There was still the problem of language. Cole could not suppress his strong Cockney accent, and in any case spoke only rudimentary French. So he obtained one more document certifying him as hearing and speech impaired. At need he "spoke as if he were a deaf-mute who could talk only with difficulty," explained Marguerite Duprez, wife of François, "stuttering, 'Uh-uh-uh-uh-uh' if there were Germans walking by."

In this way Cole could circulate in La Madeleine, Lille, and the surrounding towns, meeting the people with whom he would work closely in the months to come. Shortly after Madeleine Deram settled into the rue de la Gare, she went to the beauty salon in the rue de Turenne to have her hair done. With her was Cole, whom she introduced as her brother-in-law.

Jeannine Voglimacci, the shop's proprietress, thought Cole was "bizarre." He was employing his guise as a deaf-mute or some variation on it. Voglimacci, who would become a central figure in the La Madeleine escape organization, at first "took him for something of a simpleton."

But after some observation she revised this first impression, thinking: "This man isn't simple at all."

6

"He Was Smarter Than That"

THE YEARS Cole had spent perfecting his skills as a confidence trickster now proved a capital asset, as he cast a spell over the trustful, admiring northerners and took command of the La Madeleine network. His nationality alone had much to do with this. In that time and place, as one of his coworkers later acknowledged, "anything English was God." But Cole's magnetic personality also exerted a powerful influence on his new associates. Jeannine Voglimacci, owner of the hair salon in the rue de Turenne, observed that he was "imposing when he spoke," that "people believed in him, had confidence in him." She saw that Cole had "a way of attracting people to him, of drawing their sympathy. He made you want to help him."

Not everyone took a shine to the Cockney. During this same period, he stopped frequently at the mirror shop and home of a couple named Galant, in Roubaix. There Cole met Maurice Van de Kerckhove, still a *convoyeur* in Huyge's escape line. Though the Galants admired Cole, Van de Kerckhove found him "unsavory." But Cole's authority was such that Van de Kerckhove had to swallow his distrust and cooperate with the Cockney—though at arm's length. Henri Duprez also felt uncomfortable in dealing with Cole, though as yet this had not yet crystallized into overt suspicion. The "instinctual distrust" that he felt at their first encounter steadily increased. Cole was an *enjoleur*, a silver-tongued manipulator who was too clever by half.

Only much later did Roland Lepers fully appreciate the skill with which Cole had manipulated those following him. Lepers entered Cole's charmed circle in October 1940 and became an aide-de-camp of sorts to the freelance agent. "He knew how to show modesty," said Lepers. "I never saw him brag about being a big shot or anything. But by his attitude, and by not hiding that he was British, he would imply that he was a hero. But he wouldn't say, 'I'm a hero.' He was smarter than that."

Lepers wanted to join the France Combattante movement of Charles de Gaulle in London and hoped Cole would help him get to England. Eighteen years old, enthusiastic and solidly built, Lepers accompanied Cole around northern France. This resolved the Cockney's linguistic problem and perfectly suited the younger man who, Voglimacci realized, was "dazzled" by Cole and "followed him everywhere." A romantic figure in his young assistant's eyes, Cole had sixteen years advantage in age and a lifetime of experience in deception.

Cole met with François Duprez and other local conspirators in the small, simply furnished apartment over Voglimacci's beauty salon. French helpers and British escapers alike could arrive at this commercial address without attracting undue attention. Continual comings and goings at Cole's house in the tiny rue de la Gare soon would have provoked interest by the German secret police.

The salon was also a reassuring point of reference for women from around La Madeleine, a place where confidences could be exchanged. It was to Voglimacci that Madame Tisserand, Cole's neighbor in the rue de la Gare, had first come for advice in the summer of 1940. "Oh Jeannine," she cried, "I have an Englishman in my house!"

A great beauty and a level-headed businesswoman, Jeannine Voglimacci, thirty-six, supported herself and her son Marc with the earnings from the small shop. Her husband Jean had been taken prisoner in 1940. After his repatriation a year later he joined the Vichy Armistice Army. While François Duprez became the main source of counterfeit documents for the British escapers, Voglimacci saw to their accommodation, nourishment, and dress. Her shop provided a steady supply of women willing to shelter British escapers in their homes for weeks or even months.

Soon after meeting Cole, she brought the Cockney together with Madame Tisserand's Englishman above her shop and thereby helped set in motion the neighborhood conspiracy. She was drawn deeper into it that October, when a friend of Lepers asked her to take in a British pilot on the run. J. W. Phillips had been shot down over the Pas de Calais during a reconnaissance flight and captured by the Germans. When the leg he broke in the crash had mended sufficiently, he escaped from a military hospital in Lille by riding out the front gate on a bicycle, disguised as a nun. He remained over Voglimacci's shop until the beginning of 1941.

◆ ◆ ◆

BY THAT AUTUMN Cole developed a network of helpers extending all the way to the Channel coast through the Pas de Calais district. BEF stragglers had always been thick on the ground in this area. Now RAF pilots were crash-landing or parachuting there with increasing regularity.

In September 1940 the Battle of Britain was reaching its peak. On the 15th of that month came a critical turning point in favor of England. Six hundred British and German fighter planes disputed the airspace over London, the primary target for a flight of one hundred Luftwaffe bombers on a daylight raid. Hundreds more were engaged in combat over southern England. Inevitably, on this and other days, British pilots would be downed over French soil as they chased the bombers back to their Continental bases.

Many came to earth around Saint-Omer, a metal and textiles center twenty miles south of Dunkirk. Those who were not immediately captured by the Germans were taken in hand by Alfred Lanselle, commercial director of a grocery supply company doing business throughout the region. He in turn was forwarding the evaders to Cole.

The two had first met in 1939, when the Cockney was still in British uniform and the Frenchman was stationed at Calais with a French Army antiaircraft battery. Lanselle was a great admirer of the British: "After all," he reasoned, "they had come to France to defend us." He made a point of chatting with his cross-Channel allies whenever possible. On one occasion in November 1939, he exchanged views with the amiable Sergeant Cole in the Café Metropole, one in a row of brasseries off Lille's Grande-Place.

After the defeat, Lanselle had put the Saint-Omer food-supply company back on its feet, traveling frequently to Lille. One day in September 1940, he was in the Café Chopin on the boulevard de la Liberté, behind the train station. To his surprise and delight, he noticed Cole huddled in the corner over a beer. Rushing over to renew his acquaintance with the Cockney, Lanselle ended up by volunteering his services.

The Frenchman already was concealing British evaders. After the Battle of France was over, there were between two and three hundred British soldiers in homes around Saint-Omer. Most people kept them for just a few days, then shifted them to other hiding places. Lanselle kept a few in his own home until he could pass them off to Cole.

For his food deliveries Lanselle had obtained an English army truck from the German *Kommandantur* in Saint-Omer with the well-placed bribe of a kilogram of coffee. Along with canned goods, he packed British escapers into the lorry to shuttle them around the region. On one occasion he carried no fewer than seventeen fugitives to the Gare de Lille, where they caught the first of many trains on their voyage south. But that was later, once Cole's network was fully operational. For the moment it was simply a matter of placing the Britons in secure hiding places.

It was no longer a simple matter to dispatch this growing number of escapers to Marseilles. German control of movement between the forbidden and the occupied zones had tightened since the days when Huyge sent off gangs of Tommies equipped with the most rudimentary of documents, train tickets, and sacks of food. Escapers now needed credible false identity cards and travel documents, presentable civilian clothing and shoes, train tickets, money, and lamplighters to show them the way and deal with inquisitive officials.

Word of Voglimacci's salon had spread. Far too many British fugitives were arriving to be accommodated in the immediate Lille region. Many were sent out to the coal-mining town of Burbure, twenty-eight miles southwest of La Madeleine, where Cole had found families willing to lodge the men until their passage south was arranged.

His two principal helpers there were a young schoolteacher named Fernand Salingue and a coal miner, Drotais Dubois. Salingue became involved late in the summer of 1940, when an RAF pilot crashed near Burbure and was taken in hand by Dubois. The pilot spoke no French, and the burly miner spoke no English. Salingue was called upon to translate and ended up directing the local network.

Salingue taught at a primary school in Lillers, a larger town on the rail line running into Lille. He traveled frequently to La Madeleine to collect pilots and soldiers, escorting them back and distributing them to local families. He was helped in this by a Burbure brewer named Marcel Rousseaux, who moved British evaders in an empty beer barrel on the back of his delivery truck. Over the following months nearly two hundred escapers were to be handled by Cole's associates in the small farming and mining village.

◆ ◆ ◆

COLE INSPIRED CONFIDENCE in the Salingues, who believed he had been sent by the British to coordinate escape and evasion in the north of France. But they knew little else beyond that. Cole came and went in his own time for his own reasons. He was known to most of the people he employed as "Monsieur Paul."

Cole's work took him through the entire region. He was stitching together a complex network covering thousands of square miles, staffed by dozens of local coordinators and scores of others involved to lesser degrees. Cole recruited and encouraged these workers, simultaneously briefing and reassuring the Britons, determining what they lacked in the way of money, documents, or clothing. With him he carried a camera, snapping each man's photograph for papers to be worked up by François Duprez.

Cole's personal life, like his professional activity, was flourishing. He was acquiring a reputation as a womanizer, even if some failed to see the attraction. The identity photograph taken of Cole during his first months underground showed a gaunt, cheerless figure with horn-rimmed glasses and hair parted down the middle and slicked to either side, wearing a sweater with no shirt under a shapeless wool jacket. The only stylish touch was a handkerchief in the breast pocket.

But his wardrobe improved a few months after that picture was taken. Near the end of 1940, a tailor came to Voglimacci's shop and measured Cole for a new two-piece suit. Lepers was also fitted for clothes that would lend him respectability during the long train voyages through occupied France.

Cole also obtained an automobile that fall, a black Peugeot 302 sedan. He now could get around the region more easily than by riding the clattering streetcars or pedaling a bicycle over the cobbled highways of the north. In it, he transported evaders and delivered black-market food supplies for the fugitives living in widely scattered homes. It was important to provide food to the French families sheltering British escapers, so that deprivation would not be added to the considerable danger.

By December 1940, the pieces were falling into place. The Roubaix printer Jean Chevalier, a veteran of World War I, was running off blanks for the documents escapers needed to reach Marseilles. François Duprez completed these by applying the requisite official stamps and supplying birth certificates from the files of his town hall and others in the region. Henri Duprez, Jeannine Voglimacci, and others raised money for train fares and other travel expenses. Roland Lepers and other *convoyeurs* were ready to escort the Englishmen to the south.

After months of careful preparation, Cole's consolidated escape network was ready to swing into operation.

◆ ◆ ◆

ON CHRISTMAS DAY, Cole, Madeleine Deram, and her son crossed the rue de la Gare to dine with the Duprez family. But a few days later, they moved to new quarters around the corner from Voglimacci's shop. The owners of the small house in the rue de la Gare had returned, long after fleeing in May 1940. Cole's activities from then on would be carried on from the semidetached brick-and-stone house at 55 avenue Bernadette. It faced the grounds of a large estate rather than another row of houses, assuring an added degree of privacy. The garage underneath would conceal clandestine arrivals and departures.

At this new address, eight soldiers and airmen gathered on January 6 to begin their journey south escorted by Roland Lepers and two other young Frenchmen. Despite New Year's hopes, it was an inauspicious time to be setting out. Travel was complicated by official restrictions and made rigorous by the weather conditions. All of Europe was locked in a cold wave. There were heavy snowfalls in the south of France, Spain, and Portugal. Subzero temperatures prevailed in the northern half of France.

The war news was little better. French papers like the *Echo du Nord* hammered away on German propaganda themes. The German military communiqué, a regular feature on the front page, stated that Bristol Avonmouth, from which Cole embarked in 1939, had been attacked the night before by powerful Luftwaffe bomber formations. A prominent headline reported that "London's City Is No More than a Pile of Rubble."

Intent on rejoining that larger battle, the group of evaders rode southeast by train for about seventy-five miles to the Demarcation

Line between the Forbidden and Occupied zones, then set out on foot. The discomfort of the low temperature was offset by the ease with which the eleven men rushed across a frozen canal serving as a border between the two zones.

In Paris, Lepers led the group to a seedy hotel near the Les Halles market district. The clandestine travelers spent their first night on the road without the obligation of police formalities. The normal clientele of the Hôtel Nicolas Flamel consisted of out-of-pocket transients and prostitutes with their clients. The next morning they set out for Tours, the cathedral city 150 miles to the southwest. Lepers knew of a village called Saint-Martin-le-Beau, nine miles up the Cher River from Tours, where they could cross into Vichy France with relative ease.

Saint-Martin-le-Beau overlooked a mile-wide flood plain leading down to the fast-moving Cher. Leaving the other ten in a café near the train station, Lepers hiked through winter-bound fields to the river boundary between occupied and unoccupied France. Along the riverbank, he struck up conversation with a man who agreed to row the men across the river.

After crossing later that night, they walked for hours in the darkness to pick up a local train to the regional center of Châteauroux, where they could board a long-distance train heading for Marseilles.

◆　◆　◆

AFTER ARRIVING in the southern port, Lepers became uncertain of his next step. The Britons sought assistance at the American Consulate, where an official advised them to return the following day. Twenty-four hours later, they had located a British secret organization and bade Lepers farewell.

Yet the Frenchman lingered on, hoping to persuade the British to help him reach England. The men in the convoy mentioned his case to the unknown British agents and within a few days he was bidden to a café rendezvous.

The man who awaited him was a beefy, rubicund Englishman

with a pencil-thin, gray mustache. He introduced himself as Captain Murphy. But he was more widely known in Marseilles by the name of Murchie. Lepers had no doubt that the man represented British intelligence; Murchie looked every inch the part of an old India hand.

The young Frenchman related his group's progress from Lille, and Murchie listened attentively as Lepers explained his desire to reach London. But the captain had other plans for him. He explained that he had lived in the north of France as a reserve officer, working at a golf course near Lille. His wife was still there. Could Lepers bring her to Marseilles?

This was not what Lepers wanted to hear. But Murchie was his only link with the British. Under these circumstances, he could hardly refuse. Two weeks later, having reunited the Murchies, Lepers was summoned back to the Marseilles café. With Murchie this time was a tall Scot who introduced himself as Captain Ian Garrow.

Once again Lepers asked to go to London. Once more the British officers put him off.

"We can send you to England if you want," Garrow told him. "But they don't need you in England; you're young, and you don't have any qualifications."

He continued: "If you know the organization in Lille, why don't you continue bringing down the men we need—especially pilots who have been shot down in the north?"

It was not easy to refuse Garrow, who impressed Lepers as "a very calm man, *un gentleman*." After Lepers had made several trips, it was agreed, he might continue down the line to England. More enthusiastic, Lepers began to brief the two officers on the network in La Madeleine.

"I know an Englishman who is working for the Resistance," Lepers told them. "I think it would be good for you to get to know him."

"Bring him along," said Garrow, who was impressed to learn Cole had secured an automobile. He instructed Lepers to bring the Cockney down on his next trip and gave the young man ten thousand francs expense money.

Cole and Lepers made another trip to Marseilles in February and met with Ian Garrow. The Cockney introduced himself as Sergeant Paul Cole, foreswearing the higher ranks he had assumed in the north. He took pains to make a good impression on the sober-minded Scotsman. It was not hard to cook up a plausible explanation of how he had been left behind in France; it had happened to so many people.

Persuaded of the Londoner's good credentials, Garrow named Cole chief of the line's operations in the north and gave him another ten thousand francs. Lepers, he said, was to work under his instructions. There is no way of knowing exactly what went through Cole's mind as he joined the Garrow Organization and returned to the service of the Crown. But the confidence man in him most likely took satisfaction in knowing that the elaborate fiction he had fashioned over the previous months in La Madeleine now had become, improbably, a reality.

7

"A Great Devil of a Scotsman"

AS COLE'S TRAIN rolled north to Lille through a France in the hold of winter and the Third Reich, the wad of banknotes in his pocket must have inspired some rapid calculations as to how he might obtain more. But to assume that the Cockney was moved by no more than the desire for personal gain in his new assignment would be taking a too narrow view of his personality. He had a surpassing weakness for other people's money, it is true. His knowledge of the ten thousand francs Lepers had received no doubt influenced his acceptance of the Scot's commission.

But the stirring of some vestigial sense of patriotism cannot be ruled out. Perhaps too, Cole took satisfaction that his talent for guile and dissimulation, which once had earned him nothing but time behind bars, now qualified him eminently for service as a British secret agent.

Captain Ian G. Garrow was out of a very different mold. This towering Glaswegian with a bluff, almost homely Scottish face, noted one contemporary, "reconciled dour determination with quick intelligence and immense reserves of strength." In peacetime he had been a reserve officer in the Fifty-first Highland Division, a respected territorial formation. After the BEF had departed from Dunkirk, he and the Fifty-first fought its way to the port of Le Havre. But the collapse of a French corps nearby obliged it to surrender at Saint-Valery-en-Caux. Garrow and a small group of Highlanders slipped through the German net around the Normandy fishing port and reached Marseilles.

With his substantial inner resources, Garrow probably could have reached Spain or North Africa as other British military were doing amid the general disorder in France. But a scrupulous sense of duty prompted him to remain in France. There were many Highlanders still in Marseilles in need of leadership.

With several hundred other British officers and troops, he was interned in the Fort Saint-Jean, one of two massive sandstone fortresses looming over the entrance to the Vieux Port. Those entering this former Foreign Legion depot could read the heartening words inscribed on the escutcheon: "You have asked for death, I will give it to you." But conditions were less than rigorous. Internees were free to leave the fort after 5:00 P.M. British upper ranks parlayed their rations into cash which, combined with their personal resources, enabled them to live outside the Port.

Garrow took a hotel room near the Gare Saint Charles, the main train station dominating a hilltop over the port. Evacuating the British military fell initially to the ranking officer, a Northumberland Regiment captain named Fitch. But he moved along and it was left to Garrow to organize the escape of several hundred members of His Britannic Majesty's forces.

One of the Scot's earliest collaborators was Jimmy Langley, a young Coldstream Guards subaltern whose wounds obliged him to stay behind at Dunkirk and eventually cost him his left arm. Langley escaped from a hospital in Lille in October 1940 and, helped by the legendary Widow Samiez, reached Marseilles a week later. Invalided back to England in early 1941, Langley continued to work with Garrow as an officer in British intelligence. Assigned to the MI9 escape and evasion branch, he would play an important role in decisions on using Cole as an agent.

But in Marseilles there was, strictly speaking, no British representation. Relations between France and Great Britain had become poisoned after the defeat. Anglophobia swelled after Britain attacked the French fleet anchored at Mers-el-Kebir, Algeria. The painful preemptive measure was intended to keep the warships from falling into German hands. As a result, the Vichy French refused to allow British consular offices to reopen after the evacuation of May–June 1940.

To fill this void, each of the U.S. Consulates in unoccupied France created a British-interests section. The Marseilles consulate's British wing was directed by a Major Hugh Dodds and his assistant Arthur Dean. They had already inscribed their names in history as the British Foreign Office officials who escorted the Duke and Duchess of Windsor out of France in 1940. Britain's abdicated King Edward VIII and his American divorcée bride Mrs. Wallis Warfield Simpson had lingered dangerously long on the Riviera. Then consuls at Nice and Monte Carlo, respectively, Dodds and Dean saw the couple safely into Spain.

In Marseilles, the two diplomats saw to the "comfort and confidence" of about 3,500 British subjects remaining in France. They also monitored the living conditions of soldiers interned at Fort Saint-Jean. Dodds and Dean provided material comforts to the soldiers interned in the fortress. But they were bound at least initially by an agreement with the U.S. Department of State that they would "in no way whatsoever" help British military personnel leave France.

During 1940, Dodds and Dean appear to have respected American wishes. In January 1941, the Foreign Office would report hearing "a good deal of criticism of Dodds's attitude" toward British escapees. He had, it seems, refused to assist them in exiting France. Similar complaints were voiced about Dean. So in his first months in Marseilles, Garrow was very much on his own.

◆ ◆ ◆

BUT THERE WERE unofficial allies, British and French alike. Garrow recruited these into a secret-service post staffed more by enthusiastic amateurs than seasoned professionals. Word of this might have furrowed the brow of intelligence officials behind their desks in London. But this improvised network functioned admirably well.

Escapers, those who by official definition had broken away from enemy hands, and evaders, who remained at large behind enemy lines, entered the Garrow line through two main channels. One was Le Petit Poucet, a tiny café near the Saint Charles train station.

It was, noted Airey Neave, a Royal Army lieutenant who escaped from the Colditz prison camp in Germany and passed through Marseilles on his way home, "a small neat place with a row of painted tables down each side of a sawdust passage."

The drill was for escapists to take a seat and ask for Gaston Dijon, the proprietor. Neave and another escaper were ushered through double doors at the back into "a square room with a large skylight and ancient furniture upholstered in green silk." Neave and his companion sat down and Dijon demanded the password. "We both repeated it perfectly like a catechism," wrote Neave.

From the Petit Poucet, fugitive Britons were stowed away in private homes, in safe-houses maintained by the network, or in brothels around the Vieux Port. Men were also put in the British and American Seamen's Mission, which served as another main ingress to the line.

The Seamen's Mission had been managed since mid-summer 1940 by Dr. Donald Caskie, a Church of Scotland minister. Before the invasion, Caskie had inveighed against the Nazis from the pulpit of his Scots Kirk in Paris, taking as his text the Biblical verse promising that "they have sown the wind and they shall reap the whirlwind." But in May 1940, the Germans were still busily sowing the wind. Caskie wisely left town a jump or two ahead of them.

Days later he reached Marseilles, filled with the demoralized remnants of the scattered allied armies. Aimlessly walking the boulevards, crowded into the cafés, packed onto streetcars, French Army regulars, Foreign Legion troops, North African spahis, and Senegalese colonials mingled with the British Tommies and their officers.

On the waterfront, Caskie found confusion and hysteria as the mass of soldiers looked for a way out of the port. He observed the hunger, the fatigue, the septic battle wounds, and the downcast faces. "France had fallen, and there was no one to help the British soldiers," he later recalled. Visiting the American Consulate a short distance from the Vieux Port, Caskie agreed to take over the operation of the Seamen's Mission.

The Seamen's Mission was funded openly by the U.S. Consulate. In November 1940, the State Department allotted about two thousand dollars, to relieve the "poor dregs of humanity" lodged there. For official purposes they were destitute seamen of the United States and neutral countries with British Empire affiliations—Indians, Egyptians, Maltese, Palestinians.

But Garrow found the mission well situated as a way-station for British escapers. Caskie housed, fed, clothed, and nursed the men who arrived at his mission "footsore and bleary-eyed from days and nights on the road escaping from Dunkirk." He also offered ping-pong, darts, billiards, English books, magazines, and newspapers, a piano, and a gramophone. Caskie informed their kin in Britain of their safety in telegrams to the Edinburgh offices of the Church of Scotland.

The Presbyterian minister adapted the mission to a more clandestine vocation, building hidey-holes between floor joists, behind cupboards and under the roof. Into these his illegal lodgers scuttled at the alarm of a search by the French police.

The Vichy secret police "knew that the Seamen's Mission was becoming a clearing house for British soldiers in flight out of France," Caskie noted. "As yet they could not prove it."

This constant police pressure would in time reduce the value of the mission to the Garrow organization. Even when Jimmy Langley was in Marseilles, the mission was not known for its tight security. "An hour spent in the club was enough to make me aware of the dangers of discussing any schemes for escape with the inmates," he later wrote. The mission, he concluded, "was only allowed to remain open because it was such an excellent source of information about clandestine British activities."

For this reason, and because Caskie lacked the tight-lipped discretion of a professional agent, Garrow and his men limited their association with the Seamen's Mission. But even under close surveillance it served as a guidepost for escapers arriving with no instructions for contacting the network.

◆ ◆ ◆

MORE IMPORTANT to the line over the long run were two civilian recruits: the Marseilles businessman Louis Nouveau and Dr. Georges Rodocanachi, a French physician of British birth. Nouveau was a successful commodities trader and entrepreneur with distinctive sartorial tastes. "Louis amazed me as soon as I saw him," recalled Neave. "He was slightly built and wore a light gray suit and suede shoes, a silk shirt, and a dark red bowtie with white spots."

A fervent Gaullist, Nouveau was invited one day in December 1940 to take tea at the home of a family that regularly received British officers on parole from Fort Saint-Jean. There Nouveau met "a great devil of a Scotsman with a genial and somewhat round face and a *sacré calme*."

This marked the beginning of an entirely new career for Nouveau. That same evening he invited Garrow and Langley back to his tastefully furnished, fifth-floor apartment overlooking the Vieux Port, for a glass of Scotch whiskey. The officers returned on the following evening and others, for Nouveau "still had whiskey and . . . decided that Monday evenings would be reserved for them."

Garrow did not immediately confide in Nouveau. But their friendship was nourished by good Scotch and congenial talk. Nouveau quickly realized that Garrow was engaged in clandestine matters and offered his assistance. At first this was refused politely, but a sudden financial crisis obliged Garrow to seek the French merchant's help.

Some two million francs in regimental funds had vanished from a trunk in Murchie's hotel room under suspicious circumstances. Nouveau had registered a bad impression of the officer after he showed up one evening with his mistress, a cashier in a Marseilles restaurant. On the night the money disappeared, she claimed to have been waylaid by gunmen in the street and forced to lead them to the hotel strongbox. But her story didn't wash. After this Murchie relinquished authority to the sober-minded Garrow.

The Scot asked Nouveau if he could arrange a loan for the organization, now desperately short of funds. Nouveau immediately supplied 15 thousand francs of his own money and raised another 25 thousand francs from friends. Later he provided the line with another four hundred thousand francs belonging to a British firm with which he had done business in 1940; the funds were reimbursed to the London company by the War Office.

A much larger transfer followed a few months later. The director of a British-owned textile factory in the south of France was known to hold five or six million francs in cash. Negotiations between Marseilles and London allowed this capital to be released to Garrow's organization. Nouveau's role within the organization continued to grow, not only as a financier but as a valued and trusted agent.

Similarly, Dr. Georges Rodocanachi, sixty-four, provided indispensable help to Garrow's struggling network when every hand seemed against it. Born in England of Greek parents, Rodocanachi studied medicine in Paris. For legal reasons he could not serve in the Royal Army Medical Corps when the First World War broke out. Ardently desiring front-line duty, he turned in his British passport and swore allegiance to France so that he could join the French Army's medical service. Rodocanachi was wounded twice and gassed once, winning seven decorations and inscription in the Legion of Honor.

In 1939 he was appointed by the American consul in Marseilles to examine refugees seeking entry to the United States. By late 1940 the elderly physician was also treating the British soldiers in the Seamen's Mission and the Fort Saint-Jean. He began to invite British officers to his home on a social basis as well.

His wife, Fanny Rodocanachi, fifty-six, had been born a French citizen but was raised in England. Tall, thin, and elegant, she struck one British escaper as "a typical Victorian lady." On his first night in her home, "she came in all dressed up as if she was in Buckingham Palace" and requested he take her in to dinner. The meal consisted of nothing more than a few sandwiches.

Later Rodocanachi was appointed U.S. representative on the Medical Repatriation Board run by the Vichy authorities. He could tip the balance in borderline cases, and some wounded British soldiers and officers went home legally to fight another day. His wife noted that he called upon "all the old fraudulent and ingenious systems" for avoiding duty that he had detected in World War I. The physician drew up medical files in which he had "cleverly contrived to simulate disease and physical disabilities."

Rodocanachi's involvement with Garrow came about through a woman named Elizabeth Haden-Guest, a Jew and Communist militant of Baltic origins, who fled Germany in the early 1930s. Imprisoned at Besançon, France, after the German invasion, she escaped to Marseilles. The U.S. Consulate referred her to Rodocanachi after her young son Anthony became ill.

The enthusiastic but unconventional Haden-Guest at times shocked the staid Louis Nouveau. He noted with disapproval that she lived in a neighborhood of ill repute, while around Marseilles her son's enormous Mexican straw hat "prevented her from going unnoticed." Yet he saw that Haden-Guest was "devoted body and soul to Ian Garrow."

She confided in Rodocanachi about the Garrow escape line and asked for his assistance. Garrow, reluctant to endanger the Rodocanachis, had hesitated to do this. Rodocanachi immediately offered Garrow the use of his apartment in the rue Roux de Brignoles close to the Vieux Port.

This was of immeasurable value. The line's officers could meet in security and escapers could be hidden there until their time came to proceed down the line to Spain. Garrow maintained a fifth-floor room at the Grand Hôtel de Noailles for such purposes, but that was only a stopgap measure. The sprawling, ten-room Rodocanachi apartment and office complex provided an ideal cover for arrivals and departures.

House rules were established with security in mind. Windows were opened and closed only by the Rodocanachi's elderly maid. Toilet flushing and bath draining were held to a strict minimum. Mild English or American cigarettes were never to be smoked in halls or on the stone staircase, which was used in preference to the ancient and incommodious elevator.

In early 1941 the French government bowed to Axis pressure and transferred all the interned British troops out of Marseilles. They were sent northeast, to an old military barracks called Saint-Hippolyte-du-Fort, near Nîmes. Garrow had gotten wind of this move and went permanently off limits. On the day when the British rolled out of Marseilles singing "It's a Long Way to Tipperary," the Scots captain was ensconced in a small back bedroom of the Rodocanachi apartment.

The relatively simple early days of the Garrow organization ended as its commanding officer went underground. More than ever, Garrow needed reliable lieutenants. He believed he had found one in his new northern agent, Sergeant Paul Cole.

8

"The Antithesis of the Scarlet Pimpernel"

COLE SEEMED to live up to Garrow's best hopes in the months following his appointment as the line's northern chief. There was no shortage of men in the north awaiting transport. The mechanisms of his La Madeleine network, well-oiled through long preparation, moved all the faster for the sudden infusion of British funds. Presently Cole and Lepers were escorting a convoy of British servicemen to the south every fortnight or so.

Cole now had established an important new link in the chain of helpers extending from north to south. One of the great difficulties had been to leave the Forbidden Zone. Its southern boundary in part was delineated by the Somme River, which passed through the city of Abbeville, near the coast. Cole's organization had recruited a twenty-nine-year-old priest there named the Abbé Pierre Carpentier. With his help the Somme crossing became a routine matter.

Carpentier, a French Army chaplain, had been deeply angered by the defeat, and entered the Resistance under the cover of his work as vicar at the Church of Saint Gilles. He realized that Abbeville was uniquely situated to serve as a crossing point into the Occupied

Zone. Residents of Abbeville could cross the Somme with little difficulty once they had obtained an *Ausweiss*, a transit pass, from the
local German Kommandantur.

The *Ausweiss*, borrowed from a local resident, carried the name of
the bearer but no photograph. It had to be presented to the German
sentries on the bridges along with a French national identity card,
which Carpentier could manufacture in the study of his red-brick
home behind the church.

Identity card blanks were available in any stationer's. The requisite
gummed tax stamps were sold at every *tabac*, or café tobacconist's.
The priest duplicated the rubber stamp normally applied by the
mayor's office and learned to forge the town official's signature. All
that was required then was to apply an escaper's photo.

Once a group of British escapers was across, they dropped the
passes into the mailbox of a farm supplier whose business and home
were located along the south bank of the Somme. Then the escapers and their guides continued to Paris from the red-brick, gothic
Abbeville train station standing a few hundred yards south of the
Pont de la Gare, the main bridge into the Occupied Zone.

* * *

HAROLD COLE's efficient management of the northern escape network
earned him favor in Garrow's eyes. Garrow had plenty of other
matters on his mind in that spring of 1941. He never thought to
challenge Cole's bona fides so long as British escapers continued to
show up at Le Petit Poucet and the Seamen's Mission.

But in Marseilles, the new agent was acquiring a mixed reputation.
Cole got off on the wrong foot with Nancy Wake Fiocca, a young
and attractive Australian journalist whose marriage to a wealthy
Marseilles businessman enabled her to provide money, shelter, and
otherwise assist the Garrow Organization. One afternoon, when Fiocca
returned to her apartment, the maid informed her that Captain
Garrow and another man were awaiting her in the living room. She
took "an instant dislike" to Cole, who slouched in a leather armchair

as Garrow sat at a desk writing. "He looked, and was, very common, and did not bother to stand up when we were introduced."

Cole was sipping a glass of whiskey. Fiocca became angry when she realized his drink had come from a large bottle, until then unopened, that stood on the mantelpiece. The oversized flacon of Scotch was not to have been cracked until the day of Allied victory. She banished the Cockney from her apartment.

Donald Caskie, meeting the new agent for the first time that April, remarked on Cole's tendency to indulge in exaggeration and bravado. "He was always on the defensive," recorded Caskie, "the difficulties of the journey he had made were as nothing, he proclaimed." Caskie was not the only one to comment on the Cockney's penchant for bombast. Louis Nouveau made a similar observation after Garrow brought Cole to his apartment.

Seated on the couch in the Nouveaus' living room, Cole related a narrow escape from the German police during a voyage back to the north. "Only by kicking a German in the groin and rapidly disguising himself in blue workingman's clothes on the outskirts of some big city had he saved himself." The tale, Nouveau had to concede, was "almost well-told." But Cole lacked the force of persuasion and merely came across as a transparent liar.

Surrounded by authentic British officers was Cole overcome by feelings of inferiority and insecurity? It was one thing to pass himself off as a British officer to the French. Most were incapable of distinguishing the Cockney accent that in Britain would instantly have betrayed him. But Garrow and the other officers in Marseilles would have made short work of such pretensions.

From his prewar humiliation at Aix-les-Bains, Cole had learned the consequences of trying to gull those equipped to see through his guise. Yet he was still driven by the powerful need to be someone other than who he was.

◆　◆　◆

YET THE reputation he sought as a daring and resourceful agent was not entirely undeserved. For all of his braggadocio in Marseilles, Cole's exploits in the north were becoming the stuff of legend.

One time he and Deram had been struggling to move a heavy stove into their home on the avenue Bernadette. Never one for exertion, Cole rushed out in the street and displayed his handicapped certificate to some German soldiers passing by. They hoisted the stove up the stairs for him.

On another occasion Cole's Peugeot broke down while François Duprez was driving six or seven British escapers to the Lille train station. It appeared certain that the fugitives would miss their train. Cole leaped out and ran into the Renault dealership on the boulevard, which then housed a German motor pool. Cole, dressed in boots and a black leather coat, talked the Germans into towing them several miles to the station. The escapers hurried to catch their train while Cole dismissed their German benefactors.

Voglimacci, who admired Cole's flair and audacity, was personally in his debt. In June 1941, her husband Jean had been repatriated to Vichy France from a German prisoner-of-war camp. Voglimacci asked Cole to help her travel south to see him. The next day he came by at 5:00 A.M. with a tandem bicycle to pick her up. They pedaled to the Lille marketplace, where truck drivers were delivering produce. Cole had arranged with one trucker to smuggle the hairdresser south in the back of his cab.

Later Jean Voglimacci traveled illegally to the north, and Cole escorted him back to Marseilles. That trip was marred by an incident in a Paris restaurant, when Cole nearly got into a scrap with some Anglophobic Frenchmen at a nearby table. The Parisians, loyal to Vichy, had overheard English being spoken at Cole's table and made insulting remarks. Cole seemed ready to fight, but the proprietor intervened. Voglimacci and a British pilot followed the Cockney through several rail yards between Paris and Marseilles, witnessing Cole's extensive contacts among the trainmen. By the time they arrived in the southern port Voglimacci was full of admiration for this "improvisationist who would take any risk at all."

♦ ♦ ♦

COLE'S NERVE also impressed the British soldiers and pilots he led between the English Channel and the Mediterranean. Among them was Sergeant-Pilot F. W. "Taffy" Higginson, a Welsh RAF flier shot down over the Pas de Calais in June 1941. Higginson found the Cockney both courageous and charming. After several days' rigorous travel through enemy territory in the man's company, he concluded that "Cole was nothing but good."

Higginson was collected by the line's rural helpers after his plane crashed in the fields of the Pas de Calais. He spent several days at Cole's house on the avenue Bernadette in La Madeleine. Cole stood him up in the back garden and took his picture for false identity documents. When these had been prepared by François Duprez, the two men left for Marseilles.

The first leg of the voyage took them to Abbeville, where Higginson met the Padre Carpentier. The cleric pulled his forging equipment and supplies out of a wall safe and whipped up a pass for the flier. Cole and his charge crossed the line successfully and reached Paris, spending the night in a brothel in Les Halles.

Higginson was leery of these disreputable quarters. Before he went to sleep, the airman securely chained the door of his room, and on awakening confirmed that he had not been robbed in the night. He was carrying a change of socks and his money in a briefcase; these were unmolested. He pocketed the cash and repaired to the toilet in the hall for his morning ablutions. But when he returned to the room, he was dismayed to find that his money was missing.

The pilot retraced his steps to a dank water closet down the hall. This was equipped not with a toilet seat, but a "Turkish toilet," consisting of a porcelain hole in the floor flanked by two foot-plates. The user was obliged to crouch precariously while attempting to keep his trousers clear of the affair. While negotiating this primitive plumbing, Higginson had dropped his folding money into the filthy pit.

Setting delicacy aside, he fished the bills out, washed them, and laid the money in the sun in his room to dry. "We're going to be delayed for a while," he told Cole, explaining the mishap. They spent another night in the brothel and continued on their way to Marseilles.

The next stop was Tours, which had become the line's major jumping-off point into Vichy France. Higginson already stood in admiration of Cole's ingenuity, but his opinion was to rise even further following their crossing of the Demarcation Line.

◆ ◆ ◆

FROM SAINT-MARTIN-LE-BEAU, the two men walked along the Cher River to a farmhouse, where they were rowed across the stream by a peasant woman. But on the southern bank, a German officer accompanied by a sergeant accosted Cole and Higginson. The two Germans, seated in a café by a destroyed bridge, had observed the two Englishmen crossing the Cher.

Higginson was sure this meant disaster. He spoke barely any French. Cole seemed a dead giveaway, with his ginger hair and plus-four trousers better suited to a round of golf than this cloak-and-dagger business.

"Petrified and perspiring like mad" on this hot June day, Higginson could not keep his mind from turning to the revolver and incriminating documents in Cole's briefcase. The airman tried to keep a deranged glint in his eye, in keeping with his false identity as a French soldier discharged for insanity.

Cole took the offensive and started haranguing the Germans. "Look," he exclaimed indignantly. "You take us to the *Kommandantur*, and I'll report you for drinking in my aunt's café. That's my aunt's café up there. Come on!" Higginson could tell Cole's French was abominable, but neither of the two Germans appeared to notice.

The German NCO eyed Higginson suspiciously. "Look!" he told his superior. "He's not saying anything. He's an Englishman!" The officer examined Higginson's identity papers and satisfied himself that the flier was indeed a mad *poilu*. But the sergeant persistently challenged Higginson's papers.

The officer now demanded to see the contents of Higginson's briefcase, which included, along with the airman's dirty socks, a large bar of unwrapped French chocolate.

"I turned out my briefcase," relates Higginson, "and of course the heat of my body and the sun had melted the chocolate."

Cole seized the moment. "Look!" he said to the Germans. "I told you he was a fool." The four men examined the dark, glutinous mess in Higginson's portfolio.

"Look!" the Cockney exclaimed. "He's shat in his briefcase!"

Cole understood the power of suggestion. The German officer averted his gaze in disgust and ordered Higginson out of his sight. The flier happily complied and hid in a copse of trees down the road. Cole came along in a quarter of an hour and they continued to Marseilles without further incident.

◆ ◆ ◆

HEARING SUCH TESTIMONY from escapers, Garrow sent highly favorable reports about Cole to Major Donald Darling, his superior based in Lisbon. Darling, stationed in the Portuguese capital since July 1940 on behalf of British Intelligence, was trying to rebuild communications into Europe and re-establish Continental networks dismantled after the Germans overran the Low Countries and France. He also assisted and oversaw the lines funneling escapers south from the Netherlands and Belgium through France and Spain to the British enclave of Gibraltar.

Darling had established regular communications with Garrow, who by now was operating under the orders of MI9, the intelligence branch created in late December 1939 to aid the escape or evasion from enemy capture of British military personnel.

Peering at the distant battle from his outpost in Lisbon, Darling depended on dispatches from Garrow and occasional debriefings of escapers for his view of operations inside France. He soon became concerned about Paul Cole: there was something about this Cockney sergeant which, despite Garrow's superlatives, seemed amiss.

"He was, according to all reports, the antithesis of the Scarlet Pimpernel," Darling later wrote. "Wearing plus-fours and a pork-pie hat, speaking rudimentary French with a Cockney accent, it seemed incredible that he was not questioned and arrested by the Germans."

Darling concedes that in the first months of occupation, border guards and railway inspectors were as unsophisticated as the British soldiers moving by trial and error to Marseilles and Spain. "The rank and file of neither side spoke French," wrote Darling, "and it was not difficult . . . to bluff one's way past German sentries at check points and railway stations."

But Darling remained skeptical about Cole and sent a coded telegram to London asking for advice. Inquiries surely had been made in higher quarters about this sergeant who was piling up such an admirable record in France. But Darling's superiors merely informed him they thought Cole had "a sporting chance of getting away with it for a while."

Darling repeatedly requested his London controllers to make inquiries into the background and character of agent Cole, who "seemed too good to be true." The lack of any response from British intelligence, Darling concludes, seemed "tantamount to telling me to mind my own business."

This was a critical juncture in Cole's career as a British secret agent. He had hoodwinked the French and bluffed his way into the Garrow Organization. The lives of numerous French helpers had been placed in his hands.

It was incumbent upon MI9 and its superior service, MI6, to examine him more closely once Garrow had taken him aboard. The London headquarters of MI6 had every means of determining exactly who "Paul Cole" really was. SIS had full access to Scotland Yard and police files; Cole's photograph could easily have been identified by the escapers he had helped back to England.

The only possible conclusion we may reach is that British Intelligence had indeed decided to give Cole a "sporting chance." But this meant withholding information on Cole's criminal past from Ian Garrow, the officer most in need of such crucial information.

As a calculated risk on the part of intelligence higher-ups, this course of action might have been defended. All signs from inside France were that Cole had turned over a new leaf and was doing an outstanding job. But Cole had seemingly reformed on other occasions before reverting to type and engaging in further crimes. This new leaf would remain unblotted no longer than any of the others Cole had gone through in the past.

9

"Rumor, Suspicion, and Intrigue"

THE SUMMER of 1941 brought a flowering of Garrow's line, which by then had set down deeper roots in Marseilles and thrown off shoots in all directions. His agents were moving ever more soldiers and airmen from northern France into Spain. But this growth came only after a period of testing and heavy pressure brought on the Seamen's Mission that spring by the French police at the behest of their masters in Vichy and Berlin.

The network, and in particular Caskie's ramshackle mission, became dangerously exposed. The incessant searches, interrogations, and harassment by Vichy police agents soon flared up into a diplomatic imbroglio involving Great Britain, France, and the United States.

Even the neutral American consul, Hugh S. Fullerton, forty-eight, former first secretary of the Paris Embassy, remarked the "rumor, suspicion, and intrigue with which we are surrounded." Fullerton, writing to a London colleague, expressed anxiety over Caskie's involvement in British escapes. The United States was shortly to enter a half-alliance with Great Britain, providing arms and supplies under the Lend-Lease Act. But neutrality was still the State Department watchword.

"British secret-service agents are, of course, active in unoccupied France," wrote Fullerton. "Such agents ... must have no association whatever with our American officers charged with British interests."

Major Dodds apparently took this injunction to heart. In early March he went to Fullerton "in great anxiety to say that he had been told by Major Sawyer, a British subject who resides in Nice and was temporarily in Marseilles, that the latter had turned over a sum of 850 thousand francs to the Reverend Donald Caskie."

Dodds was "a little vague as to the origin of these funds." But Fullerton had sources of his own on the Riviera. He discovered that Sawyer had received large sums of money from Switzerland. Also, Major Sawyer and another Briton had been heard to swear that they would "under no circumstances ever allow themselves to be repatriated to England as they were remaining on the Riviera under orders of the British War Office."

Fullerton summoned Caskie to the consulate the following day. The clergyman "admitted with some embarrassment that he had the money and was at first inclined to hold onto it." Caskie also confessed that from time to time he had given money to British soldiers and civilians to help them escape into Spain. Fullerton warned that if this large sum of money were found in Caskie's possession, the consequences would be severe. The mission would probably be shut down.

Shaken, Caskie returned two days later to tell Fullerton he believed he had been victimized by Garrow and Murchie. They "came in to his mission and used it as a rendez-vous and were responsible for the activities there of which the police were complaining." Caskie, Fullerton noted, was "obviously frightened and thought that he might be made to suffer while the others made off before any actual arrests were made." The minister told Fullerton he had confided the 850 thousand francs to a priest who would return the money to Sawyer in Nice. The matter was dropped.

♦ ♦ ♦

THE AMERICAN CONSUL's concern grew, however, as he heard rumors that not only Caskie but his own British staff were in the escape business up to their necks. On March 6 he decided to call on the police and "make suitable inquiries."

The chief authority in Marseilles was a naval officer with the unwieldy name of Commandant Antoine Geoffrey Rodellec de Porzic. The story went that when he was announced to Pétain in Vichy, the *maréchal* instructed: "Show them in one by one." Fullerton was ushered into Rodellec de Porzic's office at half past four that afternoon and learned "it was quite true that Mr. Caskie was in hot water." The commandant also told Fullerton that Dodds and Dean were suspected of supplying identity papers to French Army deserters.

Glossing over this latter allegation, Fullerton assumed a tone of injured dignity. "If the French authorities had any doubts about the mission or anybody in it," he said, "the reasonable procedure would be to have the place and its occupants watched." Rodellec de Porzic backed down, assuring Fullerton that he "had not meant to convey in his conversation that the American authorities were in any way to blame for any illegal activities which might have been going on in the mission."

Fullerton again took refuge in a disingenuity that probably did not fool Rodellec de Porzic. "I suggested," Fullerton noted, "that the police must be aware that there were a good many British secret service agents in this part of France and must know who they were, and I said I wondered . . . why the police did not round up the soldiers in the Mission and around Marseilles and elsewhere and send them up to Saint-Hippolyte-du-Fort."

Their interview was adjourned until March 20. By then the crisis had deepened and Rodellec de Porzic invited Fullerton back for another "discussion of the scandal which has threatened the British Seamen's Mission."

The commandant said Caskie "had been a tool and a victim of

more designing minds," adding that the Mission "was of course under the very closest observation." Fullerton knew this well; the establishment had been raided three times in the previous ten days.

Then Rodellec de Porzic voiced stronger suspicions of Dodds and Dean, alleging their involvement in escape activities. Fullerton stiffened and objected. If the police could produce any solid evidence against any of his staff, he promised, they would be removed. The mollified Rodellec de Porzic then hinted darkly at the true source of French agitation.

"There were," he assured Fullerton, "a great many German agents in this part of France and the German government was very accurately informed as to what was going on."

◆ ◆ ◆

WHATEVER HIS personal sympathies, Fullerton had a career diplomat's distaste for the covert side of foreign policy, particularly when the policy in question was not even American. "It is quite normal that there should be in this area secret-service agents of His Britannic Majesty's Government," he wrote to Washington. But "that we should in any sense serve as a cover for British secret-service activities is inadmissable."

This precarious situation came to a head in April, when the French government invited Arthur Dean to remove himself from the national territory of Vichy, such as it was. Fullerton told Washington and London that there was "no evidence that Dean has been involved in any activities contrary to French law." But he advised that the Foreign Office employee leave as soon as possible, lest he share the fate of the Belgian and Czech envoys, who had been arrested on similar grounds. By mid-April the British envoy was safely in Spain.

An official in Washington took the philosophical view that "whether or not Dean was involved in any illegal activities" the French may have had, "in view of its position vis-à-vis the Germans, no freedom of choice in the matter."

But Whitehall disagreed and expelled one of France's last diplomats on post in London. The French had to learn, explained the Foreign Office, that "we cannot overlook it when they treat our people just as the Germans suggest merely because the Germans have suggested it."

After the departure of Dean and, soon after, Dodds, a relative diplomatic peace obtained. But in Marseilles conditions worsened, as Fullerton noted in a cable sent to Washington late in June. "Caskie's Seamen's Mission has in recent weeks been the object of renewed suspicion on the part of the police and is frequently raided," he reported, expressing the fear that it might soon have to close.

Then, he added ominously: "Heavy infiltration of German police agents in the Marseilles area and apparently growing pressure on local and prefectoral authorities impose on us increasing circumspection in our conduct of British interests. Please inform London."

10

"We Thought He Had a Mission"

THE SHADOW of the Gestapo did not weigh heavily on Cole, who prospered in Marseilles. The city was strictly controlled by Vichy France, but wartime privation and the peculiarities of life in the Unoccupied Zone fed a vast underground milieu in which mingled corruption and intrigue. In the Vieux Port, illegality was a condition of existence for the good and the bad alike.

Surveying the teeming quarter from his conspiratorial flophouse, Donald Caskie was repelled by the thieves, dope dealers, black market traders, pimps, and other "indescribable brutes" who pursued their vocations of vice in the myriad "cafés, garrets, and remoter hideouts of the district." But this was Cole's element. The Cockney moved effortlessly through this city where high-minded Resistance men rubbed shoulders with the unregenerate thugs of the mob, Vichy officers of uncertain affiliations, and a multitude of foreign agents.

The focus of intrigue was the waterfront. Reduced in maritime activity by a British naval blockade, the port stirred in a different way with its newly acquired industry of espionage. In a dockside restaurant called La Daurade, known for its superior cocktails and cuisine in this time of enforced sobriety and ration tickets, intelligence operatives forgathered to exchange information and cultivate sources.

Its owner, Charles Vincillione, was an influential Corsican mob boss who ran brothels in Marseilles and Paris, traded in black-market commodities, and engaged in other enterprises of varying illegality. His sympathies lay with the underground. This meant that he provided assistance at less-than-ruinous prices or, occasionally, free of charge.

Before Garrow's lines into Spain were fully established, Vincillione had smuggled British soldiers onto outward-bound neutral ships— at a cost of up to eight thousand francs per man. When night had fallen, Vincillione guided the men through the streets of Marseilles to the La Joliette dock area and onto darkened freighters bound for North African ports.

La Daurade was frequently a first stop when Cole arrived with fugitives. Escapers were fed and sometimes lodged at the restaurant. Another patron was U.S. consul Fullerton. The diplomat kept his distance from the likes of Garrow. But he was routinely informed if volunteer American RAF fliers were among the "clothing parcels" passing through town.

By June 1941, Cole was delivering anywhere from five to ten and sometimes more British servicemen at intervals of ten days to two weeks. Now the emphasis had been put on retrieving aviators, whose costly training and hard-won combat experience made their replacement difficult and recovery essential. But BEF troops continued to account for a significant share of the escapers and evaders.

The Cockney was receiving the lion's share of credit for this accomplishment, but he relied heavily on Lepers and other guides to carry out most of these stressful and physically exhausting expeditions. He was spending more and more of his time in Marseilles. When Lepers arrived with a convoy Cole stepped in to reimburse the French guide's expenses and take charge of the servicemen.

Lepers was not the only *convoyeur* plying the north-south route for Cole. That spring the Cockney had recruited a doughty Scotsman named James Smith. A private in the Gordon Highlanders, Smith had been captured by the Germans in June 1940. But he slipped away from his POW column of march near Brussels and reached northern France. That summer he labored on farms and moved into an abandoned house where a few other Scots were already holed up. When the Germans got wind of their presence the men struck out for the south on bicycles, but had to turn back in the face of tight controls. Smith remained in the Lille area until the beginning of January 1941.

That month one of his French acquaintances set him up with the papers needed to get to Marseilles. He and five other escapers crossed into Vichy France near Tours. But they were soon arrested by the French police and arrived in Marseilles in irons, destined for the internment camp at Saint-Hippolyte-du-Fort. But Smith and his mates escaped when their guards fell asleep while awaiting an early morning train connection in Nîmes. The French officials had been persuaded to remove their prisoners' handcuffs so they could play cards. By February, Smith was right back in the Lille area where he had started from. In April Smith was introduced to Cole.

That May Smith set out for Marseilles with Cole. In the port city Cole introduced Smith to Garrow. "It was agreed," Smith later told British Intelligence, "that I should work for him in helping to get Allied personnel to the U.K. and also to collect any military information I could." In mid-May Smith returned alone to Lille. But by the end of the month he was back in Marseilles with a Polish airman and a British soldier. He also carried airfield plans and other military information.

In early June Smith met with Cole in Lille and introduced him to his contacts in the Resistance. Smith met him ten days later in Marseilles, arriving with a convoy. A traveler of some stamina, Smith brought another convoy to Marseilles later that month, along with various military intelligence. Smith stayed in Marseilles for only four days and headed back north to Lille. But Cole tarried in the port city. What need was there for him to exhaust himself and take risks

Young Harold Cole, the dapper London East End "toff" and confidence man known as "Sonny Boy." *U.S. Army Crime Records Center.*

After Dunkirk, the fugitive deserter Cole dressed as a Frenchman. Nearsighted, he rarely wore glasses. *Courtesy Jeannine Voglimacci.*

Running swindles on the Continent in late 1938, Cole was back in English custody by early 1939. *U.S. Army Crime Records Center.*

Voglimacci's hairdressing salon in La Madeleine, where British escapers were received by Cole.
Courtesy Jeannine Voglimacci.

Jeannine Voglimacci and her husband, Jean, on the streets of prewar Lille. She was a fixture of the escape line.
Courtesy Jeannine Voglimacci

Jeannine Voglimacci in the studio apartment over the beauty salon.
Courtesy Jeannine Voglimacci.

Henri Duprez in 1940. On this forged Belgian identity card, he claimed to be a resident of Herseaux.
Courtesy Henri Duprez.

François Duprez. His forged documents were essential for Cole's escape network in the north.
Courtesy Jeannine Voglimacci.

Madeleine Damerment, a French helper. Later sent into France from England, she died in a German camp.
Courtesy Jeannine Voglimacci.

James Smith, a Scottish escaper and assistant in Cole's escape organization until his August 1941 arrest. *Courtesy A.G. Payne.*

Fernand Salingue. This country schoolteacher sheltered and guided RAF fliers and British troops. *Courtesy Elisa Salingue.*

Downed RAF aircraft fed a steady flow of British and Allied pilots into Cole's escape organization. Training, luck, and French helpers kept pilots out of German hands. *Centre de Recherches et d'Etudes Historiques de la Seconde Guerre Mondiale (CREHSGM), Brussels.*

RAF Sergeant Pilot F. W. "Taffy" Higginson. He admired Cole's daring as an escape line guide. *Courtesy F. W. Higginson.*

This Czech RAF pilot, sheltered in the home of François Duprez, posed with the official's two daughters. *Courtesy Marguerite Duprez-Beylemans.*

J. W. Philips, a Canadian pilot, was concealed over Voglimacci's salon for months in late 1940. *Courtesy Jeannine Voglimacci.*

Marscilles' Vieux Port, a focus for espionage and Cole's disreputable intrigues. *Photo Baudelaire, Marseilles.*

Captain Ian Garrow. He laid the foundations of the Marseilles escape organization. *Courtesy Helen Long, from* Safe Houses Are Dangerous.

Reverend Donald Caskie, the Scottish minister who concealed escapers and evaders in the Vieux Port mission. *Courtesy Neil Caskie.*

The British and American Seamen's Mission, where Rev. Donald Caskie hid escapers on their way to Spain. *Courtesy Neil Caskie.*

RIGHT: U.S. Consul Hugh S. Fullerton. He informed Washington of Marseilles' "rumor, suspicion and intrigue."
Courtesy Mrs. Hugh S. Fullerton.

BELOW: Escapers and helpers in the quai de Rive Neuve home of Louis Nouveau, at far right. Next to him (r–l): Airey Neave, Hugh Woolatt, Mario Prassinos, Francis Blanchain.
Courtesy Lady Airey.

Dr. Georges Rodocanachi, in his Marseilles study. *Courtesy Helen Long.*

Dr. Albert Guerisse, alias Patrick O'Leary, in a photo taken by a Marseilles street photographer.
Courtesy Count Albert-Marie Guerisse.

escorting convoys when he had reliable workhorses like Lepers and Smith?

◆ ◆ ◆

IN LISBON, Darling remained informed as to Cole's habits, particularly his "elaborate love life with a number of women." London still had not provided any background on Cole. Darling continued to fret and chafe, certain that the Cockney was "a wide boy, out for himself and a good time."

He was not far off the mark. A free man in Marseilles, Cole prowled the cafés, brasseries, and *dancings* of the half-free city, looking for recruits and developing his main personal interests: easy money and impressionable women.

With his glib line of chatter, Cole struck up a multitude of acquaintances on the docks and in watering holes up and down the broad Canebière running from the Vieux Port basin up toward the Gare Saint-Charles. They were filled with every manner of refugee and hard-luck case, for whom Marseilles was either the end of the line or, if a ship with berths to fill ever put in, just the beginning.

Marguerite Royer, twenty-five, and her brother, Gaston Peltret, twenty-two, had arrived separately in Marseilles in the spring of 1941. Married to a French Colonial Army NCO stationed in Syria, Royer had intended to join her husband at his post. But in Marseilles, hemmed in by a British blockade, passage could not be booked. She joined her brother, whose wish to join de Gaulle in London was similarly unfulfilled, at the tables along the Canebière while waiting for a ship to the Levant.

Royer drew a monthly allocation from her husband Maurice's army pay. This was almost enough to live on. But Peltret and his friends were generally out of pocket. They spent long hours nursing their drinks and chafing at the unremitting boredom.

In the far-off world outside Vichy France, the air war continued over England and northern France. General Irwin Rommel's Afrika

Corps had won a string of victories over the British in Egypt. A second German front had been opened with Hitler's June 22 surprise strike into Soviet Russia. Japanese Imperial Forces were in full expansion throughout the Far East. Peltret, like other young men on the Canebière, was eager to leap into this conflict and escape from the wearisome backwater of Marseilles.

No one noticed exactly when Cole insinuated himself into their company. But they soon noticed that the tall, thin Englishman did not stint in buying rounds of drinks. Paul, as he introduced himself, spoke little but gave to understand he was no stranger to the Resistance. This combination of generosity and patriotism was irresistible. They looked forward to the evenings when Cole would stroll in off the Canebière, order up drinks, and invite a handful of them to dine with him in one of the better restaurants.

"When Cole arrived with his pockets full he was the Messiah," said Royer. "We didn't question it." Cole, a mysterious Briton and a friend of France, was a tangible link with the noble struggle carried on by England. "We thought he was doing good work," explained Royer. "We thought he had a mission."

Cole brought his charms to bear on the young women during evenings on the Canebière and Sunday outings to the Parc Boreli, the local racetrack. But he was after more than diversion. The young people, Gaullists one and all, were ideal material for enlistment in Cole's section of the escape line.

Peltret had arrived in Marseilles eager to join the Fighting French, but was obliged to reconsider his plans after being quoted the price of 50 thousand francs for a guided trip over the Pyrenees. So he was enthusiastic when Cole sounded him out about helping the Garrow line. He met with Cole in an apartment near the Vieux Port boat basin. In a darkened room of the scantily furnished flat, shutters closed against the midday sun and enemy ears, Cole explained that England needed Peltret most in France, showing its airmen the way back home.

Enthralled by the same very British charm that Cole had applied in the north, Peltret declared himself ready to serve the Allied cause in the Garrow organization.

◆ ◆ ◆

PELTRET RECEIVED his first assignment a fortnight later, at the beginning of July. Cole, handing him a sketched map, said he was to travel to a farm near the town of Bléré, on the south side of the Cher River fifteen miles from Tours. There he would find a group of British escapers needing a guide to Marseilles.

The young Frenchman rode the trains northwest to Bléré, then located a nearby settlement called Les Ouches. The tiny, isolated hamlet of stone houses and barns crouched on a flat stretch in the low hills rising from the Cher. At a farmhouse he collected two British fliers and a suitcase filled with documents.

Tramping cross-country and riding local trains, Peltret and his two Englishmen took two days to reach Châteauroux. It turned out that the next train for Marseilles did not leave until 10:00 at night, hours away. The fliers wanted to find a hotel where they could rest and wash up. Peltret advised against this. But the two Britons were insistent and, after a few hours spent wandering aimlessly around Châteauroux, he gave in. They filled out police registration cards under the baneful eye of the hotel proprietor, manifestly a Pétainist, and obtained a few hours rest.

Entering the train station that evening, Peltret caught a meaningful glance from one of the porters. But he dismissed it and continued onto the platform. The next moment, he was surrounded by French security police wielding machine pistols. The hotel owner, Peltret concluded, had denounced the suspicious trio to the Vichy police.

The fugitives threw their hands up and submitted to arrest. Acutely aware that spying was a more serious offense than associating with Englishmen, Peltret left the valise standing on the platform as they were prodded away, hoping it would quickly be stolen. But the bag had not moved when a Vichy inspector came to his wits and sent someone back for it.

The two Englishmen disappeared. Peltret was jailed and, in January 1942, convicted of espionage on behalf of a foreign power. He was sentenced to two years' imprisonment, later reduced to eighteen months. Released at the end of 1942, Peltret went to work for another Resistance network and served the Allied cause until the end of the war.

Marguerite Royer, visiting her brother in prison, brought news of Cole and the others in Marseilles. The vivacious brunette was intrigued by Cole's mysterious air. Until her husband arrived that November, she carried out small assignments for him, such as safeguarding a packet of French identity cards while he was away. Royer once was called before the Vichy police for questioning about Cole. But she pleaded ignorance of his activities and was released.

Another woman, named Gabrielle, became Cole's mistress and traveled with him from time to time. She too was given assignments, such as seeking out Frenchmen willing to sell their identity papers for use by the escape line. But she did not stay with Cole for very long. Later she took up with a French police detective whom she supplied with information picked up along the Canebière. No doubt she also briefed him on what she knew of Cole, to be added to the dossier being kept on the Cockney agent in Vichy files. More than a few people had developed an interest in the elusive Paul Cole since his arrival in Marseilles that spring.

♦ ♦ ♦

THOUGH HIS MAIN EMPLOYMENT was with the escape line, Cole was expanding his espionage sideline. Traveling widely in France with his eyes and ears open, plugged into the burgeoning Resistance movements, he easily developed contacts in this field.

Already, in May 1941, Cole was trading on his knowledge of the Franco-British underground. In that month he bumped into an acquaintance from Lille named Eugène Dupuis, with whom he had worked in the North. Cole introduced Dupuis to a British colonel named Seagrim, who in turn presented the French agent to a Polish lieutenant named Victor Henoch. The officer was setting up an intelligence network that would tap into the large Polish refugee community in France. Henoch's network, sponsored by British Intelligence, was the forerunner of a much larger and more important intelligence network called Interallié.

Cole began collecting intelligence from throughout the north of France on his trips back to the Lille area. His burden of work in the escape line had been diminished by the efforts of Smith, tirelessly ferrying escapers out of Lille. Now Cole set about organizing his scattered contacts into a productive intelligence circuit.

At regular intervals Cole collected information on German installations and troop movements from the Lille apartment of a young woman named Marie-Louise Gallet. One of Cole's best subagents was the French railway employee Maurice Dechaumont, whose brood of ten children earned him the code name "X-10." Dechaumont obtained maps of airfields and German military transport orders. Cole also took whatever the Voix du Nord Resistance movement could provide him in the way of local information.

From the port of Dunkirk, Cole was receiving information from Raphaël Ayello, a manufacturer of rope and fishing nets who also operated a tugboat service. Ayello had retreated to the south of France in 1940 with his army unit. Still in Marseilles late that year, he was recruited by French intelligence and sent back to the Pas de Calais to carry out espionage. According to Ayello, his French employers were in close liaison with British Intelligence.

In early 1941 Ayello was contacted by "Paul" Cole, who told Ayello to collect information on German troop movements in the coastal region and to monitor preparations for the amphibious assault on England still threatened by Hitler. Later Ayello was asked to provide a detailed map of the port of Dunkirk and its defenses.

Pierre Carpentier was also feeding Cole intelligence: monthly reports on troop movements, sketches of the German airfields at Abbeville and two other locations, information on fuel and ammunitions depots, the map coordinates of a German flak battery south of Saint-Omer, and after-action reports on RAF bombing raids.

Cole had asked Henri Duprez to collect blank or used German occupation documents such as identity papers and travel permits, along with materials like theater tickets, old cigarette packs, and matchboxes. This was just the kind of shopping list that would be drawn up by an Allied intelligence service planning to parachute or otherwise infiltrate agents into the north.

Evidently a great deal of intelligence and other materials were being provided to Cole—but where was all of this going? Carpentier would later state cryptically that "the documents furnished by me to Cole never reached Marseilles." The Garrow organization had always welcomed and even solicited military intelligence. But this had never amounted to the widespread network of informants, couriers, and safe houses that Cole was setting up. There were too many risks inherent in running an escape and evasion line to add the many dangers of a major spying operation.

As of mid-1941, however, Cole personally was running an intelligence network of wide scope in the north of France. It is unclear on whose orders he was working. But the circumstances suggest that his employer was a branch of British intelligence more highly placed than MI9.

◆ ◆ ◆

BRITAIN'S INTELLIGENCE SECRETS of the Second World War have in large part been consigned to inaccessible archives or the flames. Yet we know enough about Cole and the British services operating in France at that time to work up a scenario that is not only plausible but most probable.

In the small world of the espionage professionals working in Marseilles in 1941, it was unlikely that Cole, a high-profile agent if there ever was one, would go unnoticed for long. The Vichy authorities already were tracking him. Surely he also came to the attention of the British secret-service operatives in the port—not the unlikely Sawyer or the uncautious Murchie, but more professional agents who worked efficiently at developing strings of informants.

Very likely, one of them considered Cole early on as a possible agent in the north, a region of France that was of vital importance to Great Britain. A cross-Channel invasion attempt was still viewed as possible. Night bombing of London and other cities was regularly carried out from airfields in the Pas de Calais. British bombers were carrying the war inside the borders of the Reich, so the RAF needed information on German fighter bases and antiaircraft positions in northern France. The requirements for information were endless— but there were precious few reliable agents in place.

At some point in the summer of 1941, Cole was hired by a British agency that outranked MI9, and given instructions that did not entirely square with his duties in the escape line. For Cole there was no conflict. He would now draw two salaries and win higher recognition when the war was over and it came time to weigh his actions against a larcenous past.

Cole now served two masters, though both fought on the same side of the European conflict. However advantageous this was for the Secret Intelligence Service, the new arrangement could only work to the detriment of Ian Garrow's struggling escape line.

11

"Escapers Don't Win Wars"

AT ALMOST any other point in its prestigious but, for the most part, obscure history, the Secret Intelligence Service, variously known as SIS and MI6, never would have considered Harold Cole as an agent. In peacetime, his low-caste birth to an East End family of laborers would automatically have excluded him from this upper-crust agency that ran to "metropolitan young gentlemen whose education had been expensive rather than profound and who were recruited at the bars of White's and Boodles."

It was true, as has since been pointed out, that "crooks, and fantasists, con-men and clowns, as well as dedicated patriots, abounded" in the murky world of European espionage. But even in wartime, Cole's criminal record and desertion from the British Expeditionary Force should by rights have placed him in that class of intelligence informants who are to be dealt with at the healthy remove of a lengthy barge pole. Cole was patently unreliable.

If 1940 had not been a year of major setbacks for the SIS, the very suggestion of hiring the deserter would have produced loud snorts on the upper floors of the service's Broadway, London headquarters and resulted in a rocket to the field officer advancing the proposal. But as things were, 1940 had been "a complete shambles" for the SIS. Things were not going that much better in 1941. The service was in dire enough straits to see Cole as a potential asset.

The Secret Intelligence Service was caught badly off balance when the German offensive slashed through the Low Countries and France in May and June 1940. Every major SIS station—with the exception of that in Geneva—was obliged to pack up and go home. "The fact was that none of the British secret service departments was really prepared for the situation created by the German conquest of Western Europe," concludes one historian.

The SIS was making great strides in breaking the German Enigma encryption system. This would in time yield the high-grade intelligence product that received the code-name of "Ultra" and determined the course—if not the very outcome—of the war. But SIS had all too few agents on the ground in France and Belgium at the very moment when Great Britain's very survival depended on obtaining solid information about Germany's strength and intentions across the Channel.

The Intelligence Service in London could draw on the secret services of the Allied governments-in-exile that were still in touch with underground movements in their respective countries. The Czechs and the Poles were valued partners; the latter had played a crucial role in cracking Enigma and mounted a sizeable effort inside occupied France. But inter-Allied intelligence cooperation, particularly in the case of the Free French, was strewn with political feuds and internecine rivalries. It was unsatisfactory over the long run. The SIS wanted its own people on the job.

That is why, in the late summer of 1940, soon after the rout, SIS turned covetous eyes upon MI9. The escape and evasion outfit had drawn scant interest from the senior intelligence service prior to the fall of France. Some saw it as more of a War Office hobby-horse than a significant military program. But with its Continental networks in a shambles, top SIS officials realized that the thousands of British soldiers trickling out of France carried with them a potential intelligence windfall.

Suddenly MI9—and its agents—took on new importance.

◆ ◆ ◆

IN THE FAST-SHIFTING intelligence climate of 1940 to 1941, no man played a more important role within the SIS than Lieutenant-Colonel Claude Edward Marjoribanks Dansey, sixty-three. This figure of consummate intrigue was greatly admired and equally detested inside the British espionage community. For intelligence officer and historian Hugh Trevor-Roper, he was "an utter shit; corrupt, incompetent, but with a certain low cunning." But the SIS agent and man of letters Malcolm Muggeridge considered him "the only real professional in MI6."

After a lifetime in the British secret services and military, extending from the Boer War to the Phoney War, Dansey in 1939 was named second-in-command of SIS under the eminently well-connected Stewart Menzies. But Dansey, the old espionage fox to whom even Menzies deferred, was the brains of the agency. Concluded Jimmy Langley, who worked with Garrow in Marseilles before Dansey appointed him to a key post with MI9, "What Dansey wanted done was done; and what he wanted undone was undone."

Dansey's special achievement was the creation of the so-called Z Organization. This network operated parallel to the official SIS field networks, but its channels were personal, not bureaucratic. Dansey recruited its agents himself from business, entertainment, and high social circles. He realized as early as 1936 that SIS Continental stations were badly exposed, likely to be rolled up overnight if their countries of posting were overrun by Germany. The Z Organization would be ready to provide a back-up to the SIS first team.

As things happened, the Z Organization by mid-1940 constituted the backbone of British secret service efforts on the Continent, reaching into occupied Europe from its main listening post in Geneva. By then Dansey had returned to London and taken up his post as adjutant to SIS chief Menzies. Having built the Z Organization in his own image, and with the official SIS apparatus now at his fingertips, "Colonel Z" held all the strings.

◆ ◆ ◆

BY COMPARISON, MI9 and its own chief, Major Norman R. Crockatt, were small potatoes. Crockatt had served and been wounded in the First World War, later retiring to civilian life as a stockbroker. But when the British military was gearing up for war, Crockatt was tapped by a War Office section examining the possibilities of irregular warfare as seen in the 1920 to 1921 Irish Rebellion. When British intelligence decided to create a branch concentrating on escape, Crockatt was proposed for the job. Duly appointed, he set up shop in Room 424 of the Metropole Hotel in central London.

Crockatt, forty-five, cut a dashing figure, with a "natural grace of bearing, set off by a tall, well-proportioned figure and piercing green eyes." He was the kind of man who could, without flinching, stride down Fifth Avenue in the kilted colors of his Royal Scots Regiment. A "sort of John Buchan hero," to one aide, Crockatt "could have done the Charge of the Light Brigade and the whole of MI9 would have come pattering on behind him."

Crockatt was astute enough politically to know that it his fledgling service were to develop, he would need strong allies within the fiefs and dependencies springing up between the War Office and Number 10 Downing Street.

MI9's assignment was to encourage the escape and evasion of British service personnel behind the wire in POW camps or at large in enemy-held territory. But Dansey initially appeared uninterested in escape and evasion and at times expressed clear hostility to it. "Escapers don't win wars," he declared. "Intelligence does."

Consequently, Crockatt found that the top ranks of the SIS "were determined to prevent evaders and escapers from involving them in any way. This attitude may have been correct from their own security aspect, but it was a terrific handicap to those trying to build up an organization." But with the Franco-British defeat and the resulting disarray in his own service, Dansey examined MI9 in a new light. The steady flow of escapers and evaders into Marseilles and Gibraltar put MI9 in possession of intelligence and lines of communication that Dansey badly wanted.

MI6 also faced political pressure and unaccustomed competition from the newly created Special Operations Executive. SOE's charter, drafted by Winston Churchill, instructed it to "set Europe ablaze" with clandestine campaigns of "subversion and sabotage against the enemy overseas."

Three weeks after the advent of SOE, the SIS offered Crockatt the means to establish a full-blown escape line from Marseilles into Spain, along with the radio communications to run it. Crockatt, short on funding, appreciated this largess. He also knew that MI9 would thereafter be subjected to the iron will of Claude Dansey. But Crockatt had no real choice in the matter. Those in British intelligence circles knew that Dansey "could have broken Crockatt, or anyone else in MI9, as easily as he blew his own nose."

◆　◆　◆

DANSEY EARLIER HAD dispatched Major Donald Darling to Portugal with instructions to restore overland communications links to France. In Lisbon the bearish, lugubrious Darling held the title of British vice-consul in charge of repatriation. While processing British civilians who had departed occupied Europe legally, he handled more clandestine travel arrangements.

Through Darling the SIS provided funds to pay Basque guides who led the British escapers over the Pyrenees; the official rate was forty pounds for officers, twenty pounds for enlisted men. Dansey's man in Lisbon also set up a system of couriers through to the Marseilles organization, then the principal escape network in France.

Whatever came out of France to Darling was passed along to his own superior, the former escaper Jimmy Langley. Attached to MI9,

Langley's first loyalty was to Dansey, who had hand-picked him to provide liaison between SIS and MI9.

Every inch Dansey's man—by his own admission Langley was "petrified" by the withering looks and knife-edged comments of the intelligence czar—he was set in place as a kind of interservice mole. "Theoretically you will be on loan from MI9," Dansey told Langley. "In practice you will be on my staff and under my orders in MI6."

Dansey, never one to leave anything to chance, was making sure that he not only controlled MI9's operational lines of communication but surveyed its headquarters as well.

◆ ◆ ◆

DESPITE THE LENGTHS to which Dansey went to keep MI9 under his thumb, it nevertheless remained "a sideshow, something which he supervised, controlled, and kept a wary eye on while continuing to conduct the more important business of the SIS."

The burden of these larger affairs fell on the Geneva outpost, then in the charge of Victor Farrell, who was recruited into the Z Organization while an English teacher at the French military academy of Saint-Cyr. Farrell, officially British consul in Geneva, oversaw espionage operations in much of France along with his considerable activity in Switzerland itself, the venue of choice for high-level Nazi defectors.

It was probably through the Geneva station, an important conduit for funds going to Garrow, that Cole was recruited by MI6. Evidence later would suggest that he transmitted his information to Farrell through an intermediary in Lyon, midway between Paris and Marseilles, through which he regularly passed.

There is no available documentary evidence that in the summer of 1941 Cole became a field agent for the SIS. SIS organizational structure and the names of major figures such as Dansey and Farrell are well known today. Some of the more spectacular operations— particularly SIS success stories—have gone on the record. But SIS archives of the period have remained tightly closed and are likely to continue so.

Yet it is not difficult to conceive that SIS agents in Marseilles in 1941 heard the stories about Garrow's new man in the north. Through Darling, the SIS had received copies of Garrow's first enthusiastic reports about the Cockney lance sergeant who was doing a "brilliant" job pulling BEF stragglers and downed fliers out of the Nord-Pas de Calais.

The north of France also was a critical intelligence target. Historians were to conclude that the Battle of Britain was won in September 1940, but England was still reeling from the shock of the 1940 rout, the London Blitz, and Hitler's continued successes in the Balkans and the Middle East. The most immediate threat to British home security still came from across the English Channel.

Harold Cole, Dansey's agents must have noted with interest, came and went between Lille and Marseilles with seeming impunity. He regularly brought back escapers and, not infrequently, the added fillup of raw intelligence on everything from troop train schedules to the design of the Snorkel minisubmarine under testing in French waters.

◆ ◆ ◆

CLAUDE DANSEY had resolved that MI9 should not interfere with the mission of his own SIS. But this did not mean, conversely, that he could not manipulate the junior service for his own purposes. He could, if deemed necessary, poach from the MI9 staff. An agent like Cole, for all of his faults, would clearly have caught the eye of Dansey in the dark spring of 1941.

Dansey and his aides examined Cole's history as a confidence man, thief, deserter, and most recently, escape-line operative. They weighed the risks and concluded that the Cockney could be put to even better use. He would require careful handling, and his recruitment would have to be kept a secret from MI9. But Cole had something the SIS needed: access to and abundant contacts in the north of France.

Such a decision would logically have had to reach Dansey's desk, especially given the inquiries from Darling. "Many of those who worked in the escape and evasion lines were strong personalities, who could only be controlled with difficulty," wrote the SIS official's biographers. "In every case, the final decisions regarding their recruitment and use lay with Dansey."

This undoubtedly was so in the case of Lance Sergeant Harold Cole, who now had a line, however indirect, to the very top ranks of British Intelligence.

12

"This Chap Was Running a Racket"

ONE AFTERNOON late in July 1941, Ian Garrow left the Rodocanachi apartment and descended the broad stone staircase of the building into the sun-baked streets of Marseilles. He was accompanied by a shorter man whose purposeful bearing nonetheless matched that of the towering Scotsman. Had they been challenged by the Marseilles police and security services, Garrow's companion would have produced documents identifying himself as Joseph Cartier. To officers of the escape line he was known as Patrick O'Leary. But neither of these was his true name.

Dr. Albert-Marie Edmond Guerisse, thirty, a native of Brussels, had begun the war as a lieutenant in the Belgian Army Medical Corps. But now he had set his national allegiance and his profession aside to work with Garrow.

Warily eyeing the streets around them, the two men walked for several minutes until they arrived at a public garden. After a brief wait, they were joined by a tall, blond-haired, freckled man whose eyes, slightly crossed, seemed shifty to Guerisse. Seated next to Garrow on a park bench, Guerisse listened to the Scot's conversation with this newcomer and brooded silently as he examined Sergeant Paul Cole.

The Cockney delivered a stirring account of his latest trip from the north. It featured a hairbreadth escape from a German patrol, gunshots traded in the summer night along the Cher River borderline, and quick thinking by Cole to whisk his convoy of escapers out of harm's way. Unimpressed, the Belgian studied Cole's physiognomy and decided that he "didn't like his face at all."

Cole turned to the subject of money. He needed 50 thousand francs to buy a radio transmitter, which would allow direct communication with London. But he assured Garrow that ample funds for normal operations were on deposit with François Duprez, whom he identified as a banker in Lille. "He has plenty of money in the bank," Cole said, "but I need more."

Guerisse watched Garrow for signs that his incredulity was shared. The Scot revealed no emotion then or as they walked back to the safe house. But over whiskey that evening Garrow himself broached the topic.

"What do you think, Pat?" asked the Scot.

"Ian, I don't like this man," said Guerisse.

"Why?"

"I don't know. He has a funny smell."

"He's a British NCO," Garrow said, "A good Englishman."

Guerisse deferred to his superior, but stood by the conclusion he reached as he scrutinized Cole that day in the park.

"Ian, be careful," he warned. "He's a bluffer."

◆ ◆ ◆

TWO MEN on conflicting courses, Harold Cole and Albert Guerisse had unknowingly bound their wartime fortunes with this first meeting in Marseilles. Profoundly dissimilar, the two men nonetheless shared one important trait: each exerted a charismatic influence on the men and women around them. A natural leader in whom toughness and sensitivity were alloyed, Guerisse embodied the virtues to which Cole could only pretend. RAF escaper Higginson found him "effervescent," with a remarkable ability to "raise people's morale in any circumstances."

Guerisse in time was to assume leadership of the escape line, placing his own stamp upon it to such an extent that escaper Airey Neave, later a top MI9 official, would conclude, "O'Leary always dominates the scene."

When Belgium capitulated in May 1940, Guerisse embarked at Dunkirk with the other remnants of the Grand Alliance but was shipped immediately back to France. Elements of the Belgian Army were regrouping near Poitiers—but soon it was time to leave the Continent again.

At Sete, on the Riviera, Guerisse threw in with a Czech division whose commander, hearing of the Franco-German armistice, muttered over his pastisse, "Well, the Czechs do not capitulate." His ten thousand unyielding Slavs were taken to Gibraltar aboard three British coalers, Guerisse with them. There he signed on as ship's doctor with *Le Rhin*, a captured French merchant vessel delivered by its Gaullist captain as a war prize. The British armed the vessel in England, renamed it the HMS *Fidelity*, and commissioned it as a "Q" ship for British secret-service operations. Guerisse was made a lieutenant commander in the Royal Navy and named the ship's executive officer.

In April 1941 Guerisse set out from the *Fidelity*, then sailing the Mediterranean, to land two Allied spies on the Riviera while taking off a group of Polish agents in a small boat. A combination of bad luck, poor navigation, heavy seas, and meddlesome Vichy officials landed Guerisse and two others in a French naval brig. He made the initial error of claiming to be a Gaullist on his way to join the Free French in London—an offense worse, in Vichy eyes, than being a British agent.

So Guerisse modified his story before a military judge, explaining that he was actually a French Canadian named Patrick Albert

O'Leary, serving in the Royal Navy. This story held up under questioning, and Guerisse and his men were removed to the internment center at Saint-Hippolyte-du-Fort.

That was exactly what Guerisse had hoped for.

◆ ◆ ◆

ONCE A SCHOOL for the sons of French officers, Saint-Hippolyte-du-Fort was more like a barracks than a prison. Its walls were only about ten feet in height. At many points the prisoners were separated from the town around them by just one set of steel bars. American diplomatic observers considered it "far superior" to Fort Saint-Jean. But the charms of Saint-Hippolyte-du-Fort were less appreciated by internees who, the French commandant bemoaned, were inclined to "drink too much and later cause disturbances."

Officers had the run of the town. They could leave the prison by giving their word of honor they would not bolt. This allowed them to leave the prison to make escape arrangements. They then could withdraw their parole to make a dash, honor bright. Out on parole, ostensibly to see a soccer match, Guerisse met Garrow in an American sympathizer's apartment in Nîmes. As ranking prisoner in Saint-Hippolyte, the Belgian had by then become chairman of the inevitable escape committee.

Measuring the Scot's tall frame and un-Gallic features, Guerisse bemusedly concluded that Garrow met "all the conditions to be immediately arrested when met in the streets of Marseilles." But he also found him "elegant, full of humor, and calmly determined." Garrow outlined his efforts, emphasizing the network's "brilliant agent in the north of France." Guerisse found all this "absolutely wonderful." He decided that once his crewmen, named Fergusson and Rogers, had escaped from Saint-Hippolyte, he would report to Garrow in Marseilles.

By the beginning of July, the Belgian was at liberty. Fergusson had preceded him, walking out of the prison in a French guard's uniform. Soon after, Guerisse boosted Rogers over the low prison wall and tackled a guard while Rogers pedaled away furiously on a bicycle commandeered outside the prison.

Guerisse's own escape was more complicated, as he was given two weeks' solitary confinement for his part in Rogers's evasion. The bars of a window in a seldom-used room of the prison were sawn through. An identity card in the name of Joseph Cartier was manufactured with a linoleum-cut imprint. He made his break during a somnolent Friday lunch hour. But an alarm was raised, and Guerisse was pursued through the dusty streets of the garrison town. The residents of a local convent hid him in an attic and later spirited him through an underground passageway leading out of town to the nunnery's vineyards.

In Marseilles, Guerisse found the rue Roux de Brignoles and climbed to the second floor at number 21.

"We were expecting you," said Fanny Rodocanachi. "Go down the corridor to the right and there is your flat—with the chief."

Garrow welcomed Guerisse and poured out two glasses of whiskey to celebrate.

"Well, *mon cher*," said the Scot. "I think we are going to be working together for a long time."

Intent on getting back to the HMS *Fidelity*, Guerisse was not entirely pleased at the prospect of settling into Marseilles to work with Garrow. He let this be known.

"What about helping me for a while?" said Garrow, crestfallen. His own French was halting and heavily accented, his appearance too plainly foreign. He needed a lieutenant with fluent French and the clear judgment Guerisse so evidently possessed.

In the end, a request for orders was sent down the line to Barcelona for transmission to London. If Guerisse was to stay, the BBC would broadcast an agreed-upon message during its nightly round of coded instructions to the anti-Nazi underground. The response came back inside of two weeks.

"*Adolphe doit rester*," was pronounced not twice, as was the custom, but three times. "It was very insistent," said Guerisse, who with mixed emotions listened to the message crackle across the ether that summer night. "So we shook hands and had a strong whiskey."

◆　◆　◆

SOON AFTER THIS the two men disagreed in their appreciations of Sergeant Cole. Garrow brushed off his new assistant's doubts about Cole. But misgivings about the Cockney were spreading and built through that autumn to become a pressing concern for the organization. Garrow was one of the last to see through Cole, perhaps because his initially positive impression could be surmounted only by clear evidence of wrongdoing.

There had been a subtle change in Cole's attitude through that summer of good living in Marseilles and occasional trips on the escape route. He was reverting to the cynical, unscrupulous behavior that had marked his life in the past. On first joining the organization Cole had been on his best behavior, eager to prove himself. But once established as a key agent, he could not resist the temptations.

Around the same time he met Guerisse, Cole was sent to meet one of the line's Paris agents in Marseilles. André Postel-Vinay, a senior French civil servant, had taken charge of an escape and intelligence network in the capital and had come south for consultations.

Postel-Vinay had been recruited by a fellow bureaucrat in the Inspection des Finances, Pierre d'Harcourt, who was working for the Cinquième Bureau. This intelligence wing of the French Army officially had been dissolved after the armistice. In reality it had gone undercover and established a national system of informants. But d'Harcourt, wishing to make sure his information also got to London, passed it to the Garrow line in Marseilles along with the escapers rounded up by his rural agents.

D'Harcourt was arrested in July 1941, when he foolishly tried to recruit a German officer who in a social setting had expressed anti-Nazi sentiments. Postel-Vinay took over the network and traveled to Marseilles to meet his British contacts. He wanted to ask Garrow for a radio transmitter and operator—not realizing that this was something Garrow still lacked.

Cole, still in Garrow's confidence, was sent to the meeting. The well-bred Parisian was taken aback, sensing that the Cockney agent was a man "of few scruples." No doubt picking up these misgivings, Cole began to mouth high sentiments to explain his involvement in the underground. But "it simply rang false when he talked of England and patriotism." To Postel-Vinay "it seemed obvious that this character did not believe the things he said."

Their business concluded, Cole asked Postel-Vinay for his address in Paris. Like most Frenchmen, the civil servant was loath to give out such personal information to a stranger—the more so as Cole did not inspire confidence. But Postel-Vinay felt he "couldn't show an abusive distrust" and gave Cole his address.

One day he would regret not having trusted his instincts and found some pretext to refuse.

◆ ◆ ◆

FLIGHT COMMANDER Archie Winskill, a British pilot shot down over Calais on July 14, Bastille Day, obtained more substantial evidence of Cole's unreliability. Taken in by a French family, Winskill traveled south with a Scot from the Fifty-first Highland Division, bearing false documents provided by Pierre Carpentier. French helpers gave them directions along the way, but they moved south essentially on their own. In Marseilles the two evaders were taken in hand by Cole, whom they met in the Petit Poucet.

Over drinks, he briefed them on the organization's procedures— plus a few he had worked up for his own benefit. "You are now with a British escape organization," Cole said, "so you won't need any money." He told them to empty their pockets of the funds raised by their northern hosts, miners and railwaymen, in collections through the bars and bakeries of the Pas de Calais.

Winskill gave Cole all his cash despite a strong suspicion that "in fact this chap was running a racket." Over the next few days, he learned that this was not Cole's only angle for fleecing the pilots and the Garrow Organization.

After a few days in Marseilles, Guerisse moved Winskill to Canet Plage, a fishing port near the Spanish border. He was entrusted to the care of a young Frenchman who tended the safe house there. Already present were two Polish fliers, one a sergeant pilot, the other an officer. The latter said he had been shot down in a Spitfire from the 303 Polish Squadron based in Norfolk. Winskill and the Pole chatted in French, but when the British pilot suggested they shift to English the man admitted he didn't know any. Winskill had never met a Polish pilot who didn't talk at least a little English; a bare minimum was needed to communicate with British ground controllers.

He became convinced after further conversation that the Pole had never handled the stick of a Spitfire, and by deduction, that he was faced with a German agent who had infiltrated the line. Easing away from the man, Winskill approached the Frenchman.

"Look," he said quietly. "This chap isn't a pilot, he's never been to England, and he's never flown a Spitfire."

The escape line's agent reached the same conclusion as Winskill. "There's only one thing to do," said the man. "Tomorrow I'll go to Marseilles by the first train to see Cole."

Before breakfast they agreed on the final details of their plan. Winskill was to draw the Pole into one of the bedrooms, slam the door, pull out the revolver the Frenchman had given him, and hold the man at bay. Meanwhile the other would confirm his identity with Cole.

According to plan, Winskill drew the gun on the Pole and motioned the supposed Gestapo agent to a seat in the corner. The man obeyed, but then, to the flier's bewilderment, burst into tears.

Under questioning, the Pole admitted that he was not a pilot but a Jewish refugee. A medical student in Paris in May 1940, he had fled to Marseilles and found work in a chemical plant. On the waterfront he had run across Cole, who promised him passage to London—

at a price. The young man had paid what Cole demanded and been coached in how to pass for a Polish Spitfire pilot.

To Winskill, who had felt Cole's larcenous touch, the story had the ring of truth. Persuaded the Pole was not a German plant, he decided to cover for him. The Frenchman returned late that night to report Cole had firmly vouched for the imposter.

"He knows exactly where the chap came down, he's seen his parachute, and he knows the little farm," the agent said.

"I'm terribly sorry," Winskill said, shamming embarrassment. "You're quite right. I've made a terrible mistake."

◆ ◆ ◆

SOON WINSKILL'S GROUP set out on foot to cross the Pyrenees, reaching Spain in safety despite a young and inept Basque guide who got them lost. The genuine Polish pilot whipped out a map torn from a calendar, and the group emerged from the Pyrenees near Burgos, Spain. A diplomat from the Barcelona consulate came to fetch them in a car.

There was room for only two on the first trip. Winskill, the senior officer, elected to take the Polish imposter with him. The authorities had to be informed of Cole's dereliction. But the British officials merely became irritated.

"Why did you bring that bloody Pole?" said one of them. "I understand there's some more Englishmen you've left behind." Winskill reported Cole's chicanery, expecting a reaction of deep concern.

"Oh, we know all about that," said the diplomat, brushing him off. "Don't worry about a thing—this chap is talking rubbish."

Yet if Barcelona was hearing about Cole's machinations, Garrow also had to be receiving reports of his agent's indiscretions. Sooner or later Garrow would decide that something had to be done about Cole.

13

"He Just Didn't Give a Damn"

A HEAVY MASS of clouds lay over northern France on August 21, 1941, as the RAF 610 Squadron flew east over the Channel to escort a bomber wing raiding a steel works at Lille. It was a difficult run for the Spitfire pilots: to protect the bomber wing, they had to stay below the clouds where they could keep it in sight. This conceded a tactical advantage to the Messerschmitt fighters rising up in swarms from airfields around Calais and Saint-Omer.

Flight-Lieutenant Denis Crowley-Milling was among the vanquished in the "running battle in and the running battle out" of France that day. Shortly before 3:00 P.M., as he headed home at 25 thousand feet, a bullet penetrated his Spitfire's engine. Crowley-Milling force-landed in a field twelve miles southwest of Saint-Omer. He hauled himself unhurt from the wreckage after detonating a small charge in the Identification Friend or Foe system, or IFF. This device emitted a distinctive electronic signal so that the plane would show up as friendly on British radar screens. It could not be allowed to fall into German hands. This task carried out, Crowley-Milling hurried away across the fields.

By this date, all RAF pilots were well briefed on how to avoid being picked up by German patrols after crash-landing or dropping by parachute. MI9 lecturers advised them to alter their appearance by obtaining civilian clothing, or at least to rip off RAF insignia. Fliers also carried small kits with local currency, survival rations, and other gear for living rough.

MI9 training and assistance, later redoubled by the efforts of its U.S. counterpart, MIS-X, would help some 35,000 Allied military personnel captured, downed, or otherwise stranded behind enemy lines to escape from or evade enemy capture. In Western Europe alone, more than 7,000 found their way back to Allied territory; the great majority of these were British or American. Air crews, totaling 4,361, accounted for the majority of the Anglo-American contingent. More than 4,000 of the British and American airmen who made it back to their bases before and after D-Day never fell into German hands at all.

The more foresightful pilots readied for evasion well before they were shot down. American airman Whitney Straight, beloved of the prewar British tabloids as a race car driver and socialite, flew with passport photos in his pocket and a nondescript leather jacket on his back. He already spoke excellent French. Upon crash-landing near Le Havre in July 1941, Straight, thirty, completed his ensemble by purchasing a beret from a farmer's wife. Despite these preparations, he was caught later in a restaurant in Vichy after ordering a meal without proffering ration tickets. Straight eventually was freed on medical grounds, with the help of Georges Rodocanachi, and returned to active service in Great Britain.

Plain luck was an essential component of any successful evasion. This was humorously illustrated by the experience of RAF pilot Tom Slack, shot down south of Abbeville later in the war. Slack, twenty-seven, was walking cross-country late at night when, he reported, "about 2200 hours, while I was crossing a road, I met a German soldier armed with a revolver."

Slack stood stock still and whipped his silk flying scarf over the

RAF wings on his chest. "The German seemed slightly intoxicated, and to my amazement, as he walked past me he said, 'Bonsoir, Monsieur,' to which I replied, 'Bonsoir.' I then went on quickly for about a mile, when I rested for a time." After recovering his nerve, Slack continued more circumspectly on his way.

The one essential MI9 did not provide to RAF pilots was a list of the French helpers sheltering evaders and passing them along to escape lines. There was too great a risk that this information would be extracted by German counterintelligence. Captured British fliers had on occasion identified helpers, inadvertently or otherwise. So a downed airman initially had to sort things out for himself.

Having plodded through the French countryside for "twenty-five miles, jolly nearly," Crowley-Milling chanced seeking assistance. When night had fallen, he knocked on the door of a farmhouse. Its occupants, happily, knew Norbert Fillerin, a farmer who was channeling downed airmen into the Garrow line. The Frenchman had not heard of any British craft being shot down in the past days. At first he suspected the fair-haired Crowley-Milling of being a German agent provocateur. But after interrogating Crowley-Milling, Fillerin decided he had a bona fide British escaper on his hands.

A week later, Crowley-Milling was turned over to Desiré Didry, a blacksmith and cobbler from Saint-Omer, who took Crowley-Milling into Lille a few days later. In the back of a butcher shop near the train station the pilot was handed off to Cole. Crowley-Milling, delighted to meet a fellow Briton in the middle of occupied France, followed the agent to La Madeleine. A Czech pilot and two British soldiers were already there awaiting the trip south. A few days later they set out for Marseilles under the guidance of Cole and Roland Lepers.

◆ ◆ ◆

THE VOYAGE was a constant source of apprehension for Crowley-Milling. He expected at every moment that some German authority would end the charade by arresting the lot of them. Cole was "so obviously English it wasn't true. He was always chattering away in this frightful French with Germans around, and he just didn't give a damn."

Lepers also jangled Crowley-Milling's nerves. There was, at the time, a popular English song called "Johnny Belinda," played frequently on the BBC. "This wretched Frenchman kept whistling it and showing off his English, which absolutely scared us all, because we thought we were bound to be caught."

Cole, concluded Crowley-Milling, "never should have gotten away with what he did." In Bethune the party of six had been joined by a half-dozen BEF stragglers. When the party of twelve reached Abbeville, Carpentier could not produce enough passes for the whole crowd. Unconcerned, Cole crossed the bridge with four men. Then he collected all the passes and went back for four more, including Crowley-Milling. The airman grew alarmed as he examined the pass Cole had handed him.

"But that's not my photograph!" the flier exclaimed.

"Don't worry," Cole said. "No one will notice."

No one did. Crowley-Milling and the rest passed undisturbed to the southern bank of the Somme.

The Cockney's long experience in deception was now paying off. It was a first rule of the confidence game that timidity was more likely to provoke suspicion than boldness. Whenever the group of evaders encountered German soldiers while waiting in a train station, they mingled with them on Cole's instructions.

"Whenever you see soldiers," Cole told Crowley-Milling, "you must go and join them."

In practice this strained the flier's nerves. While waiting for a train in Abbeville, the evaders mingled with a troop of German soldiers on the southern bank of the Somme. The Czech airman, taking Cole's advice to heart, drew the attention of all by whistling at the girls on the opposite bank, "much to the amusement of the German soldiers."

Evaders traveling on French trains normally remained planted in their seats, pretending to read or feigning sleep, while their French escorts dealt with conductors and watched for danger. But Cole had little patience for such caution. "Come on," he told Crowley-Milling during their train ride south. "Let's go have a meal in the restaurant."

In the dining car, the only two seats available were directly across from two German officers. Crowley-Milling sat miserably through the endless meal while "this wretched man shouted at the waiter in this appalling French." But to his amazement and relief, the Germans "didn't turn a hair."

◆ ◆ ◆

THE CONVOY reached Paris late that evening and were let in the back door of a brothel in Les Halles. Crowley-Milling first was given a room with the Czech pilot. But this arrangement was reshuffled after the brothel-keeper came around offering them each a woman on the house. "Oh, yes," the Czech replied enthusiastically. But Crowley-Milling declined the offer politely and shifted down the hall to share Cole's room.

Crowley-Milling was taken aback at Cole's dark tone as they chatted before going to sleep. He told the flier that he had orders to shoot Lepers when they reached Marseilles. He even produced the revolver with which he proposed to carry out this deed. But the whole thing seemed overly theatrical to Crowley-Milling, who did not take the threat seriously.

Was Cole merely amusing himself at the expense of the naive airman? Or was this a revelatory moment when, his guard down, Cole expressed his fear of being dispatched in a similar fashion for his own lapses? No one knew better than the Cockney how much he had cause to fear the rough justice of the underground.

Uncomfortable, Crowley-Milling changed the subject. When this was all over, what did Cole intend to do? He could not have known that Cole had little to look forward to at the war's end. But the agent seemed to mellow as he thought this over.

"I'll put an advertisement in the paper, probably in the *Times*," he said. "We can all meet for a drink."

The next morning they traveled to Tours, then changed to a local line heading southeast to a crossing point into Vichy France. At one station along the local line, the train filled with German soldiers. For the first time Crowley-Milling saw Cole become nervous. At his orders they got off at the next station and ducked into the woods until dusk. They crossed the river over a small footbridge and tramped thirteen miles to Valençay, where they picked up the train for Châteauroux, Toulouse, and, at the end of the line, Marseilles.

Inside Vichy France, Crowley-Milling felt a different sort of apprehension. In the north of France most of the population would actively help a British escaper. But it was far different in the Unoccupied Zone, where collaboration had poisoned the spirit of the French. "If they caught you near the border," the flier knew, "they would hand you back to the Germans."

Coming out of the Gare Saint-Charles in Marseilles, Crowley-Milling had one last bad moment. A spotlight played on the train station doorway, while French gendarmes examined papers and inspected suitcases. That illustrated another rule of thumb for escapers and evaders traveling through wartime France: voyagers carrying suitcases were more likely to be stopped for inspection than those clutching tattered brown paper parcels. Cole's convoy, traveling light, was not challenged. The men walked straight out into the streets of Marseilles.

After days of wearying and nerve-wracking travel, much of it rough, Crowley-Milling was relieved to attain the safety and comfort of the Rodocanachi apartment. There Fanny Rodocanachi gave him "a Victorian tea party with a little napkin and balancing a cup on one knee and a sandwich on the other."

It was, at times, a curious and not unpleasant war.

◆ ◆ ◆

MEANWHILE, Cole picked up the tangled threads of his personal life in Marseilles. When not leading a convoy or engaged in some swindle, Cole was squiring one of his numerous mistresses. He was, according to Lepers, "a man who liked women." Maurice Van de Kerckhove noted that he "had affairs everywhere" and possessed "a reputation for success with women."

Not all females were susceptible to his charm. In March 1941 Jeanne Huyge took refuge over the La Madeleine salon after narrowly escaping arrest. She met Cole several times as he came and went on escape line business. To her critical eye he "had a face like the edge of a knife."

Later, though, she glimpsed the passions he aroused in other women. Hunted in the north, she had moved south to Toulouse and gone to work for French intelligence, which sent her to the Lille region at intervals. During one such trip, she and Voglimacci were over the shop when they heard someone coming up the stairs. Huyge ducked into the closet while Voglimacci answered the door.

One of Cole's girlfriends had heard someone was staying over the salon. She concluded that Cole had returned from traveling without coming to see her. A scene ensued as she demanded to know where Cole was hidden. Voglimacci tried to allay her suspicions and maneuver her out the door. The woman insisted on looking in the closet. She carried on this way until Huyge, exasperated cried out, "No! Paul is not in here!" Cole's mistress regained her composure and left.

In Marseilles Cole cultivated romantic interests among his entourage along the Canebière. He found it a simple matter to intrigue patriotic young Frenchwomen with his polished imitation of an upper-class British officer. Most of these affairs were casual and transitory. But at the end of that summer of 1941, Cole developed a more serious relationship with a woman recruited recently into the Garrow organization.

She would become one of his most faithful admirers and, in consequence, one of his most badly abused victims.

◆ ◆ ◆

SUZANNE WARENGHEM, a dark-haired nineteen-year-old woman with classically high-featured French looks, had joined the escape line near the beginning of July, when she appeared at the Seamen's Mission with two Scottish soldiers.

Sergeant Thomas Edgar and Private James Tobin of the Fifty-first Highland Division, medical orderlies captured after Dunkirk, had accompanied a group of British wounded through various prisoner-of-war camps to the Val-de-Grâce Hospital in Paris. In the spring of 1941 these wounded were about to be transferred to Germany or invalided home. Tobin and Edgar began to think about escape.

In mid-June they clambered over a hospital roof, dropped into a courtyard and walked out the gate. Suzanne Warenghem, a regular visitor to British soldiers in Paris hospitals, and Roger Pelletier, a French student, waited outside with raincoats to cover their British uniforms. Over the next three days Warenghem and Pelletier set about obtaining civilian clothes and false documents for the two escapers. Tobin indulged in some sight-seeing, ascending the Eiffel Tower in a Paris that was "alive with Germans."

When all was ready, the two escapers and their guides traveled into Vichy France via Bordeaux. For the next two weeks they laid low in southwest France, where Pelletier worked in a Chantier de la Jeunesse, a Vichy youth camp. But that was a less than ideal hideout. Soon Warenghem, Tobin, and Edgar continued on to Marseilles.

The two soldiers inquired at the American Consulate, where an official offered no encouragement. "There's about a hundred of you guys coming in here each week," he told them. "So don't come back." They ignored his advice to surrender to the French authorities.

They had only one other address, that of a French insurance broker who proved of no help. But his secretary pointed them towards Caskie's establishment. The minister introduced them to an Australian named Bruce Dowding, who brought them to a brothel in the rue du Paradis. They stayed there for five days or so, while the passage of the two Britons was arranged. Tobin and Edgar were given five hundred francs and two hundred pesetas apiece and sent with twenty other escapers on their way to Spain.

Warenghem, much taken with the fresh-faced, wavy-haired Tommy Edgar, begged to be sent to London with them. She was refused, but not sent away. The Garrow Organization's officers had been impressed by her work bringing Tobin and Edgar south. Dowding offered her a job as a guide. In a Marseilles café, not long after she began working for the line, Warenghem was introduced to its northern coordinator, Paul Cole.

◆ ◆ ◆

BY AUGUST the two were keeping regular company. Cole brought Suzanne around to meet his friends on the Canebière, introducing her as an English student. Warenghem had heard from others in the organization that Cole had many mistresses and was considered a rake. But such a reputation might be cast in a romantic light.

Cole "had a taste, which he never attempted to conceal, for good food, fine wine, and glamorous women," writes Warenghem's biographer, Gordon Young. "He was at his best seated at a dinner table talking easily, in a low voice and impressively, though with a show of modesty befitting an English gentleman, of his past exploits as a secret-service agent."

This might have swayed any young woman in that era when Britain was a bright bastion of resistance for those held in durance vile on the Continent. But Warenghem was perhaps more susceptible than most to Cole's British charm.

Her father, Georges Warenghem, was half-English. Her mother had died in childbirth, and Warenghem was raised with the help of her father's relatives in Paris. But she spent many holidays across the Channel, where she became fluent in the language of Shakespeare and, she told Young, "learned to love England."

Her youthful attachment to Britain was strong. During the 1938 Munich crisis, she announced to her cousins that in the event of war she hoped to remain in England. But the threat was deferred, and she returned to her father's house in Le Havre, working as a secretary in a high school there. Warenghem continued with teaching jobs until the Phoney War gave way to the *Débâcle*, and bombardments obliged the Warenghems to flee to the less hazardous Normandy village of Saint-Pierre-le-Vieux.

Eager to take up the battle in England, Warenghem hitchhiked south to the Pyrenees. But, unable to afford a high-priced guide into Spain, she renounced her plan and went home. Eventually she moved to Paris to live with her aunt, Jeanne Warenghem, who lived just west of Paris. Working as a secretary in Versailles, Warenghem continued to express her indignation at the German occupation by chalking Gaullist and anti-Nazi slogans on walls around the city. She also began to visit wounded British POWs in hospitals around the capital, a course that eventually led her to Garrow and company.

Her deepening relationship with Cole was matched by increased responsibility within the escape line. One day that September, Garrow asked her to go back to Paris to work as an agent, operating under the orders of Cole. A few days later she traveled with Roland Lepers back up the escape route to Paris.

Explaining to her aunt that she had found a new job with an American journalist named Paul Cole, she plunged into the new assignment. Warenghem saw to the many requirements for bringing gangs of escapers in and out of town on their way between Lille and Marseilles.

Guerisse watched this development with concern. He could see that Warenghem was "very much attached" to Cole. He was less certain of the British agent's devotion to the enthusiastic but naive French girl. The soldier-physician understood how romances were forged under the stress of constant danger. But he sensed Warenghem was badly mistaken in placing her faith in Cole.

"I wanted to warn her that this man was a liar, a fraud," he stated later. "But what could I say? She was in love."

14

"He Was Being Closely Watched"

COLE'S MOVE to Paris may have been occasioned by the arrest in late August of James Smith, who had almost ceaselessly traveled between Lille and Marseilles that summer. At the end of July Smith had brought three RAF pilots and three infantrymen to Marseilles, for once handing them directly to the Garrow Organization without the intermediary of Cole. Then Smith returned to Lille and, after a lull of some weeks, again set out for the south with three British airmen in tow.

Stopping in Bethune, Smith met a Frenchman who previously had channeled escapers and information into the line. He asked if the Scot could take along a man he identified as a Norwegian pilot. Smith agreed and the entire convoy continued by train to Abbeville, where Carpentier made up false identity cards and gave them bridge passes. That night they slept in Paris and set out again in the morning.

In Orléans, about halfway to Tours, two German policemen and four Luftwaffe officers entered the escapers' train compartment and started questioning them in French. "The three gunners could not speak French and their game was up," Smith later reported. He managed to convince the Germans he was a Frenchman and reached the toilet compartment, where he flushed away the intelligence materials and letters he was carrying. But when he came out he was arrested and the Germans seized the attaché case which he had placed on the overhead luggage rack. The briefcase contained military information and letters addressed to Ian Garrow.

Smith's arrest was a blow to the escape line; it would not be easy to replace the sturdy Scot. But there were more serious implications. The infiltration of the escape line by a German disguised as a Norwegian meant that the enemy's counterintelligence services were on to the Garrow Organization's northern wing. Before long this pressure was to mount and focus on Cole himself.

◆ ◆ ◆

DESPITE THE massive German occupation force and a society riddled with collaborators and Gestapo informants, Cole found Paris a convenient location from which to oversee the north-south movement of escapers. His closest coworker was Warenghem, who escorted the escapers around the city and arranged their movement by train through Tours to the Demarcation Line. But Cole had also found several new agents on the Left Bank to assist him in both escape work and intelligence gathering.

The most active of these was Vladimir de Fligué, thirty-five, a Russian émigré of great energy and enthusiasm who owned an electrical manufacturing concern in Paris. Born to a prominent family in St. Petersburg in 1905, de Fligué was the grandson of one of Czar Nicholas II's most trusted ministers. After the Russian Revolution his family fled through Turkey to France, where de Fligué studied engineering. In 1936 he launched Servo-Contact, a company fabricating sophisticated switching devices for trains and other industrial systems.

After meeting Cole that September, de Fligué took British escapers into his apartment and factory, both located in the rue Quatrefages, near the Jardin des Plantes in the Latin Quarter. Agnes Kirman, a neighbor in the same building, also put them up. Kirman was the secretary and mistress of another member of Cole's Paris subcircuit: Fernand Holweck, fifty-one, a distinguished researcher with the Curie Institute.

A brilliant practical physicist, Holweck worked with Marie Curie from 1911 until 1914. During World War I, he developed radio communications for the French Army. Later Holweck pioneered in incandescent lighting, phototransmission, sonar, short-wave, gravitational measurement, and radiation therapy. Though philosophically opposed to armaments work, Holweck troubleshot for the French military. He resolved a number of prewar defense-industry headaches ranging from airplane cannons that froze at high altitudes to fogging submarine periscopes.

Holweck told Warenghem once that he wished to go to England to serve the Allied cause. He may have contributed some scientific intelligence to the espionage side of Cole's business. But his main function was to provide false documents for the escapers passing through de Fligué's flat.

The third member of Cole's Paris circuit was Édouard Bernaer, sixty-nine, a journalist. As a younger man Bernaer had worked in London for the Reuters news agency, then launched a series of publications in France. One of these was a radio magazine called, initially, the *Wireless Weekly*, later known as *France Radio*. Bernaer may have met Holweck before the war through this publication, as the scientist was then working on short-wave transmission.

French secret-service documents state that in October 1940, Bernaer "established contact with Commandant d'Honicthun of the Postal Censorship at Toulouse, to whom he provided reports." This same report says that "it was he who put Cole into touch with the engineer Fligué and the physicist Hollweck [sic], who had proposed together to create an intelligence network and to transmit the information gathered by wireless."

◆ ◆ ◆

WARENGHEM, deeply involved in all this, was drawn closer to Cole. She was "flattered by Paul's tactful attentions and impressed by her new role as the chief assistant to a British officer of high repute," writes Young. "Moreover, she was fired by enthusiasm for their common cause."

They often dined together at the Chôpe du Pont Neuf, a brasserie on the fringe of Les Halles, Zola's "belly of Paris," where appetites of all kinds could be satisfied late at night by vendors of onion soup and perfumed flesh. Escapers were brought to the Chope du Pont Neuf for a hot meal after their arrival at the Gare du Nord.

The restaurant, capacious and popular, with a reputation for hearty late-night fare, was divided into two dining rooms separated by a horseshoe-shaped bar. While German soldiers and civilians dined in the front of the Chôpe, British escapers were seated on the red-upholstered banquettes at the back by owner Eugène Durand.

The restaurateur was incorporated into the fictive life story Cole related to his admiring female assistant and companion over meals in the brasserie. As a boy, Cole told her, he often traveled with his widowed mother to Paris, where they stayed at a hotel in the rue du Pont Neuf. It was then, said Cole, that he had picked up his fractured French and become acquainted with the burly restaurant owner.

If Warenghem believed this, others were starting to challenge Cole's veracity. Lepers had "started wondering" about some of the inconsistencies in Cole's behavior. He still resented the high-handed way in which the Cockney had brushed him aside after the link with Garrow was established. Lepers was especially unhappy with the exploitative arrangement by which Cole stepped in once the French guide had led convoys through the Forbidden and Occupied zones, claiming the credit and pocketing the funds.

No longer an ardent admirer of the Cockney, the younger man

was reaching a bitter conclusion: "Cole had worked out a scheme; he used me."

◆ ◆ ◆

LEPERS WAS NOT ALONE in his dissatisfaction. That autumn brought ever more serious questions about Cole in the north and south alike. His superiors and those under his command harbored grave doubts about his honesty and trustworthiness. Some felt he was no longer of use to the escape line, posing a danger to its security. But as yet only a few believed, as did Caskie, that Cole was "half a man, and when the unresolved half was defined, he might be a traitor."

At first the suspicions concerned only Cole's finances. "He was spending far more money on women and wine than he was being paid," noted Guerisse, "and was being closely watched." François Duprez confided to his wife, "I'm starting to lose confidence in Paul. We're losing money, and we don't know where it's going."

Voglimacci also remarked on a worrisome change. As she cut and combed hair in the salon, she listened to reports of the tall Englishman spending money freely in Lille's cafés and restaurants. Gossip had it that Cole was consuming "a passable amount of champagne." He was seen speaking English in public as though he no longer had anything to conceal. The Cockney was "too sure of himself; he wasn't afraid of the Germans." Cole had always exhibited contempt for the enemy, but now his conduct was reckless.

At the same time, he became more furtive and secretive. Cole had always cultivated "an air of mystery" around Lepers. The more that was known about his movements and activities, the greater was the danger that he would be exposed. "He wanted us to know as little as possible about him," said Lepers.

Earlier, this was accepted because of the heavy responsibilities Cole had shouldered. But by late in 1941, Lepers could see that Cole was doing less and less work in the escape line while spending money freely on himself and his women.

His northern associates were deeply concerned. But from the outset Cole had been careful to circumscribe contact between the British in Marseilles and Lepers, who did not know of Garrow's headquarters in the Rodocanachi flat. "We were all worried," Lepers said later. "But what could we do? I couldn't go and knock on any door. I didn't know where the doors were."

◆ ◆ ◆

ALFRED LANSELLE also was distressed about the change that had come over Cole. The Saint-Omer merchant felt there was "something that didn't square" in the agent's behavior. He had an indirect channel of communication with Marseilles and knew that Cole was asking for more and more money. He was also hearing that "Paul was out on the town in Paris and chasing women." Lanselle concluded that the Cockney now represented a danger.

He underscored the instructions he had given from the start to his helpers in the Pas de Calais, those who had fliers to hand over to the English agent. They were to take the airmen to the house in the avenue Bernadette in La Madeleine, but were not to give their names or any other information to those who took in the evaders.

"You knock three times on the door, and you hand over the Englishmen that you are guiding, and you say, 'Here's a package for Madeleine-Marie,'" Lanselle told them. But he added, "Don't go in, don't try to make contact. Because you never know what may happen." At first this was just common sense. But now it seemed essential to limit Cole's knowledge of who had helped him.

Lanselle, who once had admired Cole, now envisioned desperate measures. Near the end of September 1941, he went to Desiré Didry and a priest named Courquin, who worked with the network. He asked them to arrange for Cole to come to Saint-Omer. Lanselle would be waiting with a car to take Cole off and shoot him.

But Didry and the priest dissuaded him from this course. Later he would regret having listened to them.

◆ ◆ ◆

LIKE A CHEAP SUIT, the Cockney's charm was wearing thin. He inspired distrust rather than confidence when, enigmatically, he paid a visit to Jeanne Huyge in Toulouse that fall.

For her work with the French intelligence service, she had assumed the identity of Claudine Breuvart, twenty-seven, wife of a nonexistent French Army officer posted to China. In visits to the north, she picked up intelligence collected by other agents. While moving from town to town by streetcar, she looked for German Army unit designations on signposts, circling page numbers and letters in a detective novel to prompt her memory when she was safely back in Toulouse. Her biggest coup was locating a tank company of which the Deuxième Bureau had lost track.

Despite her precautions, German agents began inquiring at the Toulouse boarding house where she lived, one of them disguised in the *soutane* of a French *curé*. She also was being watched by the Direction de la Surveillance du Territoire. Vichy security agents called her in for questioning after each trip north.

Early in September she received a letter from Cole suggesting they meet. When they sat down at an outdoor café table in Toulouse later that month, Cole appealed to her to come back to the north to work with him. "The convoys of Englishmen have stopped," Cole told her grimly. "Things aren't going well at all."

Huyge had no reason to suspect Cole then. But she had one thought on hearing this: "Paul doesn't know I've been back in the north." This seemed odd and triggered caution. Each time she had gone to the north, she had stopped to see Jeannine Voglimacci and stayed above her salon for a night or two. But the hairdresser apparently had not confided this information to Cole. Huyge, therefore, was not about to tell him herself or return to the north to work for him.

"If the people in the north have become so stupid," she told him, "I'm not going to risk my neck for them."

There were only two explanations for Cole's visit to Huyge in Toulouse. One was that he needed Huyge, an experienced guide, to replace Smith and enable him to dispense with Lepers and others who were beginning to challenge him.

But his overture to Huyge would later appear in a different light. For those who would conclude that he already was in the pay of the Germans at this date, the meeting would appear to be an attempt to lure her back to the north, where she could be arrested by the Abwehr. There never would appear any solid evidence to prove this. But the episode hinted that the wily agent's tangled web of deceit was starting to unravel.

◆ ◆ ◆

HENRI DUPREZ was one of the first to have proof that Cole was defrauding the network. Since the end of 1940, the manufacturer and others had financed the escapers' travel out of their own pockets. This was a considerable sacrifice for those pinched by the inflationary, shortage-ridden occupation economy. Cole had assured Duprez that British intelligence would eventually reimburse these advances. But the swindler's pledges remained unfulfilled.

The printer, Chevalier, had quickly pegged the Cockney for a sharp who, capitalizing on the goodwill extended to British troops, "duped many in the Lille region." In early 1941, Cole had asked Chevalier for five thousand francs to evacuate an English family. Chevalier agreed, but personally confirmed the existence of the family. In the same house, he found two Tommies who were "outraged at Cole's behavior." They told the printer they had "neither asked for nor received anything" from the deserter.

Some time after this, Henri Duprez received a letter from Garrow. The Scot had written to inform the northerners of difficulties in Marseilles. It had been "impossible to obtain even a partial cooperation from the French authorities." Garrow explained that "the North African route that I sometimes used has become mortally dangerous."

Some of the men sent that way "at a very high price" had been captured and thrown into French colonial prisons.

Then the Scot turned to financial concerns. "The bearer of this message will describe our present method [of reimbursement] and will explain everything to you," he wrote. For Duprez the letter "confirmed that Paul Cole was receiving money and, far from passing it on to those who were entitled or make an accounting, on the contrary asked for more."

When Cole next requested money for evaders about to depart for Marseilles, Duprez demanded receipts signed by the escapers in question, accompanied by their photos. The consequences for Duprez would be serious if these notes and photographs ever fell into the hands of the German police. But Duprez saw a crisis looming over Cole and wanted solid evidence in hand.

◆ ◆ ◆

THE SITUATION soon worsened, Duprez later noted, "as other proofs of Cole's treason were presented."

Maurice Van Camelbecke, forty-five, one of the line's most active guides, urgently summoned Duprez one day. In the apartment over Voglimacci's shop, he found Cole with a man claiming to be a Polish RAF flier shot down in the region. But the man had no papers, spoke very poor English, and knew not a word of French.

Van Camelbecke feared he might be a German infiltrator. Asked for proof, the man pulled out his shirt tails and yanked up the waist band of his shorts, where an RAF serial number was displayed. Duprez jotted this down and hurried off to see Jean Catrice of the Voix du Nord network of the Resistance, who could contact London by radio.

In a few days, word came back that the flier was a genuine member of the Allied forces. Duprez looked up Van Camelbecke to tell him the Pole could be shipped south. He was dismayed to learn that the man, entrusted to Cole, had been in the Maison Cellulaire de Loos, a prison south of Lille, since the evening after Duprez had taken his serial number. Cole, who had said nothing about the capture of the Pole, disappeared for the next ten days.

Henri Duprez's suspicions hardened after learning that Cole had shown up at Van Camelbecke's home driving one of the black Citroën sedans favored by the German security forces throughout France. Van Camelbecke thought he recognized the vehicle as one belonging to the German police authorities in Roubaix. He later confirmed this, having jotted down the license plate number. Assuming the vehicle was stolen, Van Camelbecke urged Cole to be more cautious. "Don't worry, Maurice," the Cockney responded, "I've got the Germans in my pocket."

Henri Duprez was furious at what could only be foolhardiness or outright treason. In view of other "flagrant" incidents, it had to be the latter.

"This is impossible!" he exclaimed. "We've got to eliminate Cole. Otherwise we're heading for a catastrophe."

Duprez consulted Jean Catrice, who advised him that London would have to be consulted on such a major step. Within a few days, Duprez heard that "London does not agree." But Catrice said he would arrange a meeting with British representatives to discuss the problem.

One afternoon that September, Duprez went to a house in the rue de Trentes in Lille. Catrice introduced him to two men who identified themselves as British agents. Duprez explained his doubts about Cole—the swindles, the Pole's unexplained arrest, the German police vehicle.

"Cole is a traitor," Duprez told the two agents. "He's got to be killed."

He was stupefied at the response. "If you touch one hair on the head of Paul Cole," said one of the Englishmen, "you yourself will pay the consequences." If there was a problem, they assured him, Cole would be dealt with by the British themselves.

Who were these men? What agency did they represent? Why did they protect Cole?

The first two questions cannot be answered without access to official files. But the third may be addressed. One possibility is that the British simply were unwilling to authorize the execution of an English agent, however deserving this punishment, by a French Resistance group. But it is also possible that someone in London considered Cole too valuable to be eliminated for the mere theft of funds and vague suspicions of treason.

15

"I Decided Cole Needed Killing"

AT THE BEGINNING of October 1941, Ian Garrow finally decided to take action on Cole, having concluded finally that the Cockney's fecklessness was no longer tolerable. Garrow had known for some time of Cole's profiteering, his sideline in moving paying civilians through the line, and his generally mercenary comportment. But the Scot was slow to anger. A catalyst was required to bring down his wrath and Guerisse willingly set things in motion.

It happened while Cole was in Marseilles delivering some airmen. He had come down from Paris with a couple of his female acquaintances, whom he passed off as guides. After he had reimbursed Cole's purported expenses, Garrow asked when he would return north. Cole said he was taking the train to Lyon that night, for the first leg of the trip back to Lille. The two men shook hands and that was that.

The next day Guerisse was having lunch in a Greek restaurant off the Canebière, when he saw one of Cole's female friends sitting at another table. He walked over.

"What a pleasure to see you here!" said Guerisse, who could apply charm when he wanted to. "Didn't you leave Marseilles yester-day?"

"No," said the woman. "We're going out dancing tonight with Paul and Suzanne."

"Oh?" said Guerisse. "Where's that?"

She mentioned a popular dance hall in Marseilles. Having found out what he wanted to know, Guerisse left after more friendly chat and went back to his table.

Later that day Guerisse and Garrow were unwinding over glasses of whiskey. "Ian," said Guerisse. "Where do you suppose Cole is right now?"

"Oh, somewhere near Lyon," said Garrow. "Probably crossing the Demarcation Line by now. He was taking the train last night."

"You believed him when he told you that?"

"Of course."

"Well, if you would like to meet him, come with me tonight."

◆ ◆ ◆

IN THE DANCING, the two officers ordered drinks at the bar, then surveyed the room. An accordionist accompanied by a band was playing tangoes, polkas, and waltzes. Many dancers were following a step then popular with the French mob, in which the man scowled, held one arm dramatically behind him, and flung his partner about the floor.

They picked out Cole among the crowd. He appeared to be enjoying himself. He didn't see Garrow and Guerisse until the Scot approached the dance floor during a number and made a sign. They could see the electrifying effect it had on him. But Cole pulled himself together quickly, came up to them, and drew himself to loose attention.

Guerisse could see that the Cockney was in a tight spot: "Something was broken there between Garrow and him."

The exchange between Garrow and Cole was brief. "I hope you'll be in Lille soon?" Garrow said.

"Yes, sir," Cole answered. "Tomorrow morning."

Guerisse sensed that the dance-hall encounter had altered Garrow's view of Cole. A few days later this was confirmed.

"Pat," Garrow said, "I think you had better go to the north and inquire about Cole's activities."

Guerisse prepared to leave for Lille, relieved that Garrow's eyes had been opened. He did not know how far the Scot had resolved to take the matter.

"I had discovered in my solitary wanderings, all with a purpose, sufficient of Cole's activities to be convinced of his potential danger," Garrow later wrote to Donald Darling. The Scot had no evidence of treasonous conduct. But Cole's dishonesty made him "no less dangerous" to the network. "So I decided after much thought that Cole needed killing, and I was the man who had to do it, in spite of [the] certainty of subsequent court-martial."

Seeking the medical counsel of Georges Rodocanachi, he asked how a man might be assassinated so as "not to invite a police inquiry and investigation." The physician explained that a massive injection of insulin would produce a coma in anyone other than a diabetic. Then all that would be required was "a gentle push into one of the side basins of the Old Port."

Garrow made ready to dispatch the embezzler, choosing for the repugnant task an isolated spot on the dark quays behind Fort Saint-Nicolas, not far from the Daurade Restaurant.

"All was ready," related the Scotsman, "and we awaited Paul's return from the north."

◆ ◆ ◆

GUERISSE FOUND THE situation in La Madeleine was worse than he had feared. He arrived there around the end of the first week in October, traveling with Maurice Dufour, who had been one of his guards at Saint-Hippolyte-du-Fort several months before. The two men had crossed into the Forbidden Zone of the north using a stratagem shown them by local contacts.

It was a very simple dodge. They obtained canceled tickets for travel from Arras, to the north in the Forbidden Zone, south to Amiens, where they were. Then they mingled with a crowd of passengers coming off a train from Arras. Unable to show travel permits allowing access into the Occupied Zone, they were turned back onto the very train they wanted to carry them northward.

Once in the Lille area, Guerisse was discreet in his movements. He did not want Cole to know that the Garrow organization was checking up on him. Under the identity of Joseph Cartier, Guerisse called upon François Duprez in the rue de la Gare. The meeting was revelatory and deeply troubling.

Duprez was indignant to hear of Cole's claims that money had been left on deposit with him. Cole, he said, had never given him a *sou*, and quite to the contrary had been an incessant drain upon those in the north. Cole was constantly on the road, but frequently returned with nothing to show for his long absences. The Cockney laid this to a lack of funds. His disbelieving associates guessed that their money was being spent on Cole's many girlfriends.

But there was worse. "There were men," Duprez said, "who should have arrived, but who did not reach their destination." British escapers entrusted to Cole never passed through Pierre Carpentier's hands in Abbeville. "They disappeared," Guerisse learned.

These were grave allegations. Cole would have to face his accusers. The Belgian asked Duprez to come personally to Marseilles to testify before Ian Garrow. Duprez agreed to do this, and Guerisse gave him instructions on how to contact the organization there.

Guerisse also questioned Roland Lepers. The British agent's one-time assistant explained his own doubts. Guerisse told Lepers to arrange a convoy to Marseilles as soon as possible and see that Cole escorted it to the end of the line. Once in Marseilles Lepers was to take a room in his own name at the Hôtel Paris-Nice, just below the wide stone steps leading up to the Gare Saint Charles. He would hear from the organization.

With these matters arranged, Guerisse hastened back to Marseilles to await the denouement of the affair.

♦　♦　♦

CORNELIUS VERLOOP was likewise eager to put his hands on Cole. The Abwehr agent had been picking up leads on the British sergeant for months. Verloop was all the more eager to talk to Cole for having missed arresting him on an earlier occasion.

This came about in June 1941, after he met a young woman named Henriette in the restaurant of the Hôtel Central in Lille. Verloop was posing as a British businessman overseeing his interests under the occupation. He invited the girl to dine with him. When Henriette talked indiscreetly of British escapers she had met in the homes of friends, Verloop coerced her into disclosing more.

Postwar testimony would establish that she "very rapidly became Verloop's mistress and was assigned by him to seek out the English sheltered in the region."

Henriette brought Verloop to the home of a well-to-do notary in Lille. Cole frequently stopped there for meals and other handouts. She had no objection to seeing Colson, as the deserter was known, arrested. She knew he had exploited many families in the region.

In the *salon*, she and Verloop chatted with the wife of the house, who said it was not certain Cole would come that day. Verloop, alert, caught a blur of movement behind a stained glass door. He became certain someone was standing there. The young daughter of the house came into the room a short while after and said "Harold" was not coming. He had phoned.

But Verloop could see the telephone in the *salon*, which had not rung. The Dutchman then understood that Colson was listening from the other room.

Verloop regretted that he had not called upon the Geheime Feld-polizei to surround the house while he entered. He left without trying to make an arrest. Cole might have been armed and he didn't want a shootout. But now he knew the Englishman was in the area, exploiting the patriotism of the French men and the sentiments of French women who were "proud that an Englishman was sleeping with them."

A lot of the British stragglers took advantage of this phenomenon. But Cole was in a class of his own. "Everywhere there were women," said Verloop, "and everywhere he was asking for money."

Verloop was no romantic when it came to English evaders and their French mistresses. There were the two British soldiers who had been arrested and brought in front of his desk in GFP headquarters. They had been living in the home of two French women. "One was sleeping with the mother, the other with the daughter."

He told the soldiers, "Do me a favor: don't give me the address of these two women." But the two soldiers gave out the names anyway. Two hours later the secret police had hauled in the two women. That was Verloop's work. But it didn't dispose him any more kindly towards the BEF stragglers.

Another time his agents were tipped to the whereabouts of a Canadian with ties to Cole. The GFP raid caught the Canadian in bed with his mistress, who was straddling the man with her back to the door. The Canadian saw the Germans enter. Without hesitation he fired off several shots from under the covers and killed the *Oberst* commanding the squad. The other Germans opened fire. Shortly the Canadian and his mistress were dead too.

The incident angered Verloop. But he couldn't help admiring the man's extraordinary presence of mind. "He's in the middle of screwing, but he fires at the guy!"

◆ ◆ ◆

VERLOOP ALWAYS APPROACHED his work with enthusiasm. Born in the Hague in 1909, this professional adventurer had enlisted in the French Foreign Legion in 1935. Around the same time, he went on the Abwehr payroll. Ideology had little to do with this. He was like most of the other undercover agents serving the Abwehr's counterintelligence apparatus: "Norwegians, Americans, English, French, Spanish, Portuguese, Egyptians, everything. They were people who said, *'Voila!* I'm going to see something of the world.'"

After the fall of France, Verloop quickly became a principal agent within the Lille *Abwehrstelle*, the main German counterintelligence outpost in the north of France. Besides Captain Karl Hegener, there were six other Germans in the secret-police branch. But they did little of the field work themselves. Outside work was subcontracted, in effect, to about fifty French agents, most of them right-wing or fascist collaborators.

The Abwehr agent roster comprised, by one French postwar account, "the most superb collection of hoodlums and failures." These agents were "intoxicated by the small parcel of authority they possessed. They gave free rein to their sexual and sadistic instincts, and woe to whosoever was arrested by these individuals."

Their motives were simple: "They worked for the Nazis because the risk was slight and their employer paid well." The Abwehr henchmen had fixed salaries ranging between six thousand and ten thousand francs a month plus travel expenses and whatever they could extort from their victims. Each was supplied with a false identity card and passport, a permit to carry arms, and a weapon.

The identities of these men and women were protected carefully by an Abwehr blind system; their true names were known only to their German "handler" and a secret-service bureaucrat in the Abwehr's Stuttgart headquarters. Likewise, they did not know the true names of their controllers, whom they met at anonymous offices in Lille.

These were the men and women whom the Abwehr had, by late 1941, recruited and set to burrowing into the French and British nets operating in the region. Their reports, and the small, white slips of paper coming from the Abwehr office in Lille paying cash for tips from the general public, were sent to Verloop for action.

The Dutchman had direct access to Hegener and could call out the GFP on his own authority. Under the code name of "Vindictive," he pursued the cases that interested him the most. His territory included most everything between Brussels and Paris, from the Channel coast to a point just east of the French capital.

Verloop had a confidence-inspiring smile and a talent for turning casual conversations to his own interests. He could be ruthless when necessary. His Dutch origins helped; there were too many Flamands even in French Flanders for a Low Countries accent to provoke interest or concern. Verloop's undercover identities reflected this vagueness of provenance: Philippe Winckler, Leopold Vanhout. He assumed protective covering, passing for anything from a traveling salesman to a sailor to a harmless barfly.

His most productive gambit was the eternal opening line: "Can I buy you a drink?" Café garrulousness did the rest. Human frailty was his ally. *"Tout le monde est faible,"* he had concluded. "Everyone has a weakness."

Harold Cole had more than most. This was already working in the Dutchman's favor.

16

"Everyone Seemed to Look Up to Him"

ON THE TWENTY-SECOND of October, two newspaper articles of more than passing interest to those working in northern escape lines appeared on page one of the *Grand Echo du Nord*. One reported that seven British fighters had been shot down over the Pas de Calais. The other was calculated to give pause to anyone inclined to assist those RAF fliers still at large in the region.

"Two Belgians Condemned to Death for Having Helped an English Flier," proclaimed its headline. Leon Charlier and Armand Durand had "given shelter, fed, and aided in the escape of an English aviator who made a forced landing." The death penalty, imposed under German occupation law, was "without appeal," reported the newspaper, which published under the sway of a German propaganda service.

Those helpers of the Garrow Organization still at liberty that day read this with a new understanding. Only the night before, the GFP had rounded up a score or so of MI9 helpers around Lille. Most were guilty of no more than sheltering British escapers in their homes.

Most were to be deported or executed under the same law enforced in the case of the two Belgians.

The raids were the work of Cornelius Verloop. For him and his superiors, putting escape lines out of business was nearly as important as dismantling espionage circuits. Germany had lost the Battle of Britain in the autumn of 1940. Now, a year later, the RAF was carrying the battle to the Reich. "Hitler and Goering attached importance to smashing the escape lines," writes MI9 official Neave. "They realized the impact on the Allied war effort of hundreds of trained airmen slipping through their hands."

The arrests carried out during the night of October 21 and 22 did not halt the escape activity in the north, or even slow it significantly. But it was a sign that Verloop and other agents were making inroads into the networks, moving closer to those in command.

After meeting Verbeke in June, Verloop had pressured her to help him insinuate himself into the tightly knit circles of French helpers. She introduced Verloop to a woman named Pachy in Gondecourt who was harboring British escapers. Then Verloop branched out to workers in neighboring towns: Eugène Ringeval and André Modave in Libercourt; Octave Bouchez and family in Lille; and many others.

It may have been in the hope of pulling in the elusive Captain Colson—the identity by which Verloop knew Cole—that the October sweep was launched. Verloop began with the arrest of a certain Mademoiselle Godart. He knew she suspected him of being a German infiltrator. Godart was seized as she met several other escape line workers at the buffet in the Lille train station.

Her family in Ronchin was found to be concealing three Belgian evaders. A British soldier named David Anderson was discovered in Douai. Yet Cole remained as elusive as ever.

◆ ◆ ◆

THE GFP SWEEP threw a scare into Cole's northern network. But its operations continued. Many of the RAF fliers sheltered by the escape line were not informed of the blow. For English aviator George

Barclay, the arrests simply meant an unexplained delay in his trip home.

Barclay's Spitfire was shot up by Messerschmitts over the Pas de Calais in September. He had crash-landed in a large field, pretending to be dead while an enemy fighter circled overhead. He extracted himself from the cockpit of his plane and ran for cover. A French peasant laboring in a field fifty yards away studiously ignored the young pilot.

Minutes before, he had been airborne with the expectation of returning to a British airdrome after fulfilling his mission. Now he was on foot, in a strange land, hunted. Barclay had "never felt so lost," he later recorded. Fearing capture, Barclay "peeped round hedges before turning corners and bolted flat out across open spaces so as not to be caught in the open."

Ridding himself of his starched collar and tie, the airman turned his tunic inside out and pulled his trousers down over his flying boots. He quickly grew fatigued in the heat of Indian summer. Finally he appealed for help at a farmhouse. *"Je suis aviateur anglais,"* he explained several times at several doors before a woman gave him clothes and money, and sent him with her daughter to the village *curé*.

The priest passed Barclay along to a farmer named Maurice Ghorice, who was an avid helper of downed British pilots. At the sight of a descending parachute, Ghorice would race by bicycle to meet the pilot with civilian dress, whisking him away before the Germans arrived. "One day he found a pilot with a head wound. He was just going to whip off his uniform when some Huns arrived and he discovered that the pilot was a Hun too."

Soon Barclay was transferred to La Madeleine, the eye of the storm brewing over the north. François Duprez gave him forged identification papers in the name of Georges Maurice Barrois of the rue Solferino in Lille. Then Barclay was brought to the house in the avenue Bernadette. Madeleine Deram gave him shaving gear, clean linen, and a hand-me-down suit.

Barclay, who spoke schoolboy French, learned from Deram that she and her son Marcel, thirteen, "were very afraid the Gestapo was on their tail." This translated into great tension in the household. "Tremendous fights" broke out between mother and son. Deram would scream dire threats and "rush at him, seizing any old bottle and brandishing it above her head."

In between times, she "was always talking about Monsieur Paul," Barclay noted. "Everyone seemed to look up to him, he had a great hold over the Frenchmen who knew him, owing to his fearlessness and the splendid work he was doing."

One afternoon Fernand Salingue came to the house. That day the Derams had been "working themselves into a new pitch of fury." Barclay had tried to "quell the riot" by interesting Marcel in games with the dog, Kirsch. The boy was not allowed to play outside. His mother feared he would give them away with loose talk.

As Deram served coffee, Salingue informed the Englishman of plans to move him to Burbure. "Joy spread over his face," Salingue later noted. "He looked at me and put his hands on my shoulders and said several times, 'Ah, Fernand! Fernand!'"

Two days later, Salingue came for Barclay and the two boarded a train in the Lille station. As it pulled out, the flier began intently to study the French newspaper Salingue had handed him, wishing to avoid conversation with strangers. They traveled all day and spent the night in a small-town hotel. When they reached Burbure late the following evening, Salingue's wife Elisa prepared them a meal. Barclay and his host dined on eggs and fried potatoes, the fare that the Tommies "had always asked for before Dunkirk."

In Burbure he was joined by other members of the convoy that was shaping up for the trip south. Among them was a squadron leader named Harry Bufton, who had trained with Barclay. Bufton and his crew of five had force-landed while returning from a bombing raid on Cologne with a shot-up engine. The two British pilots "hugged each other, both deeply moved, and George cried, 'Hurrah!'" Salingue later noted.

On October 11 Barclay finally met Cole, whom the airman "gathered was the mainstay of the organization getting bodies out of France." The next day Barclay and Bufton were informed that their departure was set for October 22. But then Verloop and the GFP pounced. The convoy would not leave until the end of the month.

◆ ◆ ◆

ON OCTOBER 29 Barclay and Bufton traveled by bicycle to the town of Marles, deep in the countryside of the Pas de Calais. There they picked up the local train that ran from Lille to Abbeville. For hours they trundled past smokestacks and steeples in one coal and farming community after another, from the industrial region around Bethune to fields now stripped of their hay and corn.

Cole and Lepers were already aboard with four RAF pilots and a handful of Scottish soldiers. In Abbeville they crossed the Somme bridge. By evening the convoy was dining at the Chôpe du Pont Neuf, proceeding later to the Hôtel Nicolas Flamel. After lunch the next day, they walked to the Gare d'Austerlitz to board their train for Tours, where they were joined by Suzanne Warenghem.

Cole and the convoy waited in Azay, a village one stop before Saint-Martin-le-Beau, while Warenghem proceeded ahead to make sure that all was safe. Cole, Lepers, and the British evaders continued by foot along the Cher riverbank, while Warenghem walked back to give them an all-clear signal. After a meal in Saint-Martin-le-Beau the convoy rowed across in shifts. Then the men walked through the night to Loches.

Barclay's notes of this leg reflected the mundane concerns and sustained tension of the group's long, silent hike through the dark French countryside: "Knife, gun; contents of bags. Dogs barking. Moonlight. Saw patrols. Bad fitting shoes. Haystack—very cold sleep. Farm barn—watching signposts. End of tether at station. One hour wait—train, cleanup."

They arrived at their destination at 8:00 A.M., after a night spent upright in second-class train coaches. It was the first of November,

All Saints' Day, a bank holiday in France. Barclay was accommodated at the Nouveau flat overlooking the Vieux Port. The airman, soon to be shipped through Spain to England and a fatal reassignment to the Middle East, noted simply, "Lovely view."

Lepers, following the instructions given him by Guerisse at the beginning of the month, checked in at the Hôtel Paris-Nice. Cole distributed the escapers to various safe houses. Meanwhile Guerisse, François Duprez, and other officers of the escape line awaited him in the Rodocanachi apartment. All was prepared to give the lie to Sergeant Paul Cole and decide his fate.

17

"He Is Terribly Dangerous"

IAN GARROW had decided upon the destruction of agent Cole and made careful preparations for his execution. But when Cole next appeared in Marseilles, the Scot was no longer in a position to see this unpleasant business through personally.

When Guerisse returned in mid-October after nine days' travel to the north, he found Fanny Rodocanachi in tears. Garrow had just been arrested in Marseilles by agents of the Direction de la Surveillance du Territoire. Two DST undercover agents had presented themselves as French reserve officers who were "understanding, having the right sympathies." They strung Garrow along for a while and, when he had compromised himself sufficiently, picked him up off a Marseilles street.

Garrow was locked up in the Fort Saint-Nicolas, near the very spot in the Vieux Port where he had intended to kill Cole. Some months later, he was to be convicted by a military tribunal in Lyon and sentenced to twenty years of hard labor. Guerisse took command under the code name of Pat O'Leary.

Upon learning that the swindler had reached Marseilles, Guerisse set in motion the plan he had worked out with Bruce Dowding. With Garrow's arrest, the Australian had become one of his most trusted men. Guerisse told François Duprez to come to the Rodocanachi apartment at 4:00 P.M., one half hour before Cole was expected. When Duprez arrived, one of the household showed him to the small back bedroom. Guerisse and Dowding were waiting there with Mario Praxinos, one of the line's numerous Greek agents whose activities led German intelligence to assign the network the code name "Acropolis."

Off a more remote corridor of the flat, three British escapers were stashed away in Georges Rodocanachi's bedroom. André Postel-Vinay, in Marseilles for consultations, waited in the physician's study. In the *salon*, Fanny was serving tea to three women who remained unaware of the drama unfolding a few rooms away.

Cole made his appearance at around half past four that Saturday afternoon. He took a seat at the deal table in the bedroom, facing Dowding, with O'Leary at his right elbow. Someone gave him a cigarette and a glass of whiskey. The conversation opened as it normally did when he arrived with another convoy.

"Hello, Paul," Guerisse said. "Glad to see you back in Marseilles."

Cole did not know of Garrow's arrest. Guerisse told him that the chief had traveled to Perpignan to confer with the Basque guides escorting escapers over the Pyrenees.

"Well, tell us," Guerisse continued. "Is everything all right? How many passengers did you bring down?"

Cole began to brief the Belgian. Concealed inside the toilet giving onto the bedroom, Duprez was listening. Guerisse had placed him there earlier with the instruction, "Put your ear to the door, because I am going to speak louder, about money."

Soon Guerisse turned to this sensitive issue and raised his tone. Questioned about finances, Cole delivered his standard explanation.

"We've got plenty of money in the north," he said. "As you know, we've got our banker there, François Duprez. Of course, it's better to have money in security with people like that."

Suddenly Cole's expression changed, and he leaped to his feet, dumbstruck. Unable to contain his indignation, Duprez had surged out of the water closet.

"*Salaud*!" he spat. "You lying bastard! Not only did you never give me a penny, but you owe me a lot of money!"

All six men were now standing. Cole was skewered by the reproachful stares of the other five.

"You thief!" said Guerisse.

Cole's confident facade collapsed. He fell to his knees and pleaded for mercy.

"Please, sir," he whined. "Please, sir, yes, it's true..."

Guerisse could not contain his rage. Looking down at the contemptible figure before him, he swung with all his strength, catching Cole full in the face with his fist. The Cockney went down.

"Get up, you bastard!" said Guerisse, rubbing the knuckle he had fractured against Cole's jaw. "Get up, you coward."

Cole rose amid silence. Duprez, disgusted, asked if he were needed any more.

"No," Guerisse told him. "It's all over. We now know what we had to know. Thank you for coming to Marseilles." Then he convened a drumhead court-martial to sit in judgment on the thief.

◆ ◆ ◆

"I KNEW you were a bastard from the very beginning," said Guerisse to Cole. "Now you are in front of a tribunal, and here are your two judges."

He motioned to Dowding and Praxinos. "I am the president of the tribunal, and they are going to give me their opinions on what we have to do with you."

"Pat, let me kill him," Dowding said quietly. "Let me kill him." Guerisse knew the tough Australian was prepared to strangle Cole there in the room.

But Praxinos intervened, "Can we kill a man because he's a thief?"

Guerisse hesitated. There was no material evidence, aside from the word of Duprez, that Cole had embezzled the 300 thousand francs in question. Cole was an English noncommissioned officer. In the absence of Garrow, who had not told Guerisse of his plan to liquidate Cole, no British military authority was present. They would have to get rid of the body.

Cole, terrified, was back on his knees. Guerisse deliberated, then gave his decision. "No," he told Dowding. "I cannot permit that."

Cole would be spared, but they still had to decide what to do with him. The Cockney was shut up in the bathroom while this was discussed.

Guerisse, Dowding, Praxinos, and Savinos examined the situation in low voices. Cole could not remain in France. He was untrustworthy and knew far too much about the line. The only alternative to execution was to send him down the escape line under guard so he could be judged properly in England.

A noise from inside the bathroom interrupted these deliberations. Dowding went to investigate. As he entered the bathroom, he saw Cole disappearing into a window across the airshaft onto which the toilet gave. Cole could not be certain that the proposal to execute him would not be revived. Returning to England meant certain conviction and imprisonment. Fearful of the outcome, Cole had gathered his courage and leaped across several feet of airshaft to catch onto the sill of the facing window and haul himself inside.

There was a confused rush for the door. So large was the Rodocanachi apartment that Guerisse and his men had really no idea where the other window led. There were two main corridors running into the apartment. Cole had clambered into a bathroom at the end of one of these. The bedroom in which Dowding and the others stood was at the end of the other.

Dowding walked urgently to the main door of the apartment. He could not run or raise an alarm because of Fanny Rodocanachi's guests and the neighbors. He hurried down the staircase of the building and out into the street to see Cole, running for his life, disappear around the corner of the rue Roux de Brignoles. There could be no hot pursuit; a pell-mell chase through the streets of Marseilles would further jeopardize the security of the line. The men went straight to Cole's hotel, but the Cockney had checked out.

Now Cole was a cannon loose on the deck. There was no telling what he would do. "Cole is finished in the north," Guerisse told Dowding and the others. "From this moment on he is terribly dangerous, terribly dangerous."

♦ ♦ ♦

GUERISSE AND DOWDING soon left Marseilles and hurried north. Those around Lille with whom Cole had worked needed to be warned that "they have to be terribly careful." The young Australian, whose French was perfected during prewar studies in Paris, had volunteered to replace the renegade.

Guerisse accompanied Dowding to Amiens, outlining the canceled-ticket scheme for entering the north. Douding had time before his train and told Guerisse he had always wanted to see the thirteenth-century Cathedral of Notre Dame there. In the hushed vastness of the gothic church, the two secret agents were moved by the British war decorations and other military offerings displayed in front of the side altars, "so many souvenirs of the Britishers killed in the First World War."

Then they parted company. Bruce Dowding, traveling under the assumed name of André Mason, vanished into the Forbidden Zone to take up where Cole had left off.

♦ ♦ ♦

AS HE RUSHED to Paris, Cole must have realized that he was finished in the Garrow organization. But in the north there were enough people who would take his word that he was the innocent victim of some political intrigue. He felt certain that Warenghem would also see things his way.

She had returned to Paris after seeing the convoy on its way at Saint-Martin-le-Beau, finding a letter from Carpentier hinting that trouble was afoot. "Paul came through here yesterday with his whole team of footballers," the priest wrote in simple coded language. "They were very gay and counted greatly on their speed and their team spirit to win this new match."

Then, ominously, "One of my cousins was recently very alarmed. Her neighbor Mme Deram was disturbed by the Gestapo." Carpentier had no more information than that. "I wonder what is going on in the north," he added, "for there have been several consecutive arrests or mysterious departures."

Cole, on arriving in Paris, told Warenghem of "a spot of bother in Marseilles." Painting himself as a wronged man, he told the young woman that he "had a bit of a row with somebody and had to tell them where to get off." But he did not elaborate on this story and soon was off again, speaking of urgent matters that required his presence in La Madeleine.

As Cole had anticipated, his position in the north was not reduced immediately by the confrontation that had taken place in Marseilles. Those closest to François Duprez now knew that Cole could not be trusted. But he had a far-flung network of contacts in the region. Not all would have heard of his falling out with the Garrow line. Not everyone would accept the word of Duprez against that of Cole, who still wore the mantle of the Intelligence Service. Dowding, just beginning to make the rounds, had yet to earn the confidence of the wary northerners.

Cole laid low for several weeks in the house on the avenue Bernadette. But time was running out on the Cockney. As Carpentier had mentioned in his letter to Warenghem, the home shared by Deram and Cole had come to the attention of the German police. Long in search of the elusive Captain Colson, Verloop was ready to pounce. On Saturday, December 6, he made his move.

That morning Madeleine Deram had risen before Cole and was cleaning the house. Shortly before 10:00 A.M. she put up the chairs on the kitchen table and was about to start mopping when the doorbell rang. A stranger was at the door. "I am a friend of Monsieur Duhayon," he said.

Deram knew that Marcel Duhayon, one of Cole's helpers, had been arrested several days before. She was therefore wary of this reference.

"Excuse me," she said, "but we're refugees. We don't know this person."

"Do you know Monsieur Paul?" said the man, more insistent.

"No," she replied, and repeated, "We're refugees." She tried to shut the door. But the man had slipped his foot into the jamb.

Things happened very quickly then. Deram saw two cars full of German soldiers haul up to the curb in front of the house. She was pushed backwards and pinned against the wall behind the door. A squad of GFP troops rushed in and pounded up the staircase.

Brought into the kitchen, Deram saw a piece of paper on which Cole had jotted some notes. She picked it up and moved to the stove. As she went to throw it into the fire, one of the Germans saw her and shouted. Her guard, momentarily distracted by the sight of Cole being dragged downstairs, shoved her into an armchair. He took out his revolver and drew back to pistol-whip her.

"That's not hers!" said Cole, who had seen the attempt to destroy the paper. "That belongs to me."

Cole wore a shirt and pants, but his feet were bare. One of the GFP agents carried his boots and coat. Flanked by soldiers, Cole was led out the door and across the snow-covered walk to be bundled into a waiting car. Deram was placed in the vehicle behind. The GFP convoy roared off through the streets of La Madeleine heading for Lille.

Guerisse's worst fear had now been realized: Cole, cast out of the escape line, had rushed straight into the arms of the Germans. The Cockney would have little motivation to resist their pressures and blandishments. Indeed, Cole was about to be presented with persuasive arguments for shifting his allegiance, arguments even the best of men had found difficult to resist. Cole was unlikely to fare any better.

Arrest by the GFP had not figured in the picaresque scenario worked up by Cole for Captain Paul Delobel. But with the firm prompting of Cornelius Verloop and the Abwehr, he would quickly master his new part in what was about to become a tragedy of high treason.

18

"A Monster of Cowardice and Weakness"

THERE WOULD ALWAYS remain some question as to whether December 6, 1941, marked the exact point at which Harold Cole came under the control of German counterintelligence. Many would later conclude that he had been a German agent for months prior to that date. If so, then the raid was a sham, staged to protect Cole's cover as a German informant and ease his transition to agent-provocateur. There was a good deal of evidence to support this theory—but much of it was circumstantial and none of it was conclusive. Cole had so much to conceal from his coworkers in the escape line, and was so duplicitous by nature, that nearly all of his movements were liable to incite suspicion.

There could have been more than one explanation for most of the incidents that engendered distrust: the Polish airman who ended up in Loos; Cole's appearance at the wheel of a Gestapo vehicle; his meeting with Huyge in Toulouse. Even the October 22, 1941, arrest of Raphaël Ayello, the French agent in Dunkirk, could not be clearly attributed to Cole. Ayello was told by his German interrogators that Cole had turned him in and provided evidence against him. But

Ayello learned this only in January 1942—well after Cole himself had been arrested. Others in the same intelligence network, like Maurice Dechaumont, were not arrested in the same sweep as Ayello, although they were in even closer contact with Cole.

Verloop himself maintains that Cole was not in his hands until that day in December 1941. Verloop speculates that the Cockney may have been working for another German police service in direct competition with the Abwehr: the Sicherheitsdienst or SD, the intelligence and counterintelligence branch of the SS. The SD's regional office for the north was located in Roubaix, the same town where *convoyeur* Van Camelbecke had seen Cole at the wheel of a black Citroën later identified as belonging to the local German police service.

But if this were so, then many more questions arise. If Cole were a Sicherheitsdienst agent, why did he not identify himself as such to the GFP and demand his release? Verloop suggests that Cole may have had express instructions not to reveal his SD affiliation. Cole may have wished to conceal his employment by the SD for his own reasons, perhaps hoping to extract himself without further complications. There was another possibility. Was Cole's presumed involvement with the Sicherheitsdienst a consequence—intended or accidental—of his work with the Secret Intelligence Service? In other words, was Cole pushed in the direction of the Sicherheitsdienst by the SIS for some obscure intelligence purpose? Was he a British plant who bore disinformation intended for German ears? Much later Alfred Lanselle of Saint-Omer would assert that Cole had become a double agent on behalf of British intelligence. But there is no firm evidence to prove or disprove this theory. So we can only examine it and move on, picking up Cole's traces that December day in the interrogation room at GFP headquarters in Lille.

As Cole's interrogation began, Cornelius Verloop was looking on from behind a curtain. He had supervised the operation, but preferred to remain in the shadows. Cole's captors pointed out to him that he had few alternatives, most of them unpleasant and some potentially fatal. He was a British agent in civilian dress—a spy, in other words.

For espionage in wartime he could go before a firing squad. On the other hand, he held certain information that interested the Abwehr, which was not above using more forceful methods of interrogation.

Cole may have resisted, but did not do so for long. He was not averse to being a hero. But he had no intention of becoming one under German torture. The Cockney deserter quickly made up his mind. Verloop in fact was surprised at how rapidly Cole decided to cooperate with the Abwehr—as well as how much he had to say.

"He started to tell us everything," said Verloop. Despite his eagerness to capture the British sergeant, the Dutchman had not fully realized the extent of his activities. Cole had seemed just a "funny bird," a footloose NCO who slept with a lot of women. But as Cole talked and the Abwehr stenographer strained to keep up, Verloop said that he was "a very rare bird" indeed.

The deposition given by Cole amounted to some thirty typewritten pages. It provided an almost complete briefing on the northern wing of the Garrow Organization. Cole unraveled a long string of contacts in this "incredible network," astonishing Verloop with the number of names he produced. The British agent seemed to have a photographic memory. He identified agents and helpers in the scores, even people he had met only once.

Verloop was pleased at the counterintelligence windfall. But privately he found Cole's cynical and self-serving revelations repugnant. "One should all the same maintain a bit of self-respect," he felt.

Yet there were those Cole did not betray. He apparently did not inform the Germans of the organization's disposition in the south. Cole also withheld the name of Jeannine Voglimacci, perhaps out of some selective sense of chivalry. But he had his own motives for keeping a few choice addresses up his sleeve; if he escaped he would have a refuge and an alibi. He could always say that, because Voglimacci, one of his primary contacts, had not been arrested, it was not he who betrayed the line.

But this loyalty, such as it was, did not extend to François Duprez. The town official was one of the first to be arrested.

◆ ◆ ◆

ON THE AFTERNOON of December 6, Marguerite Duprez went out to shop for food, leaving the children in the care of the maid, and returned later in the day with her arms full of bundles. When she knocked at her own door, it was not the housekeeper who answered, but a German policeman. Filled with apprehension, she entered and sat on a bench in the hallway.

"It's nothing," one of the German agents assured her. "We're just looking."

The three Abwehr men rifled the house. They took about ten books out of Duprez's collection on the First World War and confiscated the family address book. They showed a particular interest in anything bearing François Duprez's handwriting, apparently requiring samples for comparison with forged documents used by captured escapers.

Riveted to the bench in the hall, Marguerite Duprez prayed that her husband would not walk in the door. She felt relieved though, that only one day before, Bruce Dowding had left the Duprez home after a month's stay.

The Australian had arrived in the north in early November, shortly after Duprez himself got back from Marseilles. But on December 5, Dowding took a furnished room in Lille and enrolled for law studies at the university there. This provided him with a useful cover and additional identity documents.

Finally the Abwehr detachment left, giving instructions that Duprez was to report to the local military authorities. Later that afternoon Duprez arrived home. He had found some oranges for sale while in Lille on business. His driver, named Hilaire, waited at the curb while he brought the fruit inside.

Marguerite met him at the door. "Listen," she told him. "The Germans came here to search, and now they're waiting for you. You can't go back to the town hall!"

"*Je m'en fous*," said Duprez. "I don't care. I'm not afraid of them."

"No," she insisted. "Don't go back."

"*Je m'en fous*," he repeated, handing Marguerite a small packet of papers. "Take that and hide it," he told her. Hilaire would pick it up later.

Then Duprez left for the town hall. His coworkers had been alarmed to see the Germans arrive and ransack his office, knowing that he was involved in illegal activities. While the German policemen loitered in the corridors, arrangements were made to warn Duprez on his way in. He would be diverted out a side exit and concealed in the bakery next door.

This might have succeeded, but Duprez refused to cooperate; if he did not confront the Germans his family would suffer. Handing off an address book to another employee, Duprez strode off down the corridor to meet the Germans. A few minutes later he was brought out in handcuffs and driven away under the shocked gaze of Roland Lepers who, learning that Cole was back in the north, had come to seek Duprez's advice.

Held for many months in the prison of Loos, Duprez was shipped to Germany on August 5, 1942. His prison train left from the Gare de Lille, where he had expedited so many British fugitives in another direction. In April 1943, while being held at the Bochum concentration camp, he was condemned to death. The sentence was commuted eventually, but this measure was academic. François Duprez died of exhaustion in April 1944 in the infirmary of a concentration camp at Sonnenburg, Germany.

Everywhere the same pattern was repeated as, a member of the line would testify, "there followed an immediate hecatomb." The arrests numbered in the scores; most estimates place the number of people denounced by Cole at around seventy-five, a figure he may have doubled by the end of the war.

At 8:30 A.M. on Monday, December 8, the GFP arrested Desiré Didry at his home in Saint-Omer. Cole took an active part in that operation. He showed up at the leather merchant's home with two men he presented as a Polish and an English pilot. When Didry agreed to assist the two apparent escapers, they abandoned their pretenses and arrested him. Both were German agents.

One-half hour later, the German raiding party struck at the home of Alfred Lanselle. Cole did not take part in the arrest of the grocery wholesaler. Lanselle knew that his arrest was imminent; there had been attempts to arrest others in his network, but most were able to flee. He, however, was responsible for his wife and five children, his aged father, and a brother just returned from a prisoner-of-war camp in Germany. He stayed in place to await the inevitable.

Despite these multiple betrayals, few people aside from Cole's victims realized that he had talked. After his arrest, the Abwehr, anxious to protect the efficacy of its stool pigeon, undertook a subterfuge.

While Deram was held in the German lock-up at Loos, she met a Frenchwoman named Fraser who was interned as the wife of an Englishman. Fraser distributed medical supplies to the prisoners. She brought Deram tangerines, candy and the word: "Paul has escaped!"

Later she repeated the message: *"Courage, ma petite!* He has escaped."

♦ ♦ ♦

LATER ON December 8, Pierre Carpentier was picked up, despite having been warned by Bruce Dowding of the Cockney's fall from grace and advised to move from the area. "I'm not going anywhere," he said. "The good Lord put me here, and I will continue to do my duty."

But his stepmother, Julia Carpentier, with whom he lived and who loaned her own *Ausweiss* and identity to women crossing the line, took the precaution of burning most of the incriminating documents in their home. The brick row-house was located next door to the parish church and across from a German barracks.

Nearby was a bombed-out factory owned by Charles Verbroeck, a manufacturer who also lent his documents to Carpentier's operation. On December 8, Verbroeck was overseeing the salvage of equipment from the ruined factory when a group of men dressed in civilian clothes approached him.

"We're looking for a way to cross the bridge and we don't have any papers," one of them said in French with a foreign accent. "We know that somewhere around here there is a person who can help us cross the bridge."

Verbroeck recognized this as a clumsy German effort at entrapment. He advised them to address themselves to local officials, pleading ignorance of anyone matching the description they had provided.

By one account, Bruce Dowding was with Carpentier that day in Abbeville when, around 2:30 P.M., Cole appeared at the door of the house on the rue du Cimetière Saint-Gilles. The two men were wary but not alarmed. Conferring rapidly, they agreed Dowding would remain concealed until Cole's intentions were known.

In letters smuggled from his cell in the prison at Loos, Carpentier described how he was "ignobly betrayed by Sergeant Cole." These documents later were to prove indispensable in convincing skeptical officials in the upper ranks of British Intelligence that Cole should be branded a traitor.

Cole, wrote Carpentier, "presented himself at my home with five persons who had to cross the line clandestinely with him." The Cockney said he had two Belgian pilots, one British pilot, a Polish airman, and one English soldier with him, all of whom needed passes for the Somme crossing. The priest spoke briefly to the Belgians and determined that they were authentic. The English soldier spoke a little French while "the RAF captain spoke English correctly, was the perfect English type, and seemed to be a good soldier."

The Polish pilot spoke neither French nor English—but the priest did not question this. He set about making the fraudulent documents. "It was at this point," he wrote, "when German police in civilian dress arrived and took us, hands in the air, to the nearest barracks." One of the Belgians tried to flee but was easily caught; the Pole was quickly taken away.

Catching Carpentier's murderous glances at Cole, the British flier understood what had happened. As the prisoners were led to the German encampment, he bitterly cursed the Cockney under his breath. But Cole was led away after a few minutes, while the priest was separated from the escapers to be incarcerated at the prison of Loos.

Dowding did not remain at large much longer. When the Germans sprung their trap, the Australian slipped out the back door and escaped through the garden. By one account he was captured in a nearby town a short time later; by another he made it back to the Lille area and started to warn his contacts of Cole's treachery. The Germans captured him at the Marquette-lez-Lille home of Madeleine Damerment, Lepers's girlfriend. The Geheime Feldpolizei had already taken her father into custody.

◆ ◆ ◆

COLE'S TREACHERY continued the next day in Burbure. On the Monday when Carpentier was arrested, the Salingue family had heard a coded BBC message indicating that Barclay, Bufton, and others in that convoy had reached London safely. Despite confusion in the network over Cole's expulsion, Salingue and his friends had continued to expedite escapes. At the end of November, thirteen escapers set off from Burbure, loaded into the truck of a local hog farmer. They were distributed at various stations along the Lille-Abbeville train line, to avoid attracting the attention of German officials.

But the Salingues and others in Burbure "could feel that things were starting to go bad." German patrols passed their houses constantly, and the pressure mounted. The Germans closed in on December 9. Elisa Salingue, on her way to the school where she taught, saw a squad of Germans leading Drotais Dubois away from his home in the rue de Lillers. Cole accompanied the police.

Madame Salingue was certain the Englishman had seen her standing by the side of the road as the group passed. But he made no sign of recognition. Farther down the street, he encountered the brewer Marcel Rousseaux, who stood on the steps of his house. Cole passed him by. Then a woman named Vambergue, who had sheltered British evaders, called out to Cole as he passed.

"*Quoi?*" she exclaimed. "Monsieur Paul, you're doing that?"

But he made no response, and she, like Rousseaux, was ignored by the German police detachment. Witnessing this, Salingue's wife immediately sent word to her husband's school in Lillers. Fernand escaped to Lille, where he hid in the apartment of friends and fled later to the Unoccupied Zone.

Later that same day, the Germans descended on the Gare de Lille. Maurice Dechaumont, alias X-10, the French railway worker who had supplied Cole with information on troop movements, was arrested at his desk. August Dean, of Lille, one of Dechaumont's informants, had been arrested already. Fernand Treveille, who worked at a German barracks in Lille and provided not only military information but essential false documents for the escape line, was also taken prisoner. Marie-Louise Gallet, in whose apartment Cole had collected intelligence, was betrayed in her turn.

◆　◆　◆

THERE WERE THOSE in the north whom Cole did not hand over to the Germans—but he had given extremely damaging evidence in the cases of those he did name. Two days after Carpentier's arrest, he was taken from Loos to the GFP office in Lille for his first interrogation. There he found the supposed Polish pilot "in the full uniform of a German lieutenant."

This officer, who Carpentier gathered was the GFP commander, came "to jeer and ridicule" the priest for the way in which he had been captured. Carpentier learned from the officer that Cole's statement against the line had filled thirty pages. Later he learned from the German investigating magistrate handling his case that "Cole had shamefully betrayed us, not only handing us over, but in revealing in his statement many things he didn't need to say, so as to aggravate our cases and to be sure that we would not be able to come after him."

The official's questions indicated the extent of Cole's revelations: firearms had been found not only in Carpentier's own home but in the homes of friends—weapons of which only Cole, Carpentier, and the arrested parties knew the existence. Carpentier earlier had been willing to give Cole the benefit of the doubt following the Cockney's expulsion from the Marseilles line. But now, behind bars, his emotions were no longer guided by Christian restraint.

"I, a priest, would not hesitate to coldly burn him," he raged. "If you leave him breathing, he can only make every situation worse and he will remain a danger for you. . . . This man does not deserve the slightest pity; he is a monster of cowardice and weakness."

Carpentier, like many of those arrested by the Germans on the information provided by Cole, was deported to Germany. He and Dowding were sent first to a prison in Bochum, Germany. On April 16, 1943, they were condemned to death by a Nazi tribunal in Berlin. From Bochum they were sent to Dortmund. There, in the early evening hours of June 30, 1943, they were decapitated in a jail in the Lübeckerstrasse. Executed within minutes of them were Desiré Didry, Marcel Duhayon, and Drotais Dubois.

The prison register stated that "the condemned sheltered, in 1940 to 1941, English soldiers secretly present in occupied France, just as they encouraged young French and Belgians to enlist in the English Army. Duhayon and Carpentier did, moreover, collect important military information in the aim of communicating this to the enemy."

19

"Meet My New Boss"

WHIPPED ON by his German masters, Cole now moved to betray his connections in Paris. He and two GFP agents, who would supervise his work over the next several days, traveled to the capital by automobile on Thursday, December 11. He had told Warenghem by letter that on this same day he would arrive at the Gare du Nord on the train from Abbeville. But Cole did not lead the German agents to Warenghem, perhaps partly for sentimental reasons, but also to protect his own interests. Cole hoped to slip his Abwehr escort while in Paris and he would need someplace to go to ground. He knew he could prevail upon Warenghem to shelter him—provided she remained ignorant of his treachery.

His first stop in Paris was at the home of Vladimir de Fligué. He introduced his two shadows to the Russian as British pilots. One, explained the Cockney, was joining the escape-line staff. "I want you to explain to him everything he needs to know about the organization," Cole told de Fligué. "He's going to take over from me for a while. I have to go on a trip to Brussels."

Accustomed to taking orders from the British secret agent, de

Fligué agreed. He also promised to run an errand. Warenghem would be expecting Cole to step off the midday train from Abbeville. But Cole would not be there, and he preferred she not be informed that he was already in Paris. De Fligué agreed to meet her at the station to say the British agent would be delayed. The traitor left de Fligué with the promise that he would see him later in the day. He asked the manufacturer to be sure Holweck was present then.

From the Gare du Nord, Warenghem returned to the apartment in the rue Quatrefages to dine on rabbit with the Russian, his wife Simone, and their two children. She left at about 1:30 P.M. An hour later, Cole kept his appointment with de Fligué and Holweck in Agnes Kirman's fourth-floor apartment. The taciturn pair of British escapers needed false papers, Cole told de Fligué. This meant the group would have to go up the street to de Fligué's workshop. But outside the apartment building the two Germans announced that Cole and his associates were under arrest.

Cole made a show of resistance. Holweck, a large man with a volcanic temper, put up a genuine fight. He broke loose and fled across the rue Quatrefages into a parking garage, which gave out into the next street. But he was cornered, subdued, and shoved into a waiting car, his white shirt bloodied from the melee.

As Holweck and de Fligué were driven away, the Russian took a look back at the street where he had lived and worked for years. He saw Cole standing casually on the sidewalk with the two agents he had misrepresented earlier as English fugitives. De Fligué understood then that he and Holweck had been sold out by the very man who had drawn them into the escape business to begin with.

♦ ♦ ♦

PACKING OFF the inexperienced and trusting de Fligué and Holweck had been simple work. Cole now turned to the more intricate problem of covering his tracks and extricating himself from German control. This would require deft manipulation of Warenghem and Bernaer— and even more skillful deception of his GFP watchdogs.

After sending de Fligué to the train station Thursday morning to warn off Warenghem, Cole had stopped by the Chôpe du Pont Neuf. There he ran into Bernaer, who had been trying to reach him for the past forty-eight hours. Cole stalled the elderly journalist, making an appointment to see him in two days' time, again at the Chôpe. It was vital to keep Bernaer ignorant of his treachery: the writer held a large sum of money that Cole needed, and he was in contact with the Deuxième Bureau. It would not do to tip off French military intelligence to his new relationship with the German secret service, which Cole had decided would be only temporary.

Meanwhile, Warenghem was picking up some conflicting information. On Friday, having received no word from Cole some twenty-four hours after he was to have met her at the Gare du Nord, she inquired at de Fligué's factory. The Russian's wife told her Cole had been arrested with de Fligué and Holweck. Fearing that the entire network somehow had been compromised, the distraught Warenghem hurried to the Gare Saint Lazare and returned by train to her aunt's home in the suburb of Courbevoie. There she began preparing for flight to the Unoccupied Zone. If Cole had been arrested, she was also in danger. She needed the guidance of Garrow in Marseilles, who should be made aware of the bad turn affairs had taken in Paris.

Seeking to warn the others in the Paris circuit, she phoned Durand at the Chôpe. Warenghem informed him in guarded language that Cole "had an accident and has been taken to hospital." His situation was "very dangerous," Durand might be concerned to know. But the restaurateur told her Cole was not only still at large, but would be at his brasserie the following day at 3:00 P.M. She could meet him then.

The next day was December 13, a Saturday. Warenghem went to the restaurant at the appointed hour and took a seat on one of the red banquettes at the back. Durand drew a glass of beer and set it in front of her. Cole arrived later in a state of high agitation and sat down to give her his rewritten version of events.

He, Holweck, and de Fligué had just carried off a remarkable escape, Cole said, elaborating a story in which the three were accosted by the Germans outside de Fligué's house and obliged to surrender at gunpoint. They were shoved in the back of a car, with one German policeman to guard them while another drove.

Following Cole's instructions, the Cockney told Warenghem, the burly Holweck had thrown his handcuffed wrists around the neck of the police guard while Cole sprang on the driver in the front. The car was pulled over and the three captives fled amid a hail of bullets. Holweck and de Fligué now waited in a safe location, while Cole arranged their exit from the Occupied Zone.

Cole narrated the story plausibly. Warenghem, a receptive listener, believed his account. But in reality de Fligué was by then undergoing interrogation in the Prison de la Santé, where the physicist had already expired, a suicide or the victim of a savage beating. Transferred to Loos, de Fligué eventually was shipped to the Nazi camps to be liberated—in a historical irony the White Russian émigré hardly appreciated—by the Red Army in May 1945.

Soon Bernaer arrived at the Chôpe to find Cole "in a state of collapse, trembling with all his limbs." Cole may have felt obliged to feign shock and stress. Notwithstanding, the searing events of the week just elapsed would have frayed the nerves of even the most heartless villain.

Warenghem repeated Cole's story. Bernaer did not seem to doubt it. Cole asked him for a large sum of money and false documents for himself, Holweck, and de Fligué, who were in hiding at a location he would not disclose. At this point Bernaer balked, insisting that he would not part with the money until he had seen the two other men. Cole let the issue drop, seeing the beginnings of suspicion on the part of Bernaer.

Turning to Warenghem, Cole asked the young woman to obtain changes of clothing for the other two. But when she offered to bring the garments to their hiding place, Cole put her off as well. He instructed her to bring them to the restaurant, then left for another rendezvous in his round of betrayals.

◆ ◆ ◆

THE NEXT VICTIM was to be André Postel-Vinay, whose address Cole had obtained when they met in Marseilles. Late on that same afternoon, Postel-Vinay was climbing to his apartment on the avenue de Villars in the affluent *Septième arrondissment* of Paris, when he encountered Cole and another man with a "fairly sinister face." The two men were on their way down. At Cole's suggestion, they went outside and got into a black Citroën parked at the curb. Postel-Vinay noticed that the vehicle bore a German military pass on its windshield. But he shrugged this off; stranger things happened in the French underground.

Cole's partner remained silent as they drove down the tree-lined avenue de Breteuil, the Hôtel des Invalides looming behind them and the Eiffel Tower piercing the gray sky beyond the École Militaire off to the right. There were few other cars on the streets.

Cole explained his unexpected visit. Postel-Vinay knew vaguely that Guerisse and Cole "had had words about money," but had not been told of Cole's banishment from the network. The English agent said the Garrow Organization was to be split in two: one section would continue with escape and evasion, while another, to be headed by Cole, would deal in espionage. He asked Postel-Vinay to provide him with any current information he had accumulated.

Postel-Vinay hedged, mistrusting Cole as much now as he had on their first meeting. But he thought the reorganization might allow him to obtain the radio transmitter and operator he had been requesting from the British for many months.

"Maybe tomorrow," he told Cole.

They agreed that Cole would come by the next morning to pick up Postel-Vinay in front of his building.

"You can meet my new boss," Cole promised him.

After a "very bad night" Postel-Vinay readied himself by shoving an Enfield six-shot revolver in his belt. If Cole betrayed him, he would shoot the Englishman, then turn the weapon on himself. Downstairs, he met Cole in the same black Citroën with its ominously mute driver. With little conversation, they drove north across the Seine, past the Opéra, Trinité, and the place de Clichy to a hotel on the edge of Montmartre.

Inside, Cole went to the reception desk, spoke briefly to the clerk, then returned. His new employer was absent, it seemed, but Cole led his associate up to a second-floor room. Postel-Vinay was getting nervous. He was holding incriminating military intelligence that included sensitive information on the *Scharnhorst*, the *Gneisenau*, and the *Prinz Eigen*, three German pocket battleships in harbor at Brest. He was carrying an illegal weapon; for this alone, the death penalty could be imposed under occupation law.

The window of the room looked out on the bare trees and the brown and gray crypts and tombstones of the Cimetière de Montmartre. Postel-Vinay studied this discouraging backdrop as Cole told him "all kinds of stories to pass the time."

The French agent resolved to draw his weapon at the first sign of trouble. But then the door was thrown open and four or five hard-faced men rushed in. Postel-Vinay faced a "battery of revolvers" without the least chance of using his own. Without a word, Cole walked out. Postel-Vinay, regretful that he had not better heeded his instincts, was taken to the Prison de la Santé.

Fearing that he had left an incriminating notebook with the names and addresses of confederates in his apartment, he became despondent and tried to kill himself. But he survived a headlong leap from a prison gallery, sustaining several fractured vertebrae. After several days without treatment he was brought to a military ward at the Hôpital de la Pitié.

Interrogated there for the first time, he realized the German police knew very little about his network. Cole knew none of his agents, and the notebook was in safe hands. Postel-Vinay recovered his taste for life. Now only simulating mental distress, he slashed his wrists and was transferred to a mental asylum, from which, with the complicity of a French doctor, he escaped and made his way to London via the Garrow Organization.

♦ ♦ ♦

WARENGHEM returned to the Chôpe on December 14, the day of Postel-Vinay's arrest, with the clothing Cole had requested. Several hours later, when darkness had fallen over the city, the brasserie's door flew open and the Cockney rushed in. Urgently, he ordered her to get out of the restaurant and wait for him at the street corner. The Gestapo, he said, was close on his heels.

She obeyed and ran into the blacked-out street. Cole appeared a moment later. There was a screeching of brakes, and Warenghem could see a dark automobile pull up in front of the restaurant. They ducked down into the Pont Neuf Métro station and boarded the first train to come along.

According to his plan, Cole had shaken off his Abwehr handlers. This confirmed Verloop's suspicions. The Dutchman had been dead set against allowing Cole out of his Lille cell, even on a tight leash. But Hegener was taken in by the persuasive Cockney.

"Faites gaffe!" Verloop had warned the chief of the Lille Abwehr branch. "Look out! You're making a big mistake. Colson is a shit. Either get rid of him or lock him up until the end of the war."

Now Cole was loose again, fleeing from pillar to post, a man without friends on either side of the subterranean battleground. His former comrades would kill him if given a chance; he could expect little better from the Germans. His only chance lay in continued deception of Suzanne Warenghem, who continued to trust in the idealism and bravery of the cynical, craven traitor at her side.

20

"Who Are You, Really?"

GUERISSE BECAME WORRIED in January, as the weeks passed and neither convoys nor messages arrived from the north. Something clearly was wrong in La Madeleine. He suspected this was the work of Paul Cole, and decided he must travel to Lille to deal with the situation personally. Near the end of January, Guerisse arrived in La Madeleine.

His first stop was in the rue de la Gare, where he gleaned his first grim intelligence of the havoc Cole had wrought. There was little he could do for the bereaved Marguerite Duprez. For her part, she had little use for someone so closely associated with the activity that had brought about her husband's disappearance. Guerisse walked up the rue de la Gare in the failing late-afternoon light and entered Voglimacci's beauty salon.

Guerisse was even less welcome there. Voglimacci was working when he entered. She sized him up distrustfully. They had never met before. There had been many arrests and her shop was under close surveillance. Suspecting German entrapment, she curtly ordered Guerisse to wait for her in the hall while she finished with her client.

"Who are you, really?" she demanded. "I don't know you. I don't know what you want." Under the strain of events, Voglimacci was uncustomarily sharp.

"I'm Joseph Cartier," he told her. "I've just come from Madame Duprez. She told me to see you."

Voglimacci gave no sign of recognition.

"Listen," said Guerisse. "I'm going to name some names. I know Paul. I know Roland." He mentioned other persons in the network and described various operations in detail. "I can only tell you this, and I ask you to hear me out."

"Come upstairs," Voglimacci said.

In the studio, Guerisse explained his concern: the halt in the convoys, the lack of news. He described his confrontation with Cole and the agent's headlong flight from Marseilles. Then she told him of the disasters in the north, or as much as she knew.

"Where has Mason gone?" he asked. "What's become of the Abbé Carpentier?"

Voglimacci did not know. "Give me a minute to think," she said. "Mason may be at the home of someone in Marquette."

She had in mind the family of Madeleine Damerment, with whom Roland Lepers had kept company. Damerment had shown Dowding around when the Australian first arrived; perhaps he had taken shelter with her family in Marquette-lez-Lille.

By now Lepers was gone. He had been picked up twice by the police—once in Marseilles by the Vichy authorities, and again in Abbeville while trying to cross illegally into the Forbidden Zone. After extracting himself from these difficulties, he had arrived back in the north, but left for the Unoccupied Zone after Duprez was arrested.

Voglimacci and Guerisse left the beauty salon and went on foot to Marquette. It was nearly an hour's walk. It was now after dark and past curfew. A chilling rain was coming down. Guerisse was deep in his own somber thoughts. Despite his assurances, Voglimacci was still gripped by doubts.

The news in Marquette was disheartening. Dowding had been arrested there with Georges Damerment in December. There was nothing to be done. Voglimacci and Guerisse picked their way along the obscure and wet roads and paths back to La Madeleine.

"Don't give yourself away by your voice," Voglimacci warned him. "There are patrols everywhere."

When they arrived she stopped and bluntly told Guerisse she was leaving him. "I took you there, now I'm going home."

She had not slept the night before. Her nerves were frayed and she was exhausted. Voglimacci studiously ignored Guerisse's hints that he needed a place to stay for the night. At six o'clock the next morning, he arrived back on her doorstep.

"Madame, please," he implored. "Just an armchair?" He had spent the night huddled in a passageway out of the rain. Repenting her harsh behavior of the night before, Voglimacci gave him dry clothes and a hot breakfast. Later she traveled to Abbeville to seek Carpentier. She returned to report that he, too, was in German hands.

"It's not over," said Guerisse. "We've got to contact the Abbé Carpentier in the prison at Loos."

Voglimacci knew a police official in Lille and obtained from him a list of the guards at the prison. Eventually one of them agreed to carry messages to the priest. In this way Guerisse received the missive in which Carpentier scrawled his scathing denunciation of the traitor.

Inside the prison at Loos, surrounded by swamps from which a sinister fog arose in winter, the priest endured. He sang "Tipperary" at the top of his lungs during torture sessions. In his letters, he expressed great concern that Voglimacci not be incriminated by evidence seized at his house. She had given him some identity photos. But he had concealed them in a family photo album without cropping or stamping them for incorporation into false identification cards.

He sent his "respectful remembrances" to Voglimacci, whom he had met only once, but to whom he was strongly attached. She closely resembled a girl he had loved in his youth, but whom he had left to enter the priesthood. Carpentier first met Voglimacci in November

1941, when she and Madeleine Damerment had come to obtain false passes for the Somme.

The priest was so struck by the similarity that at first he refused to allow her to risk crossing the Demarcation Line. He had placed her photograph not in the drawer of his desk with those of other network members, but in his own family photo album.

In his correspondence from prison, Carpentier wrote that he was "being punished because he was a bad priest." He had never forgotten the woman whose memory Voglimacci had awakened, and felt that this was a sin. This scrupulous guilt was one of the reasons that Pierre Carpentier refused to consider a plan for his escape from the prison. Another was that François Duprez, lacking a leg, could not go over the wall with him.

Besides this, the priest had taken the entire responsibility for the Somme crossing operation upon himself in the hope that parishioners who had loaned him their papers would receive only minor punishments. Most of them served no more than a few months in an Abbeville jail.

◆ ◆ ◆

AMID THE WRECKAGE of the line, there remained airmen to move south. Guerisse remained in the north for a week or so to set the network back on its feet. Soon after he had left, Voglimacci received a disturbing message from the traitor.

Cole had always been respectful and kept his distance from the hairdresser. He had spared her while turning in dozens of others. It was one of the contradictions in his character that would gain him a reputation, largely undeserved, for chivalry. Now Cole threatened Voglimacci with dire consequences if she did not stop working for the network. "I had to stop," said Voglimacci, recalling the strange letter. "If I continued to receive members of the organization in my home, he was going to knife me."

Though postmarked in Le Havre, the letter had been written in Paris, where Cole was still in hiding after his series of betrayals in

December. Possibly one of Suzanne Warenghem's relations in Le Havre mailed the letter at Cole's request.

Ever since Cole and Warenghem had fled from what she believed to be the German police at the Chope du Pont Neuf, he had been living in the Courbevoie apartment of her aunt, Jeanne Warenghem, outside Paris.

On his arrival there, Cole developed a high fever that incapacitated him for days. Warenghem and her aunt were alarmed enough to begin making plans to dispose of his corpse. But the crisis passed. Cole later told them he had suffered a recurrence of malaria, picked up during military service in the Far East. He spent weeks recuperating, nursed back to health by Suzanne and Jeanne Warenghem.

"Gradually," writes Warenghem biographer Gordon Young, "Paul Cole recovered his strength and his customary confidence. His gentle, courteous manner . . . won the heart of Suzanne's aunt." Ever the confidence man, Cole sedulously worked his charms on the elderly woman. He knew his security depended on her good will. Suzanne also succumbed to Cole's earnest attentions. Her admiration for the man she saw as a courageous British secret agent swelled. "After de Gaulle," she confided to her aunt, "I admire him more than anybody."

There were warning signs that Warenghem failed to heed. While Cole was recuperating from his bout of fever, Warenghem lent him a sweater on which was pinned a British lieutenant's pip, embellished with rows of blue, white, and red beads in France's national colors. It was a token of appreciation from a British soldier she had helped escape. When Cole returned the sweater to her the pip was missing; when questioned he denied any knowledge of it. She realized later that the light-fingered Cole, enamoured of the trappings of rank, had stolen the emblem.

His explanation of the network's dismantlement also left much to be desired. Warenghem was realist enough to know someone had betrayed the organization. Cole agreed, casting aspersions on Roland Lepers to protect himself. "Poor Roland must have been caught and then denounced everybody," said Cole sanctimoniously. "I never thought he would have done a thing like that."

Though she implicitly trusted Cole, Warenghem found it difficult to believe the young Frenchman had agreed to cooperate with the Germans. But the alternative—that Cole was the traitor—was inconceivable to her. The question hung unresolved.

Warenghem volunteered to travel to Marseilles to locate what remained of the network there. Cole vetoed this suggestion. The Vichy secret services would arrest her immediately. Instead, he told her, he would travel to the north to pull together the remnants of the network there as soon as she could provide him with false identification papers.

When, at the beginning of March 1942, she had obtained these from friends working in the French public administration, Cole once more began to travel, leaving her behind in Paris. It suited the traitor best that she remain uninformed of his itinerary and the dark purposes for which he now moved through occupied France.

21

"I Swear I'll Cure Him!"

BY THE BEGINNING of March 1942 Guerisse and the survivors of the Garrow organization's decimated northern wing were certain that Cole was a traitor and an agent-provocateur for the Abwehr. There was the testimony of Marguerite Duprez, who had received messages from her husband in prison, and of others who had seen Cole taking part in German raids. Most significantly, with Voglimacci's help, Guerisse had also obtained the letters from Carpentier—not only a priest, but a French Army officer—which set forth Cole's iniquitous conduct in corrosive detail. But those at the highest levels of British Intelligence, in London, apparently remained unconvinced that Cole had gone over the top.

Unquestionably, Cole had made a deep impression on many of those whom he had met and assisted when he was still a bona fide British agent. Some of these people found it unbelievable that Cole could have gone over to the German side. One of these was Taffy Higginson, the RAF pilot Cole had brought down to the South in June 1941. Subsequent to his voyage with Cole, Higginson's luck had run out. His forged French credentials were challenged in the French border town of Banyuls, just short of the Spanish frontier, and he was arrested. After some months in the French civilian prison system he was transferred to Saint-Hippolyte-du-Fort and then to the Fort de la Revère, near Nice. Despite plans for an eventually successful escape, Higginson was still in the Fort de la Revère in early 1942.

Through contacts with the outside he received news of Cole's treason and of Guerisse's determination to execute the man. Believing there had to be some misunderstanding, Higginson sent an urgent message to Guerisse. "For God's sake don't (kill Cole), because I'll hold you responsible when I get back to the U.K. There's no justification as far as I am concerned to do this to him."

The RAF flyer was not alone in his reluctance to believe in Cole's treason. But there could be no such explanation for the reactions coming from London, where evidence of Cole's moral turpitude in civilian and military life was readily available. There had to be some other reason for MI6's refusal to believe the accounts of the Cockney's treason emanating from France.

For some time, the Cockney had been a subject of minor discord within the SIS. From Lisbon and then Gibraltar, Darling had persisted on the subject of Cole; when he learned of the large sum of money the Cockney was accused of having embezzled, he again became agitated. "I sent a detailed letter to London giving my reasons for suspecting Cole of dishonesty if not worse," he writes. The memo "produced a rebuff from London in the shape of a note which read 'Your summing up of the Cole ... situation is not appreciated and do not write further in this vein.'"

This cavalier attitude towards the security risk posed by a key agent in the largest escape line in occupied France was baffling. It ran counter to the ruthlessness with which SIS deputy chief Claude Dansey customarily dealt with suspected treason or even mere insubordination in his Continental circuits.

Dansey exercised "the power of life and death over countless spies, for when treachery was suspected Dansey alone could give the order" for execution. Once crossed, he was implacable. When one known traitor was spotted in Lisbon with undercover agents of the German Sicherheitsdienst, the British head of station in the Portuguese capital requested advice. Cabled Dansey: "Kill him repeat kill him."

This merciless attitude did not apply only to traitors. In 1942 Dansey learned of disciplinary problems with ninety Allied escapers and evaders holed up in Paris during a major German crackdown. British and American pilots were placing the entire network at risk by recklessly taking strolls, frequenting cafés, and visiting nightclubs. A French agent radioed Dansey for instructions. Came the SIS leader's order (which in the event was not followed): "Kill them."

In the far more flagrant instance of Cole, however, distress signals from Marseilles produced only equivocation in London. After the November confrontation with Cole in Marseilles, Guerisse conveyed to Darling "his conviction that Cole was not only an embezzler but more than possibly a traitor as well. He told me that he would liquidate him when next he had the opportunity."

But "this information did not please Colonel Dansey," reports Darling. The intelligence chief sent down word that "he did not agree to Cole being killed and to pass that message to O'Leary at Marseilles.

"It was all very well, I thought, to sit in London and issue instructions covering a situation only understood by the man on the spot, who was in danger. Luckily for Cole, he had gone once more to northern France out of O'Leary's immediate reach, but O'Leary's next communication on this subject was adamant."

Indeed, O'Leary was itching for vengeance on the traitor, as he wrote to Darling later in 1942. "If God is just, *mon cher* Donald, that bastard Paul will fall into my hands; I swear I'll cure him!"

◆　◆　◆

EVEN IN FEBRUARY 1942, with Cole out of sight and the northern line in ruins, London was reluctant to accept the truth. This lent urgency to Guerisse's efforts to communicate with Carpentier in Loos. Guerisse obtained the priest's letter explicitly condemning Cole in the first days of March 1942, just as word came that Donald Darling had called Guerisse to an urgent conclave in Gibraltar. Armed with this letter, Guerisse was greatly reassured. "The evidence was there that Cole was a traitor, for the first time, and given by a man who certainly did not lie."

The Belgian hurried to Barcelona, using the line's long-established routes and guides. In Madrid Michael Cresswell, a British diplomat code-named "Monday" to Donald Darling's "Sunday," took him in hand. He passed through the gates to Gibraltar in the cramped trunk of Cresswell's Sunbeam Talbot. Received in the British enclave by Darling, Guerisse confided Carpentier's letter to him.

But the subject of the traitor was not broached immediately. Guerisse's first engagement was to dine with Lord Gort, once commander of the ill-fated British Expeditionary Force and now governor of Gibraltar. Gort, learning that a British agent had arrived from the north of France, summoned Guerisse to his table, saying, "I wish to have fresh news from Lille."

Even when Guerisse was closeted with Darling and Major John Codrington, a central figure in Dansey's "Z" system, there was little talk of Cole. Codrington, dispatched to Paris after the 1939 invasion of Poland, was now SIS head of station in Gibraltar. In discussions with the two men, Guerisse received the impression that they were "not at all certain that Cole was a traitor." Until they inspected Carpentier's letter closely, "in fact they were in doubt." More than this, Guerisse could feel that Codrington, at least, was dubious as to Guerisse's own position in the affair. Guerisse wondered "whether at certain moments they hadn't thought: 'Well, who is a traitor? Is it O'Leary?'"

♦ ♦ ♦

IN POINT OF FACT the SIS was not taking Guerisse's word that Cole was in German hire. While the Belgian was entertained in Gibraltar the SIS went behind his back to get a second opinion. Guerisse had been gone only a few days from Marseilles when the order came from Barcelona that his second-in-command should proceed to Geneva and contact certain persons at the British Consulate there.

Guerisse's replacement was Mario Praxinos, who in November had advocated mercy for Cole. Praxinos traveled with another agent to Annemasse, in the Savoy, from which he hoped to reach Swiss territory. But no sooner had the two men gotten off their train than they were detained and interrogated by the Vichy customs police. Any illegal border crossing under such close surveillance was doomed to failure, so they returned to Marseilles. Hearing this, Louis Nouveau decided to go to Geneva himself.

Traveling to Lyon, he called upon American Vice Consul George David Whittinghill, thirty-four. Whittinghill was not out of the classic State Department mold. Born in Rome to American parents, he had returned to Italy in 1934 as a foreign correspondent. After another spell in the United States with *Time* and *Newsweek*, he became a press assistant to the American consulate general in Milan. Whittinghill arrived in Lyon in April 1941 to take up his duties as head of the consulate's British Interests Section.

There he provided discreet assistance to the Garrow organization, directing military personnel into the escape channels. But his involvement with the British seems to have gone beyond this. Nouveau had learned in late 1941 that Whittinghill was in close contact with the Geneva outstation of the SIS, directed by "Z" agent Victor Farrell. On one occasion, the French businessman-agent later noted, he carried to Whittinghill "a small piece of paper coming from the British secret service in Barcelona."

Whittinghill had established a route by which he or his delegates could travel clandestinely into Switzerland through the Savoy. But when Nouveau had inquired about this passage, Whittinghill "refused to give ... the slightest details." Nouveau now renewed his request, explaining that "the message from Barcelona had been imperative."

Whittinghill relented and divulged the procedure. In the town of Bossey, near Annemasse, Nouveau was to contact a grocer named

Vuaillat and give the pass-phrase "Maria says hello." The American diplomat also provided Nouveau with a false French national identity card. Armed with advertising brochures to support his cover as a traveling salesman, Nouveau arrived in the border town of Anne-masse the following evening. After meeting his contacts he was taken across the Swiss frontier by a local peasant and deposited at a tramway stop with only two Swiss francs in his pocket. The streetcar carried him to the center of Geneva.

"I felt like I was in another world," writes Nouveau. Just hours before he had been in the somber, blacked-out France of Vichy; now he strolled the dazzlingly lit boulevards of neutral, prosperous Swit-zerland. On the lakefront, he found the British passport office that covered the local SIS station, but his contacts were absent. Directed to a seat, he waited for twenty-five minutes until there entered a thin, astringent official who identified himself as Mr. King.

Nouveau embarked on a complicated explanation of who he was and why he was there, only to be interrupted by King. "I don't know anything about all this," said the Englishman. "I don't know what you want."

Nouveau repeated his explanation in an abridged version, again drawing a blank. The Briton "maintained his same calm and cold attitude and repeated that he didn't understand at all, that he didn't really see what he could tell me, that he didn't see what all this had to do with him."

"Good God!" Nouveau finally burst out, exasperated at this mad-dening demonstration of British phlegm. "I don't know what I can tell you, because the only instructions I was given were to get in touch with you and put myself at your disposition. After all, isn't this all about Paul Cole?"

The British diplomat cocked his ears. "Oh," he said. "You know about Paul Cole?"

They had been standing in the hallway as King gave Nouveau the brush-off. But now the Briton drew him into an office and invited him to take a seat. Nouveau, fatigued and unnerved, asked for a whiskey. He was astonished to hear that there was not a drop to be had in this secret service outpost. He took a glass of mineral water instead and submitted to interrogation.

"He began to ask me question after question, and I told him, with all the details, everything that I knew about Paul Cole's activities over the previous months."

As he talked, Nouveau reflected on King's strange behavior and the reason he had been called to Geneva. He thought he finally understood. "The secret service had been very surprised to see that—and this was pure coincidence—as soon as the organization passed under the command of O'Leary, who was of Belgian nationality, the reports on Cole had become . . . so negative that he was denounced as a traitor."

After two hours of questioning, King cabled the SIS head office in London to report, then arranged overnight accommodations for Nouveau. The following morning Nouveau met station chief Farrell. They ate lunch together in a local restaurant and talked through the afternoon about Cole and other aspects of the Marseilles escape line. Later Nouveau was plied with more questions cabled from London and asked to draft a written report.

The London headquarters of the SIS, it seemed, was more than passingly interested in the activities of Sergeant Paul Cole. It apparently did not occur to Nouveau that this intense concern might have stemmed from causes other than the sudden change in Cole's standing with Marseilles.

◆　◆　◆

IN GIBRALTAR, meanwhile, it was debated whether Guerisse should fly to London for consultations. But Codrington put the damper on this. The Belgian government-in-exile wanted to know what had become of its medical officer, and SIS wanted no complications, he said. Then too, it might have been awkward if Guerisse had inquired as to how a petty swindler had managed to humbug the most prestigious intelligence service in the world. Instead, Jimmy Langley,

Dansey's agent inside MI9, flew in from London to handle the situation personally.

On the day before Guerisse's scheduled return to France, he dined with Langley, Codrington, and Darling. To Guerisse's surprise, there was little discussion of Cole. But he sensed that his view had prevailed. By the time Darling saw Langley off to London, the latter was "determined to make no further effort to prevent Cole from being eliminated." Guerisse boarded a Spanish trawler the next day with the explicit order to execute Cole whenever possible, a directive that was forthwith transmitted to all other British circuits in France.

But London's failure to inform Ian Garrow of Cole's criminal record from the beginning had contributed to the profound damage sustained by the Scot's organization. Later, time that should have been devoted to recovery had been lost while Dansey and company in London challenged Guerisse's judgment.

"It had taken over a year," concluded Darling, "to make London realize that Cole was a traitor and was presumably collaborating with the Nazis." Meanwhile, Cole was still alive somewhere inside France, and the threat of further betrayals hung over the escape line.

22

"His True Identity Was Established"

BY THE EARLY SPRING of 1942, Suzanne Warenghem had fallen strongly under Cole's influence despite warning signs that he was not entirely trustworthy. One came on his return from a trip, ostensibly to the north, when he boasted that he was on the German wanted list. He pulled out a photograph torn from a magazine, showing what appeared to be his profile.

"The Germans are looking for me everywhere," Cole told her. Wanted posters were plastered all over the north offering a large reward for his capture, he said. Warenghem believed this until she ran across the same photograph—which in reality showed a Swiss physician of some renown—in an outdated magazine in her dentist's waiting room. Confronted with this, Cole glibly explained that someone in the north had handed him the clipping, and scolded her. "How dare you doubt the word and good will of a British officer?"

They quarreled and Cole went out in the evening, leaving a note behind. "Suzy darling," he wrote. "I see *plainly* that you do not wish to understand my state of mind at this awful moment. Why do you wish always to misunderstand things? Place yourself in my position and I am sure you will see more clearly. . . .

"However, as you always think the worst, and as I do not wish to quarrel with you, I will leave immediately I get papers for the north of France," he wrote. "I will not rest to see you unhappy or perhaps lose your esteem."

Naturally Cole was bluffing. Warenghem came into line at the threat of his departure. The bond between them tightened and in late March 1942 Cole proposed marriage. Arrangements were made for a clandestine service, with the Abbé Amy officiating; he was former vicar of the local church in Courbevoie and a trusted friend of Warenghem's other aunt, Isabelle Bureau. He was now at a church in the working-class suburb of Malakoff south of Paris.

To meet a legal requirement that a civil marriage precede the church ceremony, Cole produced a forged wedding certificate. Amy, meanwhile, obtained the authorization of the archbishop of Paris for a mixed marriage, as Cole had been baptized into the Church of England. The Cockney submitted to an interview with the Abbé, but matters of faith and doctrine gave way to tales about the life of a British secret agent. Cole "told them so convincingly that I believed every word he said," the priest later told biographer Young. "He struck me as a man of extreme psychological force, very agreeable, very attractive."

Cole and Warenghem married on April 10, 1942, in a private service carried out in the sacristy of the small Catholic church in Malakoff. Jeanne Warenghem and Isabelle Bureau served as witnesses. There was no wedding mass. Warenghem, then twenty, wore a navy-blue blazer over a beige-and-pink dress, and a blue hat. Cole was fitted out in his best gray suit and a dark silk tie, with a white handkerchief tucked into his breast pocket.

After Cole had scrawled his signature beside Warenghem's more disciplined hand, the two aunts signed the church register. Then they all adjourned to a restaurant for a wedding breakfast. That night

Jeanne Warenghem gave a party for family members and a few close friends.

"Everyone said that Suzanne had never looked prettier and Paul, at the top of his form, gave once more his celebrated rendering of 'Little Old Lady,'" writes Young. The song was a favorite of Warenghem's *Tante* Jeanne, and Cole, singing it for the group, made a favorable impression. Commented one of the guests later to Young, "Paul was a real charmer."

But marriage did not remove the apprehension with which Suzanne Warenghem faced the future. Gone was the reassuring contact with Garrow, Guerisse, Dowding, Carpentier, and the others of the escape line. Warenghem was cut off from the secret activity that had brought her together with Cole. He shut her out of that entire side of his life, explaining that he was rebuilding his organization and demanding she trust in him. Soon she was additionally bound to the Englishman by the child she carried.

Eventually he gave her missions that she undertook gratefully after the long months of inactivity. Cole sent her to Brussels to mail a letter he said was of the utmost importance. She spent an entire night on a train-station platform in Lille and came close to being arrested. Her earlier sense of involvement returned. But in fact these were only fool's errands to remove her from the scene while Cole prepared to make his exit from a situation that was less and less to his liking. In his eyes she had become burdensome and a danger to his own safety. At any time she might learn the truth or reveal his whereabouts to those in the escape line, who would surely seek to execute him.

◆ ◆ ◆

IN THE MIDDLE of May, Cole dispatched Warenghem to Tours, telling her that three British pilots would arrive there in need of an experienced guide. In Tours, Warenghem met each arriving Paris train for over a week. Her frustration and anger rose until she wrote to Cole in Paris demanding an explanation. Meanwhile, he had made arrangements to borrow the apartments of her three aunts for a day, explaining to each that British escapers would be passing through. While they were absent, he stole their money, silver, jewelry, and other valuables.

He met Jeanne Warenghem for dinner that same night, after she had awaited the nonexistent aviators all day at a Paris hotel. Under the influence of a bottle of wine, Cole grew maudlin and took her hand. "*Tante* Jeanne," he said, "please forgive me for all I have done—I would like to feel that I have your pardon." She was mystified by the remark until she returned to her ransacked home.

Cole joined Warenghem in Tours and announced that they were going to travel to Marseilles, by way of Lyon. But his actions in Paris and his subsequent behavior would suggest that he had set his sights on a destination beyond the borders of occupied France. Most likely he intended to seek passage on a neutral vessel sailing from Marseilles. The gangster Charles Vincillione had arranged such transportation for British escapers on a number of occasions.

The couple arrived in Lyon on June 8. After installing Warenghem at the Hôtel d'Angleterre, Cole set out to raise more of the funds required for his escape. One of the first to be contacted by the traitor was George Whittinghill.

The exact relationship between Cole and the American vice-consul is unclear. Whittinghill was in contact with the escape line, from which Cole had been expelled for more than seven months and which had marked him for death. Yet this did not give pause to Cole, who asked the diplomat for a large sum of money. Clearly, something more was involved. Could it have been Whittinghill who passed Cole's intelligence through to the Geneva outpost of SIS? Lyon, close to Geneva, had once been a regular stop for Cole. Perhaps Cole intended to trade on the information he had been able to collect that spring.

What the Cockney did not know was that Guerisse had informed Whittinghill of his treason. Whittinghill told the Belgian that he expected Cole might show up at his consulate. He did not explain why. Guerisse asked that the American raise an alarm if the turncoat showed up on his doorstep. The diplomat had the telephone number of Rodocanachi's office. A code phrase had been worked out regarding a patient in need of urgent medical attention—the "cure" to which Guerisse had referred.

When the turncoat appeared, Whittinghill, cool-headed, feigned ignorance of his true position. Cole told the American that he had lost contact with the escape organization because of the wave of arrests in its northern wing. Whittinghill has not divulged what transpired between himself and Cole that day. But the traitor went away, according to Guerisse, with approximately 25 thousand francs in hand.

When Cole had left, Whittinghill telephoned to Marseilles and passed on the word that Cole was in Lyon. Guerisse was in Marseilles that day. He dropped all other matters and took the night train to Lyon. In his pocket was the nine-millimeter revolver he intended to use on Cole.

The traitor meanwhile had approached other potential lenders, including an acquaintance named Jean Biche, who held a post in the Vichy administration. The Frenchman gave Cole some thousands of francs and the promise of more to come. As soon as Cole had disappeared, he telephoned the Vichy secret police in Lyon to let them know a notorious German agent was in town.

Agents of the Commissaire de la Surveillance du Territoire, the local branch of the DST, raided Cole's room at the Hôtel d'Angleterre early on the morning of June 9 and arrested him on charges of espionage. Cole was found in possession of 41 thousand francs—what remained of his Paris thefts and borrowings from Biche and Whittinghill. Identity papers in the names of Joseph Deram and Franck Delobel were found hidden behind a mirror in the hotel room. Cole and Warenghem were imprisoned awaiting trial.

Soon after dawn that same day, Albert Guerisse stepped off the overnight express from Marseilles into Lyon's Gare de Perrache, tired and dirty after a night standing in the corridor of the overcrowded train. He planned to go straight to the Hôtel d'Angleterre and pump enough bullets into the traitor to terminate his career. But Whittinghill picked him out of the crowd in the station hall. "Pat, you're not going to get him," said the diplomat. "He was arrested last night by the Vichy police."

Guerisse, eager to eliminate the Judas, was bitterly disappointed. He also was concerned to hear that Warenghem had been arrested. How was it possible, he wondered, for Suzanne not to know Cole was a German agent? Later he was to conclude, like others, that she had been taken in completely by Cole. But Guerisse's faith in the young Frenchwoman was momentarily shaken.

With Cole out of reach, Guerisse remained with Whittinghill for a brief conversation as they walked through the early morning streets of Lyon. Then Guerisse headed to the station to catch the next train back to Marseilles.

◆ ◆ ◆

COLE'S ARREST in Lyon in June 1942 was a byproduct of an imperfect collaboration between France and Germany. Vichy was preaching cooperation with the invaders, but its own secret services were deeply divided over how far this collaboration ought to go. The DST was the counterespionage police arm of the French State of Vichy as it had been for the prewar Republic. But this operational security arm was under the influence of two intelligence services, whose aims were at times contradictory.

The BMA, or Bureau of Anti-National Intrigues, had arisen from the ashes of the Cinquième Bureau, the French Army staff intelligence branch dissolved under the 1940 armistice terms. The BMA pursued the enemies of Vichy and may have been involved in the arrest of Garrow. But it also hounded German agents in the Unoccupied Zone. By February 1942, the BMA had put no less than 118 German intelligence agents behind bars. This resulted in a formal German request that Vichy "search its prisons and make inquiries of every military tribunal in order to ascertain their whereabouts." Most had been shipped to French North Africa out of reach of the German services seeking their release. A few were shot.

Even less responsive to German and Vichy wishes was the Entreprise Générale de Travaux Ruraux, or TR. The name of Rural Works was an administrative blind for a counterespionage service spun off by the more resistance-minded officers of the Cinquième Bureau. TR slipped intelligence through back channels to U.S. diplomats in Vichy, who forwarded such information to the British. It identified Axis agents in Vichy France and tipped off those DST agents who were more inclined to arrest Nazi traitors than Gaullist or British operatives.

One such patriot was Louis Triffe, the policeman who led the raid on Cole's hotel room. Chief DST inspector in Lyon, Triffe also served SOE, Britain's espionage and sabotage service. So it was that in early June 1942 he drove to Anse, fifty miles north of Lyon, where an SOE agent had just been captured. Robert Sheppard, parachuted into France in the dark of night, had landed on the roof of the Anse police station. He was captured in his first hour on French soil.

"This man belongs to me," Triffe told the local gendarmes. "I want to question him." On the way back to Lyon Sheppard briefed Triffe on his assignment and gave him the two million francs he was carrying in a money belt. Then Triffe gave Sheppard a good lunch in town and locked him up. SOE agent or not, Triffe had to keep up appearances.

Sheppard was detained in the *petit depot*, a holding tank next to the Palais de Justice in Lyon. The courthouse lock-up consisted of a central hall surrounded by large collective cells with wooden planks for sitting or sleeping. One evening he observed the arrival of a young woman, "really a poor girl, obviously pregnant, crying, miserable." Sheppard, empathizing with the girl's plight, went over to where she sat in a disconsolate heap.

"Why are you here?" asked Sheppard. His mother was French, and he spoke the language with perfect fluency. "What's wrong?"

Suzanne Warenghem poured out her troubles. She and her husband, "a British officer with a secret job," had been arrested that day in a hotel in Lyon. Sheppard could see from the first that she implicitly believed Cole was a genuine British secret agent.

He also concluded that she was "an amateur, quite hopeless." Sheppard cautioned her not to confide too much in those around her—even himself. "You don't know me," he said. "Don't talk too much." But she continued, explaining that the French police had told her Cole was a traitor, working for the Germans. Entirely in the dark, Sheppard encouraged her to trust in the integrity of her husband and unwittingly reinforced her faith in Cole.

Meanwhile the Cockney was undergoing repeated interrogation by the DST. The truth, or a rough approximation of it, emerged slowly. French documents state that Cole "successively claimed to be a captain in the English army working for the Intelligence Service; a detective of Scotland Yard; then a German officer on a mission in the Free Zone." Interrogators applied more vigorous persuasion, and "at the end of several interrogations his true identity was established." Cole would state later that this deposition was "false in many particulars." As was his habit, Cole added a number of colorful touches. But the essentials of his traitorous relationship with the German intelligence services had been extracted.

Cole claimed he had worked on behalf of Britain, functioning as a double agent. But the French secret service would note that "the information we were able to collect in the Occupied Zone unmasked Cole's underhanded conduct."

Interrogated, we may presume, none too gently, Cole said that Warenghem knew nothing of his intrigues. Triffe became convinced of her innocence when he learned how the traitor had planned to rid himself of his pregnant wife. Before arriving in Lyon, Cole had entrusted Warenghem with a map of a German airfield in the north of France. He gave her instructions to bring it to what he said was a Resistance letter-drop. But Triffe knew that the address was in fact a front for the German security forces in the Unoccupied Zone. Warenghem would have been seized, bundled north into the Occupied Zone, tried for espionage by a German military tribunal, and very possibly executed. At best, given her pregnancy, she would have been deported to a concentration camp.

Cole had arranged cynically for his wife, bearing his own child, to walk into a deadly set-up.

The day after Sheppard had met and comforted the young woman, he was brought in for "interrogation" by Triffe. "What's the story with this Paul Cole and his wife?" asked Sheppard.

"Don't touch that," Triffe said. "I can tell you that Cole is definitely a traitor—there's no doubt at all."

"But what about his wife?"

"His wife doesn't know a thing about it," Triffe said. "She's absolutely genuine."

This concorded with Sheppard's initial impressions of Warenghem. "She was completely naive," he later explained. "But she was naive because she was a real patriot." Earnest in her desire to contribute to the Allied war effort, Warenghem yet lacked the skills, sophistication and hardened judgment of professionally trained agents.

Sheppard talked with Warenghem again the next day as they shared a bowl of soup. Choosing his words carefully, he told her that he had received confidential information. "You have nothing to do with it," Sheppard said, "but Cole is a traitor."

◆ ◆ ◆

STILL, WARENGHEM clung to the belief that there was some mistake, that the French police for some reason wished to discredit a legitimate British agent. Eventually she was confronted with Cole himself. The Cockney was brought into the DST office in handcuffs, showing the effects of incarceration and repeated interrogation. For openers, one of the detectives slapped him across the face a few times.

"Now, you swine," he said, "tell this woman that you are just a dirty traitor. Go down on your knees and ask her to forgive you for what you have done to her." Cole complied, kneeling before his wife and pleading with her as he had done before Guerisse in Marseilles.

Relates Young, "He raised his hands and he cried in a piteous, thin, pleading voice, 'Suzanne, it's true, I am a traitor. Everything they say is true. I don't know why—I don't know why I did it. But you know I love you, really. I'll do anything, anything, if you'll only forgive me.' "

Her illusions torn away, Warenghem was leveled by this confrontation. She had nothing to say to Cole.

The next time she saw him was July 21, when they were tried for espionage by the five-man Permanent Military Tribunal at Fort Montluc in Lyon. As husband and wife, they were allowed a few moments alone in an anteroom of the court before the session began. Cole had regained his former presence; he brushed off the earlier scene as having been staged for the benefit of the DST.

"Good acting, wasn't it," he told her cockily. "All I ask now is that if you have any doubts about me, wait until you get out of prison, then go to Geneva and contact the British Consulate there. There's a colonel who works there who can tell you that I am truly a British agent. And you can tell him everything that has happened to me."

Was this just another of Cole's many fabrications, this purported link with the Geneva Consulate? Or was there a grain of truth in it—that Cole was not only a traitor to the escape line, but a renegade agent of the SIS who had once been controlled by the Geneva outstation?

The military tribunal sitting at Fort Montluc—soon to become a Gestapo prison under the control of the infamous *Obersturmführer* Klaus Barbie—found Suzanne Warenghem innocent. The court followed the recommendations of the DST, one of whose officers concluded that if she was "a young person, unstable and an adventuress," she was not a German agent. The few letters she had been allowed to exchange with Cole during their weeks in prison seemed "sufficient assurance of her good faith."

But the evidence against Cole was plentiful. The court heard police testimony that Cole "accepted, perhaps under threat but also in the certitude of being richly rewarded, to enter the service of the Gestapo." There were no extenuating circumstances to temper the indignation of the court, which deplored the British traitor's "cynicism and refinement" in accompanying the Germans to the homes of those whom he had betrayed.

Found guilty of espionage, he was condemned to death, civic degradation, and the confiscation of all his possessions, "present and to come, of whatever nature they may be." French documents state that Cole "listened without blanching" as the sentence was read. Then he was led away in irons to await execution of the sentence.

23

"He Was Backing a Losing Cause"

SUZANNE WARENGHEM had been acquitted of espionage by the Lyon tribunal, but her future could not have seemed much bleaker if she had been convicted and sentenced with Cole. She was penniless, homeless, with child. Under the threat of arrest in the Occupied Zone, she could not return to Paris.

Upon leaving the prison gates she turned to Jean Biche, who had set the DST on Cole. Biche, living in the Hôtel Royal on the place Bellecour in central Lyon, put her up in his rooms for a few days. Then he sent her into the countryside to rebuild her health, undermined by six weeks on a French prison diet. Two weeks later Warenghem traveled south to Marseilles, hoping to escape to England.

In Marseilles the hapless twenty-year-old girl was rebuffed by the Garrow Organization, now known as the Organization Pat. This was primarily a matter of security. She had been arrested and interrogated by the Vichy authorities, who were tainted by collaboration with Germany. There was also her close association with Cole. Later

Guerisse would become certain that she was simply another of the Cockney's victims. But in the late summer of 1942, he had too many security worries to take on another potential risk.

She was not entirely abandoned. Georges Rodocanachi attended her during the last months of her pregnancy, and the line provided some financial assistance. But this was not enough, and Warenghem fell into a slough of despondent poverty. She took an attic room in a wretched hotel just below the train station in the rue Parmentier. On October 31, 1942, she gave birth to a male child who received the name of Alain Patrick Warenghem.

The hotel did not allow children, so Warenghem had to entrust Alain to the care of a midwife. She went to collect the child each morning, and with him in her arms she wandered the streets of Marseilles, one more sad figure amid so much misery. The child did not thrive. Suzanne had obtained a milk ration which she provided to the nurse, but learned that the woman, heartlessly greedy, was selling it off on the black market.

Warenghem appealed to the hotel owners, who let her keep the child in her room. There she attempted to nurse the child back to health. But it was the middle of winter and there was little or no heating. After the New Year the child's condition worsened, and he died in the hotel room on January 12, 1943.

There was little to hold Warenghem in Marseilles after this loss. Now the city only evoked tragic memories. She returned to Lyon to live in the home of a man named Roger Berthier, whom she had met while in prison. Berthier was part of the same network as Sheppard, to whom Warenghem had written from Marseilles. Her letters reflected the hopes and fears of a "very miserable" young woman who "wanted to keep alive and get moving." She sent Sheppard a photograph of herself, which he kept beside his prison cot.

Sheppard had also had news of Cole in this period. The SOE agent was held in the officers' compound of Montluc Prison, with a private cell, a batman, and a guard who carried in his breakfast each morning. Informed through the prison grapevine and his sessions with Triffe,

Sheppard knew Cole was sequestered in the main prison building. They crossed paths one day in the prison showers. Cole, the hail fellow well met, greeted Sheppard.

"You're a British officer!" he exclaimed. "So am I!" Sheppard realized the traitor was "hoping to turn me around in his net and so have his story confirmed that he was a British officer."

"That's all right," he said, snubbing Cole. "I know who you are, and that's enough for me."

Meanwhile, larger events had made Sheppard's position less comfortable. On November 8, 1942, an Allied beachhead was established in North Africa with the success of Operation Torch, a joint Anglo-American effort. There was only half-hearted resistance by the Vichy French defenders in Casablanca, Algiers, and Oran. Three days later, the Germans brushed aside their Vichy partners and seized control of the hitherto Unoccupied Zone. The Gestapo set up shop in Lyon soon after, under the direction of Klaus Barbie.

Triffe and Sheppard had conspired earlier to feed a pack of lies to the Gestapo. Under the terms of the armistice, the Germans could question Sheppard only through the intermediary of the DST. With Triffe's help the Briton cooked up answers calculated to mislead German intelligence analysts. But now Sheppard faced an infinitely less enjoyable encounter with German counterintelligence.

In a sort of administrative shell game, Triffe moved Sheppard to a civilian prison, from which the prisoner obtained a transfer to a Lyon hospital by simulating diphtheria. One midnight in February 1943, Sheppard drugged his guards with spiked wine, clambered out into a courtyard, hopped a wall, then shivered in his hospital gown until his welcoming committe arrived at 3:00 A.M.

It was a successful escape in all respects but one: Warenghem's letters to Sheppard had given the authorities a line on her, and she was arrested in March. Some weeks later she was transferred to the prison of Castres, in the Tarn province northwest of Marseilles. From its inmates were selected the French hostages executed by the German occupation authorities in reprisal for Resistance attacks.

◆ ◆ ◆

THE GERMAN INCURSION into Vichy France had prompted another escape—that of Ian Garrow, held since early 1942 in the Meauzac concentration camp in southwest France. A Vichy tribunal had condemned him to twenty years of hard labor. But the Australian journalist Nancy Fiocca, who claimed to be his cousin and traveled to the Dordogne to visit him, kept Garrow abreast of Cole's treason and other developments.

Soon after the German invasion, Fiocca learned Garrow was scheduled to be transferred to German custody. She called Guerisse to insist that action be taken. "What are you going to do for Garrow?" she demanded. "Are you going to free him?"

Guerisse was equally concerned. The Scot had not fared too badly under French custody, but he could expect far worse treatment once in German hands. Most likely he would disappear into the Reich. But Guerisse hesitated. The escape line was his first concern. Garrow himself would have insisted nothing be done to endanger its operations. "Let's think it over," he said. "We can't take too many risks."

As Fiocca steamed on the other end of the line, Guerisse's own deep affection for Garrow prevailed. "No," he said. "I'm going to take the biggest possible risk. But I must see Ian Garrow before we do anything. He is in this jail and he is the only person able to give me good information about means."

Equipped with the modified identification papers of Henri Fiocca, Nancy's French husband, Guerisse obtained entry to the visitor's room of Meauzac. Garrow was at first astonished, then outraged to see Guerisse peering through the bars.

"Why did you risk coming here?" he stormed. "You never should have done this for me!"

"Shut up," Guerisse told him. Then he asked Garrow to identify a prison guard who might be persuaded to help. Garrow named a man whose outlook and opinions were encouraging, and the Belgian left to set his plan in motion.

Visited at home by Guerisse, the prison guard was sympathetic but hesitant: if he were caught and arrested, his family would be left with no means of support. Guerisse overcame this objection by offering him the equivalent of three years' salary, with an equal sum to follow when Garrow was free.

On December 6, 1942, Garrow strolled out the prison's front gate in a gendarme's uniform that the compliant guard had smuggled into the camp. Guerisse had posted armed men around the compound entrance to create a diversion if Garrow were challenged. But this proved unnecessary. Garrow was driven to a remote farm to wait out the ensuing manhunt before traveling down the escape line to Gibraltar and London.

In the farmhouse, Guerisse sent a radio message to London informing British intelligence of Garrow's freeing, then brought the Scot up to date. They spoke of Cole, whose betrayals had begun exactly one year before.

Garrow was rueful. "You were right," he told Guerisse. "He was a bastard, and I didn't realize it in time."

◆ ◆ ◆

IAN GARROW's rescue gave proof of the expanded means and ambitious scope of the line he had founded, but which Guerisse now commanded. After the Belgian's meeting with Langley in Gibraltar, the line received far more material assistance than Garrow had ever dreamed of. When Guerisse slipped back into France aboard a Spanish trawler, he was accompanied by a radio operator. This crucial link with British intelligence enabled better coordination with outside forces. Ships and submarines were called in to take escapers straight off the beach, eliminating the rigorous and expensive Pyrenees crossings.

Canet-Plage, seven hours by train from Marseilles on the same stretch of coast where Guerisse had been captured by the French Navy in 1941, became the principal departure point for the escape line's clients. The organization rented villas there to hide the British and Allied servicemen until all was ready to embark them. On one occasion in late 1942, no fewer than thirty-two escapers crammed into a summer vacation home on the Mediterranean coast to await departure aboard a trawler.

Guerisse's agent networks extended from Marseilles to the Spanish and Italian borders, and up through the north into Belgium. A sub-network had also been established in the Brittany peninsula of the west. The line now had 250 workers—rural helpers, *convoyeurs*, forgers, radio operators. Its efficiency was such that one pilot, who crashed in France sixty miles north of Paris, passed through Paris, Marseilles, and Gibraltar to England in just twelve days.

The Organization Pat was well on its way to effecting six hundred successful escapes, before its wholesale betrayal by a French traitor in Gestapo harness. Guerisse already sensed "the danger looming over the entire network, because it had gotten too big. I didn't control it any more."

The seeds of destruction were planted soon after Guerisse and Garrow celebrated the Scotsman's escape in December 1942. Gestapo pressure and the continuing threat of more disclosures by Cole obliged Louis Nouveau to close his Marseilles apartment and take up other duties in Paris. In early 1943, he recruited a young veteran of the French Foreign Legion as a guide on the Paris-Marseilles and Paris-Toulouse runs. Roger Le Neveu, already in the pay of the Gestapo, was to become infamous within the French underground under the name of "Le Légionnaire."

The irony was that he came to Nouveau, the most cautious of men, with the best of recommendations. The French merchant considered that service in the Legion amounted to "a certificate of courage and the virtue of resourcefulness." In addition, Le Neveu was engaged to a woman whose brother had been executed by the Germans; she herself was held by the Germans.

Nouveau and two other agents interviewed Le Neveu in a café across from the Bibliotèque Nationale in Paris. Despite the intuitive misgivings of Norbert Fillerin, an agent from the Pas de Calais who had seen Cole's depredations, Le Neveu was hired. Doubts arose after his second mission, from which he returned to report that his Australian charge had been captured. But his next convoy of four airmen reached Marseilles in safety.

Only after Le Légionnaire's fourth convoy did Nouveau realize he had made a mistake—and Nouveau paid for it himself. The crew of a Flying Fortress shot down over Brittany had been brought to one of the line's safehouses in Paris. Le Neveu and two other men escorted the Americans to the Gare d'Austerlitz for travel southwest to the Demarcation Line. There was a delay at the station entrance when sentries demanded passes from the group. Le Neveu volunteered to obtain the necessary papers and came back with them five minutes later; at the time, no one wondered how he had done this.

Nouveau, accompanying the Americans, was arrested with the evaders and two other *convoyeurs* near their destination. Clearly, they had been set up by Le Neveu.

Le Légionnaire was not through. In March 1943 he arranged the arrests of most of the line's principal agents in Paris, then traveled to Toulouse, where Guerisse was trying to fend off this growing disaster. Claiming he could identify the traitor who had penetrated the line, Le Neveu arranged to meet Guerisse at an American-style café called the Super-Bar.

"Do you know who has been giving us away in Paris?" asked Guerisse, already suspecting what the answer would be.

"I know him perfectly well," said Le Légionnaire.

At that moment Guerisse felt the barrel of a gun in the back of his neck. "Hands up," someone barked, in English. Le Neveu had brought along the Gestapo, which knew that "Pat O'Leary" was a British agent.

Interrogated, Guerisse gave his name as Joseph Cartier, an engineer from Marseilles. But Le Neveu had already blown his cover. The Germans knew they had captured Pat O'Leary, chief of a major escape line. Then commenced the torture and interrogations that would continue for several months. Guerisse remained in German hands until the final days of the war, shipped through prisons in Toulouse, Marseilles, and Paris, then deported to the concentration camps of Neuebrenn, Mauthausen, Natzweiler, and finally Dachau.

He managed to pass word of Le Neveu's treachery to British intelligence along the way. In transit from Marseilles to Paris, Guerisse helped one of his lieutenants, Fabien de Cortes, escape from the train as it pulled into Paris. De Cortes contacted SIS station chief Farrell in Geneva, who cabled London that Le Neveu, a suspected associate of Cole, was to be shot on sight.

Le Légionnaire was duly executed by a French Resistance group, which discovered him in its ranks. But he had already wrought terrible damage. Cole had badly damaged the network; Le Neveu, working with a more powerful and experienced Gestapo force, was the instrument of its final destruction.

◆ ◆ ◆

AS GUERISSE'S FORTUNES declined, Cole's were momentarily on the rise. The heart of the traitor no doubt was gladdened by the German takeover of Vichy France in November 1942, although he must have faced the wrath of the Abwehr with some trepidation. The threat of execution was removed the following July, when his sentence was commuted to forced labor for life. The French had transferred Cole from Lyon to the Prison Militaire de Montron in the Dordogne. The Germans shipped him to the prison at Compiegne, north of Paris, where he remained on ice until nearly the end of 1943.

The Germans knew Cole was a valuable intelligence asset, if only he could be exploited properly. He was kept on a tight leash, penetrating escape and intelligence networks in Belgium and the north of France. British reports from inside France had an Englishman working under the name of Jean Masson, which was close to an alias Cole adopted later, "posing as a guide on an escape route plying between Brussels and Paris, during just the period which is missing in our knowledge of Cole."

Between operations Cole was probably held at Compiegne. The

Abwehr, burned once by the swindler, knew he was, as one British agent later concluded, "a runner." Given half a chance, Cole would vanish. So he was kept under wraps. In a prison like Compiegne, one of the largest Gestapo holding tanks in France, there was plenty of work for him. He likely served as a *mouton*, or "sheep," posing as a fellow prisoner to draw out otherwise uncooperative subjects.

Eventually the Germans allowed Cole to circulate more freely, perhaps on the understanding that another fugue would hold dire consequences. Besides, Cole was too deeply implicated as a traitor to expect anything but swift death from the French underground. With all of France under Gestapo jurisdiction, there really was no place else for him to go.

Back on the loose in Paris, Cole continued his betrayals. Probably in the interest of winning the trust of his German handlers, he returned to the Hôtel Nicolas Flamel, where he and his convoys once had lodged, turning owner Jean-Baptiste Delsol over to the Gestapo. Eugène Durand, proprietor of the Chope du Pont Neuf, also was denounced by the Cockney, who until the early months of 1944 had withheld information on the restaurateur's role in the escape line. But Cole spent much more of his time trying to pick up the traces of Suzanne Warenghem, newly free from German custody.

The previous September there had been a mass breakout from Castres. Warenghem was among those who escaped when the Resistance inmates seized control of a prison wing. She lived in a monastery near Carcassonne until the end of 1943, then returned to Paris. Working with various Resistance groups, sheltered by friends, Warenghem heard reports that Cole had been visiting their old haunts inquiring after her.

Under the false identity of Aline Le Gale, twenty-three, she moved from safe house to safe house and slept with a revolver under her pillow, determined to shoot Cole if he reappeared. But this confrontation never came about. That April Warenghem finally reached England after being taken off a Brittany beach by the Royal Navy. She never saw Cole again.

◆ ◆ ◆

THE EARLY SUMMER of 1944 brought, along with the Allied landings in Normandy, the culmination of a battle between the Abwehr and the Sicherheitsdienst. Admiral Wilhelm Franz Canaris, head of the Abwehr, was outmaneuvered by Heinrich Himmler, czar of the RSHA, or Central Security Department of the Reich, which controlled the SS and its dependencies, the SD and Gestapo. A downturn in German military fortunes gave Himmler the leverage he needed to oust Canaris. By June 1944 the Abwehr had been swallowed whole by the Sicherheitsdienst.

Sicherheitsdienst ascendancy translated into heightened brutality against captured British and French agents. Abwehr officers were no Boy Scouts. But they retained some sense of military discipline and restraint in contrast with the pitiless Sicherheitsdienst, which tortured freely and "dredged its way through muddy rivers of treachery and denunciation."

That summer, Cole entered the service of one of the most highly-placed Sicherheitsdienst agents in France: SS *Sturmbannführer* Hans Kieffer. A policeman in Karlsruhe before the war, Kieffer enrolled in the Nazi party in 1933 and had been an SS officer since 1936. Stocky of build, with curly hair and a bristly mustache, Major Kieffer, forty-three, was a "modest and calm man without personal ambition, who lived only for his trade." By early 1944 he had become one of the British secret service's most wily opponents.

By July, Cole was ensconsed in a top-floor room at Sicherheitsdienst headquarters, at 84 avenue Foch in Paris, working with the wireless subsection of Kieffer's counterespionage department. Kieffer's job was to ferret out Allied intelligence and sabotage networks and intercept agents parachuted or airlifted into France. With his wireless specialist, Josef Goetz, Kieffer attempted to turn captured radio sets and operators back against the British in a life-and-death battle of wits the Germans called the *Funkspiel*, or wireless game.

The object of a *Funkspiel* was to conceal the captive status of British agents transmitting under duress and to persuade their London handlers to parachute more agents into Gestapo snares. These agents in turn would be "played back" to London. Strategic disinformation was also fed over the airwaves in this whispering war. Errors in operators' hand-sent Morse-code transmissions could flag London to the danger. The British would then convey selective disinformation of their own to the Germans.

But this game could be fatal to the pawns involved, the captured radio operators. One of those who perished in German concentration camps after their interrogation by the Sicherheitsdienst was Madeleine Damerment. Her family in the north had been deeply involved in Cole's network. Her postmaster father, by all indications, was betrayed by the Cockney traitor. Like Lepers, she had escaped to England via Gibraltar, and eventually was recruited into the Special Operations Executive. Having worked in France as a switchboard operator and telegraphist, she was well qualified to work as a secret radio operator. But Kieffer, outwitting the British in one round of the *Funkspiel*, learned of her scheduled parachute drop in February 1944. With two other SOE agents she fell straight into the hands of the Paris Sicherheitsdienst. She later was sent to Dachau and executed in September 1944.

Precisely how Kieffer used Cole is, outside of Britain's intelligence archives, a matter of speculation. Cole is known personally to have interrogated British agents captured on missions related to the steady progress of the Allied armies across western France. He may have helped Kieffer to dismantle the important Prosper network of the SOE. French secret-service documents suggest he helped the Germans break English ciphers, but this is unlikely given their complexity and Cole's lack of familiarity with cryptography. But Cole could have made himself useful as a kind of English-language consultant in the formulation of *Funkspiel* messages. It was, after all, a kind of high-stakes confidence game.

♦ ♦ ♦

THE DISTANT TRUMPETS of judgment day sounded louder for Cole as German resistance collapsed and the Allies approached Paris. Most of the occupation troops and their French collaborators left the city on August 17. On every major artery leading east, one participant later recorded, "hundreds of trucks, loaded cars, mounted artillery, ambulances full of wounded on stretchers, were in file or overtaking and crisscrossing each other," while "monocled generals sped past like shining torpedoes."

Cole's transformation became complete as he donned a Gestapo uniform for flight and slipped out of Paris. Kieffer's staff retreated into Belgium, along with a handful of captive British radio operators who informed London that Cole was in the Gestapo van. He was still tagging along with Kieffer when the SS major was assigned to a commando group based near Nancy in the east of France. After the last ditch assault in the year-end Battle of the Bulge, orders came for retreat behind the Rhine. Cole followed his German masters along the downhill road to defeat.

"From that time on," states a U.S. Army report, "his career cannot be too closely plotted, other than to state he continued collaborating with the Germans until it was apparent to him, in the spring of 1945, that he was backing a losing cause."

24

"The Widest Latitude to Operate"

FIRE AND BRIMSTONE, in the form of concentrated artillery barrages, heralded the turncoat's day of reckoning. As the Reich's boundaries shrank in the month of April 1945, the outlook worsened for those who had betrayed their countrymen and allies. Cole, with an assortment of other Quislings and an army of once staunch Nazis who declined to share the Führer's fate in Berlin, fled south into the region near the Swiss and Austrian borders.

He was still with Kieffer, Goetz and a half dozen other former staff members of the avenue Foch Gestapo headquarters. Upon the fall of Kempten, southwest of Stuttgart, Kieffer's band regrouped on a promontory and saw columns of Allied armor approaching in a valley below. They loaded into three cars and hurried east toward Wald, then drove furiously southwest in a futile attempt to outflank the rapidly progressing American and French front.

North of Lake Constance, in a town called Worndorf, the German Army column in which they were traveling was pinpointed by Allied artillery fire. Those who survived the barrage rushed up and down in the road, which was jammed with gutted and burning vehicles.

Cole was hit in the leg by shell fragments, but his heavy military boots absorbed the worst of the damage. Cool-headed amidst the panicky crowd, Cole retrieved some money and the official Gestapo seals from one of the destroyed cars and got another going again. With a soldier named Stork at the wheel, Cole, Kieffer, and two other SS men named Hauk and Gandicki drove off at top speed in search of a place to ride out the end of the world.

For two days more they struggled on along the clogged and muddy roads. Then Kieffer decided it was time to take to the woods. In the depths of the Black Forest, Cole and his cronies changed into mufti, burned their incriminating documents, scattered their arms and ammunition, and moved constantly, trying to stay out of the way of Allied cannon fire.

The end seemed to be in sight when Kieffer announced he had thought of a scheme by which he, Cole, and Hauk—the others had struck out to fend for themselves—might escape Allied prison camp. Cole heard him out and concurred. The bedraggled trio set off in search of the nearest representative of the U.S. Army.

◆ ◆ ◆

DURING THE LAST TWO WEEKS of April, the U.S. VI Corps, the cutting edge of the Seventh Army, had thrust southeast more than two hundred miles into the Black Forest and the very foothills of the Alps. Ahead of the American forces loomed the white-blanketed peaks of the Austrian Tyrol. The GIs and their officers scanned the horizon and wondered what Armageddon the Third Reich was preparing in those heights. From Allied agents, secret intelligence sources, and rumors in the Swiss press, noted one American intelligence officer, "came unending reports on the preparation of a last great defensive bastion in the mountain fastness of Austria."

But the National Redoubt, as it was named in Allied councils, turned out to be more of an imaginary creation of U.S. intelligence than a final hope of the Reich. Other than a few diehard Waffen SS units, there was little military resistance to speak of left in southern

Germany. The main German formation, Army Group G, had been "completely slashed into a state of disorganization." Nearly 79 thousand prisoners—eight divisions worth—were rounded up in one six-day period.

This surfeit of prisoners became a problem for American units like the 117th Cavalry Reconnaissance Squadron. This mechanized, lightly armored formation served as the eyes and ears of VI Corps. Its five troops, fanned out along the border region, probed the collapsed German line, and policed the endless columns of POWs and displaced persons. There was no question of forcing capitulation: on any given morning a cavalry troop might "wake up to see two thousand fully armed Germans waiting to surrender."

Cole and his mates, too, were more than ready to come out of the woods. They had been ducking American shells for weeks and now faced unseasonably low temperatures. A cold front moving in from the Alps covered the Black Forest with three inches of snow on May 1. Another inch of the stuff fluttered down the next day as Cole, Kieffer, and Hauk presented themselves to the 117th Cavalry, which had established three roadblocks around the town of Wald.

Summoning up all his powers of dissimulation, Cole spun a new character out of whole cloth. He identified himself to the Americans as Captain Robert Mason, a British secret agent captured in France by the Sicherheitsdienst. The name was borrowed from his stepfather in London, Robert Thomas Mason. Kieffer and Hauk he introduced as two relatively decent Staatspolizei, civil policemen. He said they had been ordered to bring him to the concentration camp at Dachau but, in the hope of obtaining preferential treatment, had allowed him to rejoin the Allied forces.

Just about everything had passed through the U.S. lines in the previous weeks: "Bulgarians, Hungarians, Romanians, the works," one participant recalled. The officers of the 117th had no particular reason to disbelieve Cole. The confidence man laid on his very best imitation of a British officer's clipped diction, making light of his ordeal at the hands of the SS. But even this bravura performance might have gotten him no further than the next higher headquarters if not for a tremendous stroke of luck.

In conversation with the doctor who dressed his leg wound, Cole mentioned that he had worked with the French underground in the south of France. That was interesting, said the doctor, so had one of the junior officers of the 117th Cavalry. It soon turned out, by an amazing coincidence, that this officer had met Cole when the latter was still a legitimate British agent circulating in Marseilles.

♦ ♦ ♦

U.S. ARMY Second Lieutenant Lloyd Moore had a reputation within the 117th Cavalry as someone who was "a little bit different than a normal commissioned officer." He was the son of Clarence Moore, a prominent Washington, D.C. businessman and socialite, and Mabelle Swift Moore, of the Swift meatpacking fortune. In 1912, after Clarence Moore went down on the Titanic, Mabelle took her children to the Old World. Lloyd was raised in Paris and London and educated in the best British schools.

In September 1939 he joined the American Volunteer Ambulance Corps and was attached to various Allied units on the northern front. After the 1940 defeat, he drifted down to the south of France and ran across Cole in Marseilles. Moore had by then become involved with a Resistance group that by one account specialized in the assassination of Gestapo agents. When the German net began to close in on the underground network, Moore fled to the United States, where he secured a second lieutenant's commission. In late 1943, he was shipped to North Africa and joined the 117th Cavalry.

After his unit landed on the French Riviera in August 1944, Moore proved his worth. His commanding officer, Colonel Harold Samsel, considered that he possessed "unusual bravery." But his talents did not lie in combat command. Regarded as "an amazing character" with a great deal of personal charm, Moore was made a liaison officer. As the VI Corps advanced up the Rhone Valley, he was constantly running into old friends and turning up undiscovered sources of good wine and cognac. This duty was not without hazards: in September 1944 he was hospitalized when a land mine exploded under his jeep. He rejoined the 117th in January 1945, several months before his encounter with Cole.

Cole quickly determined that the American officer knew nothing of his career as a German informant and made capital of this lucky meeting. The affable Moore vouched for Cole to the unit's intelligence officer, Captain James Shenk, who put Cole and the two Germans in a jeep to VI Corps Headquarters in Garmisch-Partenkirchen, thirty or forty miles away. The U.S. Army had just occupied the Alpine resort town. Amid the general confusion Cole came before Colonel Don W. Dixon, head of VI Corps G-2, its counterintelligence section. Dixon read the note that Shenk had scribbled and given to the driver of Cole's jeep. Then he scrutinized the man before him.

Cole was not an imposing figure. His wrists and ankles stuck out of the old suit he had been given by Kieffer. But this only served to support Cole's tale of capture and maltreatment by the Nazis. The American colonel heard the same story Cole had narrated to Moore and Shenk: the parachute drop into occupied France, contact with the Resistance, capture by the Gestapo, months of interrogation and torture, deportation to Germany. The months Cole had spent in Kieffer's employ enabled him to embellish the account with detail that encouraged belief.

Dixon bought it. The intelligence officer congratulated Cole on his survival and escape. Then he asked Cole what he wanted to do now that he had been liberated. Careful to remain in character, Cole said that of course he wanted to go home, but hadn't thought about how to do this. Dixon promised to radio the British with the news of Mason's recovery.

The intelligence officer's next remark must have rung even louder alarm bells for Cole. The 206th Counter Intelligence Corps, attached to VI Corps Headquarters, might be interested in Cole's former guards, said Dixon. Why didn't Captain Mason take them over to the Hotel Badenheim so Major Harry Costello could look them over?

Cole was obliged to find this an excellent idea and reluctantly sought out the counterintelligence detachment.

The CIC proved no more perspicacious than any of the other American units Cole had met so far. CIC special agent Paul Martin questioned Kieffer and Hauk, inspected their papers, pronounced the two SS men harmless, and provided them with Allied-approved identification documents. Cole left the two Sicherheitsdienst agents heading for the Garmisch town hall to pick up permits for travel back to Karlsruhe, Kieffer's home town. Cole's former boss said that when things settled down, he planned to retire to Algeria and open a bar. But the British had something else in mind for Kieffer, who was arrested in 1947, tried for his part in the execution of an Allied commando, and hanged.

When Cole returned to the G-2 offices, Dixon invited him to stick around for a while, working on temporary duty with the American Army. Cole readily accepted this offer. "I had decided," he later would explain, "to get some of my own back." The turncoat was provided with an American lieutenant's uniform and a revolver, receiving about eighty or one hundred marks in occupation currency for the eight thousand Reichsmarks he had been carrying in the pockets of Kieffer's suit. At the Hotel Badenheim, Martin had given him an official CIC identity card. Cole had everything he needed to embark on yet another fraudulent career as the eminently respectable Captain Robert Mason of Allied Intelligence.

◆ ◆ ◆

COLONEL DIXON and Special Agent Martin might have been faulted for not having questioned Cole at greater length. But on May 3, 1945, four days before the German surrender, American officials were more on the lookout for the Nazi bigwigs, war criminals, and other scoundrels who had flooded southern Germany in the closing days of the war.

The officers in Garmisch might have taken a closer look at Cole if he had been an American. Just a few days after he had hoodwinked

The Abbé Pierre Carpentier. A priest and French Army officer, he helped escapers cross the Somme River borderline. *Courtesy Philippe Duclercq.*

This photo of Cole was probably taken from one of the identification cards he was carrying when arrested by the French in Lyon in June 1942. *Courtesy Henri Duprez.*

A wartime scene in the Gare de Lille, the train station from which escapers set out for Marseilles. *CREHSGM, Brussels.*

Major Norman R. Crockatt, wartime chief of MI9, the escape and evasion intelligence service. *Courtesy Susan Broomhall.*

Colonel Claude Dansey, the MI6 spymaster. Did he authorize Cole's recruitment as an agent? *By permission Hodder & Stoughton.*

James Langley. He served as Dansey's eyes and ears inside MI9. *Courtesy Mrs. J.M. Langley.*

Major Donald Darling. Stationed in Lisbon, he worried about the unlikely agent "Paul" Cole. *By permission William Kimber.*

Vladimir de Fligué, a Russian émigré, was recruited as an agent in Cole's Paris network.
Courtesy Mme. Simone Alix ex de Fligué and Mme. Ghislaine de Fligué, her daughter.

Fernand Holweck. This eminent French physicist died in the hands of the Germans after he and de Fligué were betrayed by Cole.
Courtesy Jacques Holweck.

The Chôpe du Pont-Neuf. Cole brought aviators in transit through Paris here for a square meal.
By permission MacMillan Co. and Studio Vista.

RIGHT: Cornelius Verloop. This Dutch agent for the Abwehr was a formidable opponent of the northern escape line. *Courtesy Cornelius Verloop.*

BELOW, LEFT: Hauptsturmführer Karl Hegener, Abwehr counterintelligence chief for Lille and the north of France. *Berlin Document Center.*

Sturmbannführer Hans Kieffer, Cole's Sicherheitsdienst boss until the war's end. *Courtesy Jacques Delarue.*

Suzanne Warenghem, the woman Cole married in April 1942 and betrayed two months later.
By permission MacMillan Co. and Studio Vista.

ABOVE, RIGHT: George D. Whittinghill, a U.S. vice consul in Lyons. Was he a link between Cole and British Intelligence?
U.S. National Archives.

RIGHT: Robert Sheppard. A British agent held by Vichy, his French Resistance contact informed him of Cole's treacherous past. *Courtesy Robert Sheppard.*

In August 1942 Cole was held prisoner by the French in Lyon.
Courtesy Marguerite Duprez-Beylemans.

Widespread confusion and mass surrender by German
troops enabled Cole to win the confidence of U.S.
counterintelligence officials. *U.S. National Archives.*

Cole in American uniform, posing as
Captain Robert Mason of Allied
intelligence. Behind him is the stove
in the Kneussles' kitchen; the circular
porcelain plates radiated heat.
U.S. Army Crime Records Center.

The Kneussle villa at Gut Krumbach,
commandeered by Cole and his bogus
counterintelligence squad. *Photo by author.*

Georg Hanft, former Nazi official of Saulgau and victim of Cole's lust for money and revenge. *U.S. Army Crime Records Center.*

Hanft was murdered 300 yards down this isolated forest road. *U.S. Army Crime Records Center.*

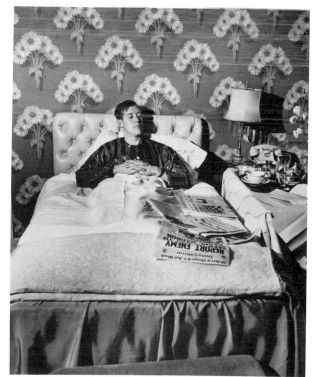

After his encounter with Cole, U.S. Army Captain Frank L. Lillyman appeared in *Life* magazine as an exemplary returning G.I. and guest of a New York hotel. *Yale Joel, Life Magazine.*

The Paris Detention Barracks. An escape artist, Cole strolled out of this Allied prison in late 1945. *By permission Roger Schall.*

LEFT: The traitor's death made the front pages of the Paris newspapers, accompanied by his 1939 photograph. *By permission Le Parisien.*

Freed from Dachau, Albert Guerisse honored Cole's victims in the north and identified the traitor's body in a Paris police morgue. *Courtesy Marguerite Duprez-Beylemans.*

Dixon and Martin, the 206th CIC arrested an American traitor named Douglas Chandler who had broadcast from Germany under the name Paul Revere. An American intelligence report described him as "a quiet fanatic" whose "warped point of view harped on the thesis that America was being forced into a war pact with England when it should remain isolated from the rest of the world."

But British traitors simply did not concern the U.S. Army for the moment, and most of the British forces were at the opposite end of Germany, far to the north.

The picture-postcard town of Garmisch-Partenkirchen, laid out under towering Alpine peaks, was filled to overflowing with American troops, POWs, displaced persons, and every manner and nationality of black-market operator. Cole could not have been more at home, and quickly found his own niche. In a visit to military government headquarters, Cole mentioned his familiarity with the French underground and was asked to examine a list of liberated French prisoners awaiting repatriation. The ever-helpful Captain Mason made himself useful foraging for victuals to supply the badly organized French relief office. In the course of this work Cole had another stroke of luck in acquiring a chauffeur-driven automobile for his personal use.

Strolling about Garmisch displaying an American lieutenant's insignia on his new khakis, Cole was hailed by U.S. Army MPs who had detained a young man at the wheel of a Mercedes convertible. They needed a French interpreter and Cole obliged. It was soon established that the driver was one Fernand Auguste LePage, twenty-two, a metal worker from Limoges brought to Germany as a forced laborer. Until the German defeat he had been employed as a driver by a Garmisch firm. LePage had taken the Mercedes from a local garage and gone for a spin with the ultimate intention of bringing it back to France with him.

Cole examined the tall, skinny Frenchman, whose lower teeth showed several gaps and whose upper denture was blackened by nicotine. Then he inspected the Mercedes, which was in better condition: a black Model V170 with red leather upholstery, its only apparent flaw was that it lacked a backseat.

Cole sent the MPs on their way with assurances that everything was in hand, then made LePage a proposition. If the Frenchman would go to work as his chauffeur, Cole would. see to it that he was back in Paris within three months. In the bargain, the Mercedes would be his to keep. LePage jumped at the offer, and Cole kept his part of the deal by immediately arranging the proper auto registration documents with the Garmisch military government.

In a few days, VI Corps, Dixon, and Cole's CIC unit moved on to Innsbruck, Austria. The Cockney grew worried that the radio message the American officer had sent out might bring an unwelcome response. It was time to get out of town. At the end of the first week in May, Cole and LePage drove northwest to Heimertingen, a small town on the edge of the Black Forest. Along the way, Cole explained to LePage that he was an agent in the British Secret Intelligence Service. On arrival he began interrogating Germans. Acting on their denunciations, he arrested three alleged members of the SS and handed them over to the American authorities in the regional center of Memmingen a few miles to the south.

No one had questioned Cole's credentials yet. But he realized they would not hold up very long if officials in Memmingen thought to ask what he was up to. So the Cockney drove north to Tuttlingen and sought out a printing company. Flashing his credentials to the submissive German proprietor, Cole ordered two rubber stamps— one bearing the seal of the military government, the other a copy of the CIC stamp on the identity card.

Not for nothing had Cole spent years in the French underground falsifying German occupation documents. He improved on his CIC identity card by typing in an additional phrase along the bottom: "The above officer is on special service for this office."

During the week to ten days he spent in Heimertingen, Cole added another Frenchman to his retinue. Georges Robert Jousset, twenty-four, transported to Germany for obligatory labor in a Messerschmitt factory, signed on as a guard. Then the Cockney prudently moved on to the west, passing through the village of Benenberg, where LePage and Jousset recruited two French women, Marguerite Gaubert, twenty, and Suzanne Votier, twenty-one, who joined Cole's staff as secretaries. Then the group again took to the highway, for the Cockney now had chosen his destination.

♦ ♦ ♦

IN WURTTEMBERG PROVINCE sixty miles to the south of Stuttgart, beyond the rugged Danube gorges, amid the rolling hills and well-tended farmland of Upper Swabia, lay the town of Saulgau. It was a prosperous burg of several thousand inhabitants, whose baroque churches, fifteenth-century market hall and thermal baths gave it to boast of a certain culture. But Saulgau was for all of that eminently obscure; in the opinion of one American criminal investigator, Saulgau and environs was "a forgotten corner of Germany; there was nothing down there." It was everything Cole required.

Additionally suiting the Cockney's purposes, Saulgau lay in the French zone of occupation. It was just fifteen miles or so from Sigmaringen, where Pétain and the remnants of his Vichy regime had waited out the end. The British and the Americans were too well organized to be taken in for long by his charade. But the French were still recovering from the effects of war and a four-year German occupation. They were far too preoccupied with re-establishing their government and administration, and with settling accounts among themselves in a national purge of collaborators, to worry about one British traitor.

A similar confusion reigned in the French-controlled areas of Germany. Three million Frenchmen were in Germany at the end of the war, having arrived there as prisoners of war, deportees or laborers. A million were to be found in the French zone, along with 120 thousand Russians, 80 thousand Poles, and 20 thousand Yugoslavs. It was, then, among the very people he had worst betrayed that Cole would find safety.

The Cockney arrived in Saulgau on May 15, in the afternoon. He quickly ascertained that the town was under the control of the Third Battalion of the Ninth Zouaves Regiment, whose headquarters was located six miles to the south, in Altshausen. He presented himself to the commander of the Third Battalion, a captain by the name of Chevauchée, in the military government offices located across from the town hall and marketplace. Informed that Cole had an intelligence assignment in the area, Chevauchée sent for his own security chief, Lieutenant Jacques Dureng de Maisonneuve.

In the presence of Chevauchée, Dureng and Camille Allart, the lieutenant's civilian aide, Cole once again told the story he had invented for the benefit of the American officers in Garmisch-Partenkirchen—with some additional flourishes. Parachuted into France as an agent of the Intelligence Service, Cole related, he had been captured and tortured by the Gestapo. He held out his hands, the fingers of which appeared to be deformed from ill-treatment by the SS. Faced with the choice of cooperating or going before a firing squad, Cole said, he had gone along with the enemy counterespionage service. But throughout his captivity he had played a double game, "working as much for the English as for the Germans."

Allart, looking on, could see that the tall, ginger-haired Captain Mason, dressed in a crisp, new American Army uniform, had a "commanding presence." The man spoke with obvious expertise of intelligence and other military matters. Despite his ragged French, the British captain seemed a most agreeable fellow. Cole explained that he had been detached by the Intelligence Service to the CIC in Heidelberg, producing documents to back this up. Having satisfied himself that these were genuine, the French security officer assured Captain Mason that he would be given "the widest lattitude to operate."

Cole immediately got down to cases, producing a sheet of paper with an official stamp on which were listed about a dozen names. These, he said, were important SS officers and war criminals whose whereabouts he hoped to discover.

At the top of the list was a Gestapo officer named Georg Hanft. Dureng was pleased to inform the British officer that he had personally arrested the man just two days before. Hanft was at that moment cooling his heels just a few streets away in the local jail, to which Dureng and Cole repaired immediately. In the small lockup Cole produced some photographs and made a show of confirming the captive Nazi's identity. Then they went back to the officers' mess, where Cole wolfed down a meal and pumped Dureng for information.

Was there by chance an American unit in the area? No, Dureng informed him, but there was an American liaison officer named Major Smith. Cole turned the conversation to Dureng's own job. He learned that the French lieutenant was alone on security duty in Saulgau, a market town of several thousand inhabitants. That was surely a lot of work for one man, Cole said; maybe he could use a hand.

The inexperienced Dureng, named to the security post simply because he had some prewar legal experience, was delighted at this generous offer. They agreed to work together, beginning with the case of Hanft. Dureng did not realize that in fact he had just become the latest addition to Cole's personal staff.

25

"The March of Prisoners Began"

WITHIN A MATTER OF DAYS Cole had insinuated himself into the daily routine of Dureng's Third Battalion. The tall, thin Englishman with reddish-blond hair became a familiar sight in the French military offices of Saulgau, with an American Army helmet on his head, a Walther P38 in his side holster, a Sten gun slung over his shoulder. The Cockney cut a curious figure. He walked with a slight forward stoop, his head sunk into his shoulders, the right one of which was always held lower than the left. Some discerned an "ardent look" in his eyes. But these idiosyncracies only encouraged belief in the sterling credentials of Captain Robert Mason. Every Frenchman knew that eccentricity was one of the more salient features of the British national character and a byword of the English officer class.

Dureng had introduced Cole to Major Pierre Laze, forty-seven, the local military governor, citing the great advantages of "exchanging mutually valuable information" with him. Laze was momentarily taken aback by Cole's American uniform, remarking that the collar insignia of the British captain's uniform was "a trifle strange." It was

that of an ordinance, not an intelligence officer. But Cole soon overcame Laze's reservations by paying his respects frequently, "always
coming in person and walking straight into his office." The same
principles of diplomacy applied in the French Army as in its British
counterpart, Cole knew.

Soon Dureng was deferring to the seasoned Captain Mason in even
the smallest of matters. When Cole had first arrived, Camille Allart
was working in civilian dress. But Dureng ordered his aide to wear
a uniform after Cole had remarked that it was bad form to have an
assistant slouching around in mufti. Allart himself could see that
Cole was getting the upper hand in relations with the Frenchmen
running Saulgau. He had, as the expression went, "put them in his
pocket." It wasn't so much that Mason dominated Dureng and the
others; to Allart it seemed more like Mason had seduced them, "by
the way he spoke, by his gestures, by his smile, by everything."

Working with Dureng on a daily basis, Cole quickly focused his
attentions on Georg Hanft. Cole first heard of the man in late 1944,
after he and Kieffer had retreated from Paris and were assigned to
the rear action commando based near Nancy, France. The smell of
defeat was in the air, and the Sicherheitsdienst was preparing for the
ultimate contingency. "In the event of dispersal," Kieffer and others
were to regroup in Saulgau under Hanft, whose photo was passed
around. When the end came, most SS men were too intent on saving
their own skins to think of rallying to the defeated cause in some
remote corner of Swabia. But Cole had not forgotten about Saulgau—
or Hanft.

Cole knew he could not continue his masquerade indefinitely;
sooner or later someone would catch on. By then he intended to have
moved along to the next stop in his postwar itinerary. But this would
require money. Cole had always needed a lot of money, but now he
needed more than ever. He deduced, or perhaps he had heard scut-
tlebutt among the SS officers in his unit, that a man in Hanft's position
would have been given funds, maybe even gold bullion, to finance

Nazi resistance. The Third Reich were finished; now those funds would go a long way to financing Cole's personal program of postwar recovery.

The problem was how to extract the Gestapo treasure from Hanft without Dureng's knowledge, or at the very least, with his complicity. Long a student of human nature, Cole began to manipulate the young officer.

◆ ◆ ◆

EVEN FOR A FRENCHMAN, Jacques Dureng de Maisonneuve had strong feelings when it came to Germans. Members of his family had been executed in savage German reprisals while the young legal clerk was off with the Maquis of the Corrèze region, in southwest France. When that region was liberated, Dureng and his Maquis comrades joined the French First Army. Eventually they became part of the Ninth Zouaves, a distinguished territorial outfit raised in Algiers. Dureng fought his way across the Rhine and into southern Germany, where, at the war's conclusion, he was assigned to the security detail in Saulgau.

Dureng's mission was to identify, detain, and question the former Nazi masters of Saulgau. From local informants he had learned of Hanft's role in the local Nazi party and arrested him. Georg Hanft, owner of a local gas station and auto parts store, was a local Nazi party boss straight out of central casting. Sixty years old, he was heavy-set and broad-shouldered, with thick eyebrows and a ruddy complexion. His dark-blond hair, now graying, was cut short and slicked straight back. A resident of Saulgau since 1926, Hanft had been named local Nazi party chief—*Kreisleiter* was the title—in 1941. Under interrogation by Dureng he admitted having been attached to the Stuttgart Gestapo service, working for the Sicherheitsdienst during the war in Luxembourg, Belgium, and northern France.

Cole and Dureng, interrogating Hanft together, extracted the names of a dozen others in the area who allegedly had worked for the Gestapo. Then they took Hanft to his house on the Hauptstrasse.

Maria Hanft, wife of the official, was placed under the guard of the gun-toting LePage. Cole and Dureng took Hanft into his study and remained there with him for half an hour. Afterwards Cole undertook a top-to-bottom search of the house, confiscating two portfolios of the Nazi's papers and documents, his wife's jewelry, two men's suits, two leather valises, and other sundry items.

Cole was not satisfied with the results of these preliminary interrogations. He told Dureng he wanted to take Hanft into his own custody, citing special Allied intelligence requirements, and proposed to give a receipt for the prisoner when he picked Hanft up. This arrangement seemed reasonable to Dureng, who knew that "other Allied officers operated in the same manner."

Cole's group meanwhile had found temporary quarters at a farm in the nearby village of Kleintissen. One day soon after their arrival in the region they drove up and told farmer Franz Widenmann that they wanted to question one of his farm workers, a Czech. But the next day they came back and informed him that three men and two women were taking over two rooms in his house.

That Sunday, which was the Pentecost, LePage and Jousset drove off and returned around 4:00 P.M. with Hanft, who was in handcuffs. Widenmann immediately recognized the prisoner, having once seen him overseeing operations at a local agricultural cooperative. Jousset hauled Hanft into the farmhouse, ordered Widenmann to bring him two stools, then took his prisoner into the cellar. Widenmann could not see what was happening, but was alarmed by Jousset's bellowed instructions. "Somebody bring me a carbine and some bludgeons," Jousset shouted in German from below. Then he ordered one of Widenmann's Polish laborers, "If this man moves, kill him!"

Widenmann, seventy-two, was terrorized by this. When one of his workers came to say Hanft wanted to talk to him, the farmer would venture only as far as the cellar door. Hanft was seated on one of the stools, using the other as a desk to write on a sheet of paper. He asked for the name of a certain baker in Saulgau; Widenmann gave it, then backed nervously away.

Fifteen minutes later Hanft was brought up to the dining room and given food, drink and a cigarette. Soon after, LePage and Cole returned with Hanft's wife and daughter, Waltraud. The man was allowed to spend three-quarters of an hour with his family. Hanft was held at the farmhouse for two or three days, sleeping on a sofa in the dining room after promising not to try to escape. He was not harmed, but to Widenmann, the Nazi appeared badly frightened of his captors. Once Hanft confided to the old farmer that "if what the captain had told him was true, he had nothing to fear." But if what Captain Mason had told him were untrue, "he would be in a most serious position."

◆ ◆ ◆

THE WIDENMANN FARM was only a temporary accommodation while LePage located better quarters. Near the end of that week before Pentecost, the Frenchman had driven the black Mercedes into the courtyard of a farm near Saulgau called Gut Krumbach. Its owner, nurseryman Anton Kneussle, forty-four, immediately noticed the driver's neglected personal appearance. This negative first impression was quickly reinforced. LePage abruptly told Kneussle he had come for schnaps, wine, and fuel. When Kneussle said he had none, the young Frenchman drew his pistol and ordered the farmer to take him to the cellar of the farmhouse, threatening to kill him if he were not quick about it.

At this point, a female Polish farm worker intervened and managed to calm LePage, who holstered his weapon and became more tractable. Having inspected Kneussle's comfortable villa, LePage asked if his captain could move in. With the memory of LePage's threats still fresh, Kneussle "could not do otherwise than to accept this proposal." After demanding three bedrooms, a bathroom, and a dining room, LePage leaped into the Mercedes and contentedly roared off.

Cole himself appeared the next day, on foot. He was helmeted, with a red silk scarf around his neck and captain's bars on the epaulettes of his uniform. Two pairs of handcuffs were attached to his belt. In his broken German, Cole demanded schnaps, wine, and fuel, then accused Kneussle of belonging to the Gestapo. Kneussle denied this vehemently and Cole did not press the accusation. Instead he moved to the business at hand and announced his intention of moving into the villa. He inspected the three rooms and told Kneussle to reserve them.

On the following Tuesday, the Mercedes cabriolet deposited LePage, Jousset, Votier, and Gaubert at Gut Krumbach. Kneussle cursed his luck as he examined the collection of strays and misfits that had arrived on his doorstep. He already knew LePage's temper. But Jousset worried him more, expressing himself with "extremely brutal gestures," seeming "moved by a sort of fear."

This violence was tempered, however, by the presence of the two women. Suzy Votier in particular struck Kneussle as calm and pleasant, though he noted she had a dull complexion and bad teeth. She went about dressed in an American Army uniform without insignia. After Cole showed up an hour later, the group moved in. Kneussle concluded that Suzy was Cole's mistress, as she shared the captain's quarters. Magny moved in with Jousset, while LePage was alone in the third room. But he quickly befriended one of the Polish women on the farm, marrying her some weeks later.

Of sterner stuff than Widenmann, Kneussle was not about to yield up his home without protest. He sent Dureng a note of protest in the morning. But a motorcycle courier came straight back from Saulgau with the message that Mason was perfectly within his rights. Kneussle gritted his teeth and resigned himself to putting up with Mason and his entourage. It was plain already that they were not going to be the most exemplary of tenants. But Anton Kneussle did not know the half of it.

♦ ♦ ♦

THE TALL, THIN British captain in the American Army uniform, Kneussle gathered over the next few days, had been assigned to round up the most notorious Nazis of the district around Saulgau and bring them to justice. Serious cases would be referred to an Allied court in Innsbruck, Cole informed Kneussle, while minor offenders would be handled locally. Mason alone would decide whether to hold or release the suspects brought before him. The Cockney's staff having installed itself in the Gut Krumbach villa, "the march of prisoners began shortly thereafter."

Over the next three weeks, Cole's gang brought between forty and fifty alleged Nazis to the villa for interrogation. At times, Kneussle stated later, discussions between Mason's cohorts and their captives were "of a most violent nature." One of the first subjects of Cole's "nefarious interrogations and beatings" was a Saulgau dentist named Doctor Eugen Krug.

Krug's name figured on the list of alleged Nazis that Hanft had drawn up while being held at the Widenmann farm. Cole and Allart appeared at Krug's home on the Wednesday after their move to Gut Krumbach. Cole rifled Krug's briefcase and confiscated his identity papers. Then he and Allart searched the house, taking wine and schnaps as well as soap and cigarettes. After Krug had been dropped off at the jailhouse, they came back for more booty, seizing five packages of tobacco, about fifty bottles of wine, several bottles of schnaps, and some champagne. Cole also grabbed whatever else caught his fancy: a fountain pen, a manicure set, hunting boots, cutlery, a wristwatch.

The day after Krug's arrest, his captors brought him face-to-face with Hanft in the town hall conference room. Also present were seven other residents denounced by the former *Kreisleiter*. The kangaroo court was convened. Cole, the judge, announced that Hanft had accused the other Germans of being Sicherheitsdienst agents. When Hanft denied this loudly, one of Cole's lackeys silenced him with several resounding slaps across the face.

Each of the Germans was interrogated in turn and confronted with evidence—such as it was. In Krug's case the main exhibits were two knapsacks packed with food and spare clothing found in his attic and deemed suspicious. The dentist received a fist in the left eye as an inducement to frank testimony; nevertheless, he continued to deny ever having belonged to the SS. After more of this, Cole left the courtroom to confer with his legal aides. He returned to say that five of the Germans would be released. But he had other plans for Krug and Hanft, and returned them to the Saulgau jail.

◆ ◆ ◆

ON FRIDAY EVENING, LePage collected Krug from the courthouse lockup and brought him out to Gut Krumbach. As the evening's festivities began, wine and cigarettes were passed around. These were offered to Krug, who at first declined, but finally accepted "upon renewed urging." Cole, Dureng, LePage, Jousset, and the two women, conversing among themselves, ignored Krug initially. But eventually they turned to the affair at hand.

Questioned again about his supposed adherence to the Sicherheitsdienst, Krug maintained his innocence as "the tone of the conversation became more serious." Cole and the others had just begun to apply persuasion when they were interrupted by the arrival of two American officers.

Captain Frank Lillyman and Lieutenant William King Richardson were U.S. Army paratroopers assigned to an airfield outside Mengen, a town some miles to the northwest. They had dealt with Dureng through official channels, but had never met him in person until their arrival this evening at Gut Krumbach. The two officers had stopped in Saulgau on their way back from a trip with a wireless operator named Yenn. Allart had directed them to the villa. Dureng started to make introductions. But Cole, instantly recognizing the threat to his position which the two officers represented, seized the initiative.

"How do you do," said Cole. "I am Captain Mason, British Intelligence Service, excuse the uniform."

Despite his American lieutenant's uniform, Cole said, he had just been promoted to captain. The Cockney "extended the usual officer courtesies," apologetically explaining that he was in the midst of questioning a very stubborn suspect. Lillyman could already see the marks of abuse on Krug's swollen face. When Cole invited him to take part in the questioning, the American captain accepted.

The evening that had begun so congenially with wine and cigarettes now took on a sadistic tone. As Cole started beating the dentist, the two women left the room. From the kitchen Anton and Else Kneussle listened to the sounds of punishment from the living room.

"Doctor Krug," someone demanded, "do you know how to box?"

"I am a German officer," he replied, "but I have not learned to box."

The table was pushed aside and Lillyman began sparring with the helpless dentist. A few minutes later Krug went across the front hall to the kitchen to wipe the blood from his face. He returned to the dining room, and the interrogation session continued. Krug was passed from one Allied soldier to another.

"While Richardson would 'caress' Krug's ribs and head with his pistol's butt," Dureng stated afterwards, "Lillyman would box him and Yenn, after making him take his shoes off, would beat the sole of his foot with the flat part of a bayonet."

At this last punishment, Krug "threw up his hands and exclaimed 'Mein Gott,' and then rattled off a lot of German."

With occasional breaks, during which Krug was given more wine and cigarettes, this abuse continued until about 1:00 A.M. Then the two women returned. One of them brought eau de cologne to bathe his head wounds. The dentist was given some bread, butter, salami, and wine, then taken upstairs where he collapsed onto a bed.

In the morning, someone knocked on the door of Krug's room, telling him that washing and shaving materials had been laid out in the bathroom. After breakfast he was taken back to the Saulgau jail. Later in the day, Cole collected him and they went to the dentist's home. Demanding more wine from his wife, the Cockney went through his personal papers but found nothing incriminating.

Krug remained under house arrest for another two days, after which Cole came back for another search. At the end of the month, Cole returned Krug's identity papers and told him his case had been closed. With this, Krug's ordeal ended. But Cole had other plans for Georg Hanft, whose real torment had not yet begun.

26

"I Decided to Bump Him Off"

SOMETHING HAD HAPPENED to Cole in the three-and-a-half years he spent under German tutelage: he developed a taste for sadistic violence. No doubt this had been encouraged by the Sicherheitsdienst officers who, once Cole was too well known to be sent down the rabbit hole, put him to work interrogating prisoners. By then he was in too deep to refuse to acquiesce in the torture of his countrymen. He may not even have cared. If the SS brutalized Allied prisoners while Cole was present, that was not his fault. If the captured agents were not smart enough to do as he had done and tell the SD everything it wanted to know, that was not his lookout either.

Yet the revulsion surely festered deep inside. Cole was too intelligent not to see the irony—that he who for so long had coveted the pips and prerogatives of a British officer was now a Gestapo flunkey. But now he could put the humiliation behind him. Dealing improvised justice as Captain Mason, he could exact revenge and get, as he would have put it, "some of his own back." Now the SS would be brought low, beginning with the *Kreisleiter* Hanft.

There was another change: Cole's personal presence had been

magnified, not diminished, by his experiences over the previous several years. Perhaps this was because the illusions that had enabled him to rise momentarily to heroism in La Madeleine were now entirely stripped away. Now only the swindler, the cheat, the imposter, the traitor, the manipulator, and the sadist were left. Everyone who had passed through the unspeakably brutal war just ended had been marked by the experience. But Cole had been to the very dark heart of the evil and returned. His aura had fed upon the violence and grown; Cole thereby drew others into his decaying orbit.

Morally disarmed by the agreeable Captain Mason, Dureng and Lillyman began their descent into the dark spiral. Only Cole knew that murder waited at the bottom.

♦ ♦ ♦

A SOLDIER'S SOLDIER, Frank L. Lillyman had earned a paragraph in *The New York Times* and a line in the history books by jumping out of a C-47 transport over France shortly after midnight on June 6, 1944. Commander of a U.S. Pathfinder Group, he was the first paratrooper out of the lead plane in the airborne prelude to the Normandy invasion. That made him officially the first man to hit French soil on D-Day. A few hours later, he won his first Purple Heart and was evacuated to England. But he could take satisfaction in knowing that the ten years he had spent in the U.S. Army had not been in vain.

Son of an upstate New York veterinarian, Lillyman joined the Army in 1934 straight out of high school, not having the money to go on to college. Six years later he was still a sergeant, but the climate of war brought him a second lieutenant's commission in 1940. After Pearl Harbor advancement came quickly in the new airborne infantry. He was a first lieutenant by the time he sailed for England in September 1943 with the 101st Airborne Division.

Recovering from his Normandy wounds in a British hospital, Lillyman went AWOL to rejoin his unit in France. General Maxwell B. Taylor called him on the carpet, waved the papers for a captain's promotion under Lillyman's nose, and then ripped them up. But his bars came along anyway as Lillyman distinguished himself in the Netherlands and the Battle of the Bulge, where his commander at Bastogne, General Anthony C. McAuliffe made history by answering "Nuts!" to a German demand for surrender of his encircled U.S. forces. When the war ended, Lillyman had collected twelve decorations, including the Distinguished Service Cross, the Bronze Star with Oak Cluster, and two more clusters for his Purple Heart.

While most of his buddies were shipped home, Lillyman stayed on in Europe. Occupation duty was regarded as a thankless chore by most American soldiers. But for Lillyman it represented a chance to hold onto the brevet rank of captain that he stood to lose if he were reassigned to a stateside post.

He was also attracted by the promising new job offered by the Office of Strategic Services, or OSS, the American spy agency that within a few years would evolve into the CIA. As the Allied victory approached, the OSS had assembled an airborne task force for the swift evacuation of U.S. and British prisoners of war and displaced persons. Lillyman was given command of a three-man evacuation team that was flown into Germany in early May with a jeep and a radio transmitter. He, Richardson, and Yenn set up their base at an airfield one mile outside Mengen.

Two weeks later Lillyman had his first taste of sadism under the instruction of Cole.

◆ ◆ ◆

LILLYMAN WAS PARTICULARLY susceptible to Cole's bogus British officer's airs. He had stood in admiration of the coolly professional British Pathfinders with whom he had trained, emulating them by incorporating the mild expletive "bloody" into his speech and using the scale of stones in estimating a man's weight. So he felt an immediate affinity with the congenial Captain Mason.

Lillyman nonetheless had some initial misgivings about the unconventional officer. He gave the matter "quite a bit of thought, especially in view of the fact that the alleged Captain Mason contin- ually wore American uniforms." This was something Lillyman had "never seen with the British Army," in which things ordinarily were done by the book.

Accompanying Cole on his rounds, Lillyman noticed that the man "spent considerable time in seizing anything that struck his fancy— cheese, wines, perfume, clothes, jewelry, and automobiles." He handed these last out to various Allied officers in the region in the interest of better relations. Learning that Dureng did not have a vehicle of his own, Cole graciously presented him with a sleek, black Union, one of the more luxurious prewar German automobiles.

There was Mason's brutality too, conduct which hardly seemed becoming of a British officer. One time Lillyman accompanied Cole to the Hanft house, where the Cockney confiscated a radio, some jewelry, and a large wad of German currency. "When Frau Hanft attempted to hold onto the money," Lillyman stated afterwards, "Mason backhanded her."

On another occasion, Lillyman saw Cole thrash a prisoner in the Saulgau jail despite the presence of numerous witnesses. "The man was pounded about the body by Mason with his fists until Mason got tired." In connection with Mason and his band, the American officer heard the stories going around that men had been beaten to death in a small jail in Saulgau or Altshausen.

Hardened by his wartime experiences, Lillyman avowed having "absolutely no consideration" for the defeated enemy. Yet these fla- grant violations of U.S. military code should have warned the career officer to steer away from Mason. But he had already overstepped his OSS brief by taking part in Cole's sessions. He was empowered to interrogate local SS and Nazi party officials—but only if this were necessary to locate Allied POWs. Lillyman had already far exceeded these bounds, plunging into what he described in letters home as the work of "chasing war criminals."

The American captain briefly considered having Yenn, his radio man, transmit a message to higher headquarters in London, asking for confirmation of Mason's status. But in doing so, Lillyman would "risk the military embarrassment of being told not to interfere." So the radio message was never sent.

Lillyman resolved the dilemma—or so it seemed—another way. At Gut Krumbach one morning, he inspected Mason's credentials surreptitiously while the officer was in his bath. With some relief, Lillyman noted the CIC document and what looked like a British Army officer's I.D. There was also a card signed by an officer of Sixth Army Group's intelligence branch, in Heidelberg. All this seemed incontrovertible proof that Mason was on the level.

◆ ◆ ◆

HIS OWN DOUBTS laid to rest, Lillyman went a step further and vouched for Captain Mason to others. The question came up in a conversation with Major Edward O. Smith of the European Civil Affairs Division, who served as American liaison with the French in Saulgau. Smith was "dubious about Captain Mason due to his British accent and mannerisms and due to the fact that he was dressed as an American officer." Lillyman assured Smith he had not only checked the man's papers, but had been told by London headquarters that Mason "had full authority, and his work was not to be interfered with." Smith in turn told Jacques Dureng that "all confidence could be placed in Mason," removing whatever traces of suspicion that may have lingered in the French lieutenant's mind.

Thus no one ever confronted Cole or queried a higher authority. Everyone took much the same view as Richardson, who believed Mason was "more or less in the pipeline back to his own forces." The American lieutenant, in his own words, "never had any reason to doubt his identity."

Lillyman by now was spending a lot of his free time with Cole. As far as Dureng could see, the American captain was virtually inseparable from Captain Mason. Technically, Lillyman outranked Cole, whose "promotion" to captain had only recently come through. But to Dureng, "it seemed as if Mason took the initiative."

This association was having a pernicious effect on Lillyman, who aped Cole's rendition of a British officer, strutting around with a riding crop in his hand and whacking his boots with it as he spoke. To other American soldiers based at the Mengen airstrip, he boasted of his prowess in interrogating case-hardened SS officers. Brandishing the swagger stick, Lillyman bragged to one NCO at Mengen of having "beat an SS man down and picked him up and beat him down again."

Smith and a French interpreter were in the Saulgau town hall one evening at ten o'clock when Cole and Lillyman came through on their way up to the second floor, where some Germans were being held. "They had these prisoners whipped," Smith's translator later related, "and we heard their screams from downstairs."

Lillyman, the professional warrior, had become intoxicated by the violence that Cole organized and sanctioned. He was, in the estimation of one American investigator who reconstructed these events, "still looking for the thrills" he had found in the heat of battle. Lillyman was "one of those fellows who just couldn't quit when the white flag was waved."

Cole, recognizing the violence pent up in the American, had not hesitated to exploit it. A report by the U.S. Army Criminal Investigation Division later would conclude: "Whenever Mason's name was mentioned in connection with atrocities, arrests, brutal treatment, and pillage, Lillyman's name was mentioned also."

◆ ◆ ◆

COLE DETAINED dozens of suspected Nazis and brought them to the Gut Krumbach villa for questioning. But Hanft remained the prime focus of interest. At the end of May, Cole brought the former *Kreisleiter* to the farm for more questioning.

Anton and Else Kneussle watched as Hanft, whom they had known for twenty years, was brought into the dining room. Cole first offered the German a cigar and a drink, and conversation began to flow somewhat normally. But then Hanft, failing to answer a question to Cole's satisfaction, was worked over with revolver butts.

For the rest of that afternoon, the Kneussles listened to Hanft "cry out and even howl at times" under Cole's tender mercies. Occasionally he stumbled into the hallway to wash the blood from his face at the washstand, and the couple, seated in the kitchen, could measure the effect of the beating. Later on, Frau Kneussle gave Hanft a meal and talked to him as he ate. The official "found himself in a very dangerous position and . . . was expecting death."

The questioning was still going on when the Kneussles went to bed at 11:00 P.M. In the early morning hours, their son Wolfgang, thirteen, came to tell them he had heard two gunshots. Anton Kneussle lay awake for the rest of the night as automobiles came and went outside. But he did not venture out of the bedroom to investigate.

In the morning Else Kneussle found the grim evidence of the night-long binge: bullet holes in the floor and ceiling of the dining room, spatterings of blood on the walls around the divan on which Hanft had been seated, bloodstains on the bathtub upstairs. Hanft had been in such a pitiful condition that Suzy was moved to patch up his cuts and abrasions.

When LePage roused himself, Frau Kneussle asked him about the shots. He muttered truculently that they had been taking care of "a big Nazi pig." Seeing bloodstains on his white sweater, Frau Kneussle let the matter drop. She took it up with Cole when he appeared an hour later. He laughed off the shots and assured her that Hanft, unharmed, had been taken to Innsbruck for trial.

But in fact he was still in Saulgau. Later that day, Cole's assistants brought the Nazi to his house on the Hauptstrasse to pick up clean clothing. Maria Hanft was distressed to see that her husband could hardly speak, so much was his face puffed out with the bruises that ran down the entire right side of his body. When he had changed his blood-soaked clothing, Cole's men took Hanft away again.

Cole still had not learned what he wanted to know. The imposter conducted private interrogation sessions, closeting himself during long hours with the German. He explained to Dureng that he "thought to obtain from Hanft some indications concerning Gestapo members of other regions." But Cole was not after further denunciations. The traitor now was gripped, an American investigator later concluded, by the "constant fear that Hanft would learn his true identity and so uncover his masquerade." Cole also yearned to lay his hands on the Gestapo treasure trove Hanft surely possessed.

Was Hanft informed of Cole's past? Was the former *Kreisleiter* sitting on a fortune in gold, gems, or currency? Cole could not obtain satisfaction, beat as he might the stolid Hanft. The man was ignorant on both counts or simply one tough and recalcitrant Nazi. The Cockney decided it was time to get rid of Hanft and confided his intentions to Dureng in the Saulgau officers' mess one evening in the first week of June.

"I have nothing more to learn from him," Cole told the French lieutenant. "Can you indicate a spot to me where he could be done away with?"

Dureng nodded his agreement; and murder was afoot.

◆　◆　◆

ON THE EVENING of June 8, Cole and Allart collected Hanft at the Saulgau prison. Cole told the French guards their prisoner was to be turned over to an American court and signed a release. At the local military security office, they were joined by Dureng and Lillyman. Then they took Hanft to the Hauptstrasse and allowed him to see his wife. Allart told Frau Hanft that Georg was being turned over to a military court; she might kiss him goodbye. But she knew what was happening and wept, despite Cole's assurances that her husband would be back in just a few days.

From Saulgau they drove south for eight miles to the headquarters of the Ninth Zouaves Regiment in Altshausen Castle. This splendid eighteenth-century chateau, seat of the royal family at Wurttemberg, had once served as the headquarters of the Order of Teutonic Knights. Its massive baroque gatehouse, topped by ornate gables and a clock tower, sat on a promontory overlooking the road south to Ravensburg.

When the four men reached the castle they locked Hanft up in a cellblock off the central gatehouse and went to eat dinner in the officers' mess in the opposite wing.

Cole, Lillyman, and Dureng installed themselves at one table, while Allart sat at another some distance away. The long French meal lasted through the evening and into the night. As the company called for bottle after bottle of wine it degenerated into a drinking bout. Cole and Dureng discussed the ways and means of doing away with Hanft. Lillyman, his head fuddled, speaking French poorly, followed the conversation with some difficulty and did not realize Cole's intentions.

These became clear when the men staggered across to Hanft's cell. The prisoner was ordered to strip. Cole ordered that every identifying mark be removed from the German's clothes. Lillyman understood from this that murder was on the agenda. This was more explicitly confirmed by Cole who, pointing out the SS tattoo under the man's left arm, told the American that he was "proposing to bump him off."

Lillyman grew uneasy but made no objections to the proposed killing. The three inebriated men with him were heavily armed— Cole with the Walther pistol and his Sten, Allart with a Thompson machine gun, Dureng with a Colt revolver. The American, armed only with his Colt .32 sidearm, remained silent for fear that he "might meet with bodily harm."

Then they were back on the darkened Highway 32, heading south towards Ravensburg. Dureng was at the wheel, Lillyman next to him, while Cole and Allart sat in the back on either side of Hanft. Cole questioned the prisoner about his supposed war booty as the automobile sped along through the warm summer night. Hanft persisted in denying that he had any such wealth.

Four miles down the road, Dureng slowed, then swung off the paved two-lane highway onto a forest road. Two hundred yards down the graveled track he pulled off to the right and stopped. The headlights, left burning, stabbed into the beech forest and threw reflections on the Häcklerweiher, a small lake about twenty yards away. Lillyman stood by the car as Hanft was put up against a large tree; Cole, Allart, and Dureng faced the Nazi in a semicircle from left to right.

The questioning picked up again. Where had Hanft hidden his treasure? Cole beat the German about the head with the barrel of his handgun. Hanft again protested that he had no money, and no more information on the Sicherheitsdienst to provide.

"I can still see the poor little bastard standing there," Lillyman stated later. "He was asked something in German and just threw his arms out in a shrug as if to say, 'What can I say?'"

Cole struck him again with the pistol, while Lillyman, who had approached, kicked him in the groin.

"Mason asked him if he would finally tell the truth," related Dureng. "Hanft replied that he had nothing more to say."

Backing off, Cole raised his Sten gun and squeezed off a burst that cut through the Nazi official's midsection, doubling him over with the shock. Then Dureng and Allart, by their own later admissions, opened fire and riddled the man's body with bullets.

Cole walked over to where Hanft lay face up. Unholstering his P38, he placed it to the man's temple and fired off a coup de grace. Then he recovered his handcuffs from Hanft's wrists.

It was sometime around midnight. The forest was silent and the air was moist.

Hanft was left where he had fallen. The three men got back into the car, and drove out to the main road, turning right on Highway 32 in the direction of Saulgau.

27

"You're Cole, Aren't You?"

HIDDEN IN PLAIN VIEW in the depths of Swabia, Sergeant Harold Cole was nonetheless very present in the minds of British security and intelligence officials. He was, one of these relates, "at the top of the list of traitors that were wanted, because of the evidence that was coming in that he'd behaved so badly." Stories of the Cockney's wickedness had trickled into England even before D-Day. As the end of the war approached, his description and record were distributed to the appropriate authorities, indicating that he was "an arch-traitor and highly dangerous to the Allied cause."

Outside of Allied counterintelligence, however, Cole was virtually unknown. Far more notorious was William Joyce, who for years had railed at the British public over the airwaves under the title "Lord Haw Haw." A "thug of the first order," if the British press was to be believed, this prewar fascist rabblerouser was assigned a priority that was out of proportion with his actual misdeeds. Whatever his effect on British wartime morale, he was never accused of having cost a single English life.

The largest group of traitors were British POWs who, unable to withstand the rigors of captivity or resist the blandishments of their captors, collaborated with the Nazis in one manner or another. Some betrayed the escape plans of their fellow prisoners or revealed the locations of contraband radios. The most flagrant offenders had left the camps entirely to follow John Amery, son of one of Winston Churchill's cabinet ministers, into the ranks of the British Free Corps— known more sensationally on Fleet Street as the Legion of the Damned.

But Cole was in a class by himself. He had worked actively for the Germans in the sensitive area of counterintelligence, compounding this offense by personally interrogating Allied prisoners. A lot of people wanted to find Sergeant Cole.

Scotland Yard, which held his prewar criminal file, and the British Security Service, better known as MI5, were on his trail. The principal agent on the case was Major Peter Hope, nominally attached to the Royal Artillery, 108th Special Counter Intelligence, but in fact an agent of MI5. Educated at Cambridge, Hope had worked on home security during the war, vetting refugees from the Continent. He was assisted in his search by Inspector Reginald Spooner of Scotland Yard. Spooner had begun his police career in London's East End in 1928, when Cole was a young toff of twenty-two. He may have had first-hand knowledge of the early exploits of "Sonny Boy." In cases like the infamous Riddle of the Sands murder, Spooner had gained a reputation as a meticulous investigator and a master of detail. When the war came he was seconded to MI5.

It was an assignment potentially more difficult than locating a needle in a haystack. Finding Cole meant sifting through the debris of a Continent turned upside-down and filled with twenty million displaced persons. There seemed little chance, given Cole's wiles and the opportunities for concealment in postwar Europe, that he would be captured quickly. But the turncoat's dossier was "pushed out into the field for people to try and get a hold of him."

There was no such thing as a computer; the main investigative tools were massive card files filled with tabbed entries bearing photographs, reports of criminal or treasonous activity, and brief descriptions. Thus Cole was rendered: "Height 5 ft 11-1/4 inches. Very thin. Narrow, bent shoulders. Reddish-fair hair, parted at side. Small moustache. Blue-grey eyes, very short-sighted. Rarely wears glasses. Small mouth, all false teeth. Prominent Adam's apple. Left lobe of ear undeveloped, scar at base of left thumb, scar under chin."

His many aliases were listed and cross-indexed: Paul Anderson, J. Paul Christin, Captain Colson, P.R.N. Corser, Paul Delobel, Joseph Deram, Richard Godfrey, Paul Rook. The names of Anderson, Christin, Corser and Rook were probably used by Cole in the 1930s and extracted from his Scotland Yard file.

Related and encouraging news came on May 28, when Lord Haw Haw was picked up in Kupfermühle, a German village far to the north near the Danish border. After trying unsuccessfully to reach neutral Sweden, Joyce and his wife had settled in, surrounded by British occupation troops. While strolling through the nearby woods one day, Joyce came across two British army officers who were foraging for firewood.

"Here are a few more pieces," Joyce called out to them, first in French, then in English. It was the age of radio. The doomsaying Lord Haw Haw's speech characteristics had been engraved indelibly on the memories of millions of British listeners. One of the officers, a Captain Alexander Lickorish, consulted rapidly with his fellow and then both came in pursuit.

"You wouldn't happen to be William Joyce, would you?" said Lickorish's interpreter, named Perry. Joyce reached into a pocket for his false papers, made out in the name of Wilhelm Hansen. In the belief that the suspect was reaching for a weapon, Perry fired and wounded Joyce in both legs. Lord Haw Haw was arrested, and all Britain exulted.

But Joyce's capture had taken place in the British zone of occupation. It involved a suspect whose voice was eminently identifiable and who, by the time he was captured, had lost most of his will to continue flight. In the case of Cole, adept at disguise and quick on his feet, it was more likely that the investigators, for all their experience and determination, would have to wait until the mechanisms of military occupation and the vicissitudes of life on the run brought Cole to the fore.

Then the Cockney, overconfident, made a mistake.

♦ ♦ ♦

'NO AGENCY desired more to see Cole brought to justice than MI9, and few within the escape-evasion service hoped more ardently for the traitor's downfall than Donald Darling. At the end of the war, he had been transferred from Gibraltar to Paris, where he headed the MI9 Awards Bureau. This office, located in a hotel near the Palais Royal, compensated and rewarded those who had incurred expense or, more important, risked their lives to help Allied escapers.

One frequent visitor to the MI9 bureau was a Swiss woman named Lotte, who had been one of Cole's mistresses during the war. She did not know of his treason and believed he had been seized by the Gestapo and deported. She was not disabused of this notion by the MI9 staff, who told her that they, too, were hungry for word of Cole.

Knowing of Cole's multiple entanglements, Hope and Spooner in liaison with the French security services had established a mail and telephone watch on those women known to have been the traitor's mistresses. Through this net slipped the postcard that Cole had sent to the lovely Lotte.

"Cherie," Cole had written. "You see I am safe and well and hope to see you again. Much love, Sonny Boy."

Eager to share this news, the woman showed the card to Sylvia Cooper Smith, an MI9 staffer who was nursing Guerisse back to health after his liberation from Dachau, and was to marry him in 1947. Guerisse, strangely, had heard of the traitor's progress while a prisoner in the Mauthausen concentration camp. One day in April 1944 the Belgian was called to the dreaded SS interrogation section. Guerisse, known to the Germans as Patrick O'Leary, was promised comfort in a special Irish POW camp if he would cooperate with the Germans. This offer was not unusual. But he was astonished next to hear that "Paul Cole has a very happy life in Berlin." The traitor, he was told, was installed in the luxurious Hotel Adlon in the Nazi capital. Guerisse made mental note of the conversation as he rejected the SS offer and returned to his barracks.

Cooper Smith now listened attentively as the traitor's mistress shared her happiness at this unexpected message. "Sonny Boy," said Lotte, enraptured. "I always used to call him that."

Telling the woman that Major Darling would be most interested to see the card, Cooper Smith brought it into his office. Darling jotted down the military address given on the missive and got on the phone to Hope. Cole had given his mistress the mail coordinates of the Third Battalion of the Ninth Regiment of Zouaves, at Saulgau. Hope immediately contacted his opposite number in the DST and the two officials hurried to southern Germany in search of Cole.

◆ ◆ ◆

UNAWARE of having set this train of events in motion, Cole was reaching the apogee of his career in Saulgau. Some of the French and American officers in the area looked askance at his looting and vicious interrogations. But no one challenged the freewheeling Captain Mason. Even the disappearance of Hanft did not provoke many questions, nor did Cole attempt to cover his tracks.

The imposter often shared a mess table with François Finas, a thirty-six-year-old captain in the Ninth Zouaves. Over a meal, Finas "learned from Mason's own lips that he had carried out an expedition during the course of which he had executed a German." But Mason spoke of it in a joking manner and Finas let the matter drop. "In view of the particular times and the important job which Mason seemed to hold," Finas said later, "I did not, through discretion, attempt to find out more about the affair."

Trusted, admired, and liked, Cole had thoroughly persuaded the French that he was an authentic agent of the Anglo-American intelligence services. The Cockney enjoyed the best of relations with the local military government. He had appointed himself the mediator of disputes arising between the French occupation troops and the local peasantry, conflicts which, one Zouave officer noted, "were always settled through his good offices."

Cole routinely socialized with the highest military authorities of the region. Many of the ranking Allied brass accepted invitations to his villa at Gut Krumbach. There was always plenty to eat and drink at Mason's house. No one thought to ask how his groaning board was supplied. Such was the esteem in which these officers held Captain Mason that on May 31, Cole and Lillyman approached the British Major General Leslie Nicholls, then in the area, to ask that he obtain the transfer of Dureng to the U.S. VI Corps as a liaison officer.

Nicholls later informed Cole this was not possible. But he nonetheless presided at a dinner for about twenty hosted by Cole on June 10 at Gut Krumbach. In attendance besides the British major general was Military Governor Pierre Laze, U.S. liaison officer Major Edward O. Smith, two French majors, three American majors, Lillyman and another U.S. Army captain, three French captains, a handful of French lieutenants, including Dureng, and Lillyman's second-in-command, Lieutenant Richardson.

The party was a success. But Cole that evening had an intimation that his position was less than secure. During the evening Cole fell into conversation in the farmyard with Anton Kneussle. "Mason confided in me," Kneussle later reported, "that he felt ill at ease, and that he had noticed Major Laze looking at him in an odd way, which seemed to indicate that something was going to happen."

Cole was not the only one with misgivings. Smith, of the U.S. liaison office, had waited at his hotel earlier that evening to be picked up by Lillyman after the American captain had met General Nicholls at the Mengen airstrip. But Smith grew impatient when Lillyman was delayed. After asking directions he drove out to Gut Krumbach alone. It seemed strange to Smith that Mason's quarters were situated so far out of the way. He resolved that night to make further inquiries despite the assurance he had had from Lillyman. But by now events were moving faster than Smith.

♦ ♦ ♦

THE MORNING AFTER his dinner party, Cole left the Kneussle farm at around noon, dressed as usual in his American lieutenant's uniform with captain's bars, the red silk ascot at his neck. Over his shoulder hung the Sten gun and at his waist was slung the Walther P38 semiautomatic.

His first stop was the Mengen airstrip. Lillyman, who was being transferred to Heidelberg, took Cole around to meet U. S. Army Lieutenant Louis J. Desantis, commander of a unit evacuating German POWs and American and British internees. Desantis, whose outfit supplied Lillyman's detachment, was informed by the American captain that Cole was taking over for him and should henceforth be provided with rations and fuel.

Later in the afternoon the Cockney had an appointment with the military governor in Saulgau. Pierre Laze was not having a very good day. He had already received disturbing inquiries from higher headquarters about the British captain who had battened onto the Third Battalion. Now he was confronted with the disconcertingly tall Peter Hope, who informed him that "Mason" was in fact a British renegade named Cole, wanted for collaborating with the SS.

The military governor showed "considerable astonishment" at this news. Laze protested that Cole was "highly regarded as running a counterintelligence exercise" with an American officer. But after examining Cole's dossier, Laze was persuaded of the truth. He then had to confess that the British imposter was coming for tea that very afternoon in his office, the requisitioned home of a German sculptor.

"Thank you very much," said Hope, "we'll wait for him."

It was about 3:00 P.M. when Cole entered, Sten gun slung over his shoulder, ready for tea.

"You're Cole, aren't you?" said Hope, stepping forward.

"Not very keen on admitting it," Cole issued a denial and started for the door. He was jumped by Hope, Lefort, and their driver. A struggle ensued, in which Cole and a French soldier rolled together under a grand piano. The traitor managed to get off a shot that grazed Hope in the leg, but he was finally subdued.

"Well," said Hope, "we're taking you back to Paris because your name is Cole."

Realizing that the game was finished, Cole admitted his identity. Then Hope stripped him of his borrowed finery, dressed him in mufti, and brought him back to the Kneussle farm in handcuffs to settle the rest of his affairs. After that, he was returned to Paris and locked up in an OSS prison on the boulevard Suchet. This was a former Gestapo lockup with which the traitor likely had more than a passing familiarity.

◆ ◆ ◆

IN PARIS Hope began a lengthy interrogation of Cole, aiming to establish a coherent account of the traitor's wartime activities. Reconciled to his new circumstances, Hope states, Cole was "perfectly at rest" and a "most agreeable" subject in these extended conversations. It would not be easy to con Hope, who had a way of looking straight through a suspect. But Cole was willing to try. Unmoved by the traitor's arguments, Hope nonetheless had to acknowledge that the Cockney possessed an "incredibly likeable personality."

Pinning Cole down was not easy. Superficially amenable and helpful, Cole agilely danced around Hope's verbal snares. The traitor was prepared to talk all day long if that was what the MI5 agent desired— but "in a very sort of egregious way; he always had a reason for everything he'd done."

Cole had submitted to and conducted enough interrogations to know the rules of the game. He "didn't tell lies that could be refuted at once—or if he verged near them he'd always wriggle out of them sideways," Hope recalled. Presented with a set of apparently damning facts, Cole would "turn them around with great rapidity into his own favor. If it looked as if he'd been working for the Germans, he'd try and explain that he wasn't working for the Germans. Something happened while he was there, which was not really his fault."

Cole could not, of course, deny everything. When faced with irrefutable evidence, he simply told Hope: "You know, I had no other option."

"Well, what about this?" Hope demanded, pointing to another undeniable transgression.

"I still had no option," Cole responded. "Either I was going to be shot, or I had to go on working."

Cole knew he hadn't a leg to stand on. Yet the confidence man in him refused to give up hope. If he talked long enough, perhaps he could talk his way right out of it. "I make this statement fully realizing its implications," said Cole in conclusion, after more than a week of interrogation. "I hope that it will demonstrate my true sentiments, which have always been for England."

28

"The King's Enemies"

RESISTANT TO incriminating himself on the score of treason, Cole had no compunctions about confessing to another capital offense. He provided Hope with a detailed account of Georg Hanft's murder and named his accomplices. On June 21, only thirteen days after Hanft's execution, Hope contacted Major John R. Miller of the OSS to inform him that Cole, "a notorious British traitor," had implicated a U.S. Army captain in the killing of a German citizen. With that conversation began a U.S. Army investigation that would not close until more than a decade later.

Miller handed the case over to the U.S. Army Criminal Investigation Division. CID Agent William L. Mulcahy left for Saulgau on June 24 with Peter Hope, Reginald Spooner, and Jacques Dureng de Maisonneuve, who had been posted to Paris. After the interrogation of various witnesses, Dureng led the investigators to the scene of the crime. Hanft's body was no longer there, but the Allied investigators found the torn sleeve of his shirt, four spent nine-millimeter shells, and one unfired .45-caliber bullet.

Hanft's corpse had been discovered on June 11, the very day of

Cole's arrest. That afternoon, two young German women were walking a forest path on their way to the Häcklerweiher when they saw a man lying off to the side of the track. He seemed to be asleep, and they did not stop then to look closer. On their way home after swimming they saw a cloud of flies buzzing around his face and settling on the nape of his neck. They noticed that the man had no shoes on his feet and his face was jaundiced. The two girls by this point had "presumed he might be dead."

Polizeimeister Clemens Haas was called from the nearby town of Mochenwangen, along with the medical examiner, who determined that the body, already decomposing, had been lying in the woods for several days. Haas found a single spent nine-millimeter bullet lying on the man's stomach, and picked up the victim's hat, which lay nearby. But he made no immediate identification. A local farmer took the corpse on his horse-drawn wagon to Blitzenreute, the farming community within which the Häcklerweiher lay. On the morning of June 13, Hanft was buried in a pauper's grave in the churchyard of Saint Lorentzius Church.

◆ ◆ ◆

AT 10:00 A.M. on June 29, several military jeeps pulled up to the simple stucco church in Blitzenreute. A dozen or so American, French, and British officers trooped into the walled churchyard, where a wooden coffin had been disinterred. A row of German policemen held back curious villagers on their way to mass. The town's gravedigger removed the coffin lid to reveal the gaping skull and badly decomposed body of Georg Hanft.

Present at this ghastly scene were Jacques Dureng and Camille Allart, the latter already under arrest in connection with the Hanft killing. The day before, by the side of the forest road leading around the Häcklerweiher, Allart and Dureng had exchanged recriminations over their respective culpability. The French lieutenant had just identified the place where Hanft was executed to the investigators.

"Here's the place where Hanft was cut down," Dureng told a

security officer named Lassalle, who was representing the French in the inquest.

"Who fired?" asked Lassalle.

"Everybody fired except myself," said Dureng. "I was only an onlooker."

Allart protested. "Lieutenant!" he exclaimed reproachfully to Dureng. "You fired along with everybody else, and I don't want to take the rap alone." Dureng merely shrugged and walked away from the French party, joining the Americans.

Lillyman also was under investigation for his alleged complicity in the murder. On July 10 he was interviewed at a U.S. Army base in Marseilles.

"So far as I can remember," he told the CID officers who came to Camp Tee-Dee, "Mason fired a full clip of P38 ammunition into the prisoner and the civilian Frenchman fired three or four bursts with the Tommy-gun."

"I did not take part in the shooting," Lillyman swore then, as he maintained steadfastly thereafter.

In the Blitzenreute churchyard, Captain André Blavoux, a medical officer with the Ninth Zouaves Regiment, performed a rapid autopsy on Hanft's remains. Blavoux had applied a chemical to his nasal passage that blunted his sense of smell. But the strong odor of putrefaction quickly got to others in the investigating party, who made haste to "put a few more meters between themselves and the corpse."

The medical officer found a total of twenty-eight bullet holes in the chest and skull of the German. Death, he pronounced, seemed to have been caused by "firearm slugs lodged in the cerebral cavity." He dug out some of these and handed them to one of the American officers present.

Dureng, having examined Hanft's remains, approached the group of French officials. He declared that "this was indeed the body of Hanft." Lassalle looked at him meaningfully.

"There are twenty-eight holes," said the French investigator. "You fired too."

"No," he denied. "I was only an onlooker."

Allart spoke up. "No, lieutenant, tell the truth. You fired along with everybody else."

Under this double pressure, Dureng finally relented and confessed. "Alright," he said. "I fired along with the others." Then he stalked back to the American group.

On July 24, CID Agent Mulcahy filed his report on the Hanft murder, which consisted of a seventeen-page summary accompanied by various exhibits and statements. "Three eyewitnesses in statements assert that Frank L. Lillyman took part in the murder of one Georg Hanft, alleged SD agent, near Ravensburg, Germany, on the night of 8 June 1945 by shooting him with a sub-machine gun," he wrote. "Lillyman in signed statement admitted being present at scene of murder on night of 8 June, but denies any participation in killing."

No criminal charges were brought against Lillyman, and with that report, the case seemed closed.

◆　◆　◆

CAPTAIN FRANK LILLYMAN returned to the United States that November aboard the troop ship *Stetson Victory*. He achieved immediate national celebrity as a war hero and exemplary returning G.I. A hotel in New York City offered him a luxury suite free for a week. Lillyman, his wife Jane, and their daughter Susan were written up and photographed for the pages of *Life* magazine, *The New York Times*, and newspapers across the country.

Lillyman was living out a fantasy that had begun for him on Christmas Day 1944 at Bastogne. It was during the Battle of the Bulge when, as one Manhattan reporter so colorfully put it, "the Germans were adding hot scrap iron to the bitter holiday menu." On that day Lillyman began drawing up a list of all the good things he wanted to enjoy when he got home—the "good food, and soft home lights, and roses, and Strauss waltzes."

Later, reassigned to Heidelberg after the episode in Saulgau, Lillyman put his wish list into letter form and sent it to the Pennsylvania

Hotel in Manhattan. An astute public relations man, cognizant of the national mood and appreciating the potential for free publicity, laid on every last request when Lillyman showed up in November 1945—on the house.

Lillyman did not speak of the Saulgau episode to his wife that week or at any time thereafter. He remained silent on the matter even when, in 1952, the U.S. Army Office of the Provost Marshal General requested that the CID "thoroughly re-investigate" his role in the death of Georg Hanft. Lillyman was by then a major under consideration for promotion to colonel. His superiors found it necessary to deal with the as-yet unresolved allegations that he had "participated in the murder of a German national."

Working in close liaison, CID Agent H. Rex Smith and French Judicial Police Investigator Jacques Delarue added twenty-five additional sworn statements to the handful taken in 1945, seeking out witnesses in Germany, France, and the United States, and piling up hundreds of pages of testimony and evidence. Dureng and Allart were again brought face-to-face at Chateauroux in October 1953. Under intense questioning Dureng, who had recanted his graveside confession, again acknowledged his participation.

In September 1953 Smith drew up his report. He concluded that Cole, Lillyman, Dureng, and Allart "did . . . with premeditation, murder Georg Hanft, a German national, by means of shooting him with a pistol, sub-machine gun and sten-gun."

By then, however, the French authorities had closed the case against Dureng and Allart with a *non lieu*, a determination of insufficient cause for prosecution. The logic of the military tribunal handling the case was that "Hanft was killed by the initial shots fired by Cole, and that the other members of the party fired only at Hanft's corpse."

But this did not get Lillyman off the hook. On July 20, 1954 he was reinterrogated at Fort Bragg, North Carolina, and insisted that he had not participated actively in Hanft's killing. In 1955 he traveled to Germany in connection with the case and in early 1956 was asked to resign his commission. Instead Lillyman appealed his case to the highest military authorities in Washington, D.C. He prevailed. That September he was reassigned to an important counterintelligence post in Italy and promoted to lieutenant colonel.

The assistant judge advocate general of the U.S. Army added a memorandum to Smith's report. "A review of all the evidence presently available against the accused discloses that there does not now exist any admissible evidence legally sufficient to support the charges and accordingly the charges have been dismissed."

Eleven years after that moonless night by the Häcklerweiher, Frank L. Lillyman finally had finally shaken off the consequences of his ill-considered association with Harold Cole.

◆ ◆ ◆

THROUGH THE SUMMER of 1945, Cole was held under lock and key in Paris. After the interrogation by Hope, Roland Lepers formally identified the traitor. The last time the two men had met was in November 1941, when they arrived with the Cockney's final convoy in the Gare Saint Charles in Marseilles. Since then, Lepers had fulfilled his ambition and become a pilot. He was stationed now in Holland with the Groupe Lorraine, a French bomber formation. Word came down through channels that Lepers's presence was required in Paris. On his arrival at Le Bourget on June 21, the young flight lieutenant was brought to a villa in the wealthy suburb of Saint Cloud, near the OSS prison on the boulevard Suchet.

There he found Cole sitting under guard in a small basement room. Squinting in the poor light, Cole resembled nothing so much as a caged ferret. It was not a pleasant reunion. Lepers heaped abuse on the pale, chapfallen traitor. The Cockney had no word of defense, other than to offer a weak reproach. "You know that I knew the address of your parents. But I didn't hand over your parents." Lepers had to acknowledge this was true. But it didn't in the least diminish the evil Cole had done.

Lepers took his leave feeling scant sympathy for the Cockney. On his way out he had a word with the guards. "Be careful," he said, "or he'll be gone."

"No, no," the guards told him.

"You'll see," said Lepers.

Soon after, Cole was transferred from the high-security OSS prison to an Allied detention barracks under the authority of SHAEF—Supreme Headquarters Allied Expeditionary Forces. It had come to the attention of the British military that a sergeant of the Royal Engineers was being held in a prison the inmates of which were principally SS members and accused war criminals. Hope got a phone call at his office, instructing him to transfer Cole to the Caserne Mortier, a prewar French barracks at the Porte des Lilas on the northeast periphery of the capital. It now served as a military prison, under U.S. control, called the Paris Detention Barracks.

"That's wrong," Hope protested. "This man's an escapee and you'll find him escaping."

"No," came the answer. "Leave him to us."

◆　◆　◆

IF COLE had access to newspapers in that summer of victory, he would have found little cause for cheer in the frequency with which the French and British press reported the conviction and, very often, the execution of yet another Nazi henchman.

France was in the throes of the *épuration*, the purging of those who had led the nation into the shame of collaboration. The bloodletting continued through that summer and into the autumn. Pierre Laval was convicted and sentenced to death on October 10. That same day Joseph Darnand, head of the collaborationist Milice, went before a firing squad at the Fort de Chatillon outside Paris. Laval's appeal was rapidly tossed aside, and he was dispatched on October 15.

Civil and military courts in London and other English cities heard a series of cases concerning alleged treason by British and Commonwealth subjects. They fell into two main groups. The smaller of these included the radio propagandists, the men and women who, like William Joyce, had broadcast to their homeland over the Reichsrundfunk. There was Thomas Haller Cooper, twenty-six, accused of "committing high treason in Germany and parts of the Continent of Europe occupied by the King's enemies." Born of an English father and a German mother, Cooper had belonged to the British Union of Fascists before the war. In early 1940 he joined the Waffen SS. After being wounded on the Russian front, he was assigned to write pamphlets on National Socialism aimed at British POWs.

On a visit to a POW camp he met a British NCO, Quartermaster Sergeant John Henry Owen Brown, who had been assigned to collect information on men like Cooper. At that time Cooper "showed himself to be anti-British and said England was bound to lose the war," Brown testified. But after the June 1944 landings in Normandy "a new light appeared to break in Cooper's mind" and he told Brown he "had been a fool." Found guilty and condemned to death, Cooper was later reprieved.

Theodore John William Schurch, twenty-seven, was less fortunate. Born in London of Swiss extraction, he nonetheless spoke with a strong Cockney accent. He had joined the British Union of Fascists at the age of sixteen because, his military judges were told, "he was persecuted in school." Captured in September 1942 during the desert campaign, he worked for the Germans obtaining information from other British prisoners of war. Schurch claimed to be Swiss, and his defense attorney pleaded that the young man had been misled by fascists at home. "Many more illustrious people than himself held these views," said the defending officer. But the court, unmoved, condemned Schurch to be hanged—which he was.

There were strange characters among the traitors. Perhaps the oddest of all was Norman Baillie-Stewart, "the Officer in the Tower" known to British newspaper readers even before the war. A graduate of the Royal Military Academy at Sandhurst, Baillie-Stewart had been arrested in 1932 and charged with giving military information to the Germans during a trip to Germany in 1931. He was said to have done this after falling in love with a young German woman named Marie Louise, whom he had met in London. Later the officer received ninety pounds from her in the mail. Baillie-Stewart became a figure of ridicule as well as opprobrium when he explained that this was in appreciation for his intimate attentions in a Berlin park. "Tears ran down people's cheeks as they read the reports of the case, so madly ludicrous was Baillie-Stewart's story," reported one observer. He was convicted and sentenced to five years' penal servitude.

Released in 1937, he sought German citizenship, but did not receive it until 1940, when the war was already in progress. Hired for broadcasts similar to those of Joyce, he was, ironically, disdained and distrusted by his German employers, who were convinced that he was in fact a British spy. So he spent a miserable war and, when it was over, fled to the mountains of Austria, where he was arrested, a comically sad figure in Tyrolean *lederhosen*. Baillie-Stewart was shipped back to England, tried, convicted on a charge of violating defense regulations, and sentenced to five years' imprisonment. His efforts to abandon his British nationality worked on his behalf. "When you shook the dust of England off your feet, you desired to have nothing more to do with it," the judge told him. "You were not . . . one of those despicable creatures who will go to and from a country and sell it."

A similar issue of nationality became paramount in the trial of William Joyce, which opened in London's Central Criminal Court on September 17, 1945. Those expecting to hear a lurid tale of evildoing inside the Third Reich were disappointed. Joyce never denied that he had broadcast messages hostile to the British people and their leaders. Not only were recordings available of his work on behalf of the Reichsrundfunk, but he had published a collection of his broadcasts called *Twilight over England*. Courtroom debate turned on the question of whether Joyce, born in the United States to an Irish father, could be considered a traitor to Britain. The court found that Joyce, having held a British passport that was renewed in 1939, could be tried for having "adhered to the King's enemies" contrary to the Treason Act of 1351. Joyce was convicted and condemned to death before the month was out.

His fate was shared by John Amery, arraigned that October and tried in November 1945. It was said of Amery that he had "packed into thirty years every kind of folly and dissipation." Bankrupted in 1937 at the age of twenty-four, he had left England to take up the Fascist cause on the Continent. He ran guns for the Nationalists during the Spanish Civil War and moved in extreme-right circles in France. In 1942, Amery accepted an invitation to Berlin where, for a time, he was "the most-petted and best-advertised English propagandist that had ever been put on the German radio." Later Amery created Saint George's Legion, which he intended to be an anti-Bolshevik unit similar to the Waffen SS brigades raised in France and other occupied countries. It would be deployed strictly on the Russian front, "fighting with the best of Europe's youth to preserve our European civilization and our common cultural heritage from the menace of Jewish Communism."

Amery, swayed by his own propaganda, had extracted a promise from the German Foreign Office that if he could draw 1,500 men to his tatterdemalion banner, he would be allowed to establish a provisional British government on the Channel Islands. But by mid-1943, Amery was in bad odor with the Nazi authorities, and he was packed off to France and Italy. Saint George's Legion was renamed the British Free Corps and came under the influence of a New Zealand Expeditionary Force NCO by the name of Roy Nicolas Courlander. This lance corporal, taken prisoner in Greece in 1941, had in 1943 given a series of broadcast talks on German radio. He had been compelled to do that, he later would testify in the Central Criminal Court in London, just as he had joined the British Free Corps "to control it and use it against the enemy." Courlander made eight or nine tours of the stalags attempting to recruit British POWs into the Free Corps. He informed one prospect who later took the stand against him that 150 thousand Nazi sympathizers were on the way over from England to sign up.

But Amery, Courlander, and the men they attracted were merely deluded and manipulated by the Germans, who "had far too much sense to keep on with the Legion because they thought they could raise enough men to form a fighting unit for use on the Russian front or anywhere else," writes Rebecca West. "They wanted them for quite another purpose. They put these men in villas in various pleasant parts of Germany and dressed them in German uniforms with flashes with the letters B.F.C. and the Union Jack to show that the wearers were British soldiers, and let them go rotten with idleness and indiscipline and debauchery."

Most of these recruits were to be pitied as much as despised, and few of them went to the gallows. Their common trait was a weakness of character and, as often as not, intellect that allowed them to be used and then cast off by their German sponsors. Only a few, like Amery, committed treason with a full knowledge of what they were doing or out of genuine political beliefs. At parties in their barracks in Pankow, Hildesheim, and Dresden, they would toast the Duke of Windsor, the abdicated Edward VIII, whom they still recognized as king. His late-1930s flirtation with German Fascism comforted their own dereliction. But when the rumor flashed through their numbers in late 1944 that they were to be posted to the Eastern Front, "the British Free Corps took to its bed as one man."

As the end of the war approached, these pathetic troopers of the Legion of the Damned "daily grew more drunken, more desperate, more maudlin amorous in the arms of their whores." Their motto was stamped out many years before by Rudyard Kipling in his *Barrack-Room Ballads*, in reference to the "gentlemen rankers" who served below their station in life. "We have done with Hope and Honour, we are lost to Love and Truth; We are dropping down the ladder rung by rung."

29

"A Fantastic Chain of Events"

MEANWHILE Cole languished in the Paris Detention Barracks awaiting his own trial, judgment, and almost assured hanging for the large collection of misdeeds he had assembled over the previous five years. The question remained, however, as to which nation would first have the pleasure of judging the traitor. The French authorities "wanted him like mad," according to Hope. But the British were not about to hand over the Royal Engineers sergeant for trial in Paris. Thus Cole, by one account, "lay there week after week while the French, English, and Americans wrangled over the priority of their respective claims to bring him to justice. Each felt they had the more serious charges, and each wanted to try him first. The wrangle became a bureaucratic duel. Presently it developed into a pitched battle. At its height, news came through that Cole had escaped."

Security arrangements at the Caserne Mortier were less than rigorous, despite the many indications on Cole's record that he was a talented escape artist. By the month of November, Cole had worked his way into the confidence of the mixed Anglo-American guard details keeping watch over him. At some point in the autumn of

1945, Cole announced to his jailers that he was setting to work on his autobiography. He obtained the use of a typewriter and, complaining of the chill in his cell, the privilege of working in the guardroom.

Late on the evening of November 18, Cole was at work on his opus when the opportunity arose for him to depart the confines of the detention barracks. Shortly before eleven o'clock that Sunday evening, the Cockney gathered up his papers and announced that he was going back to his cell, at the same time requesting permission to use the toilet in an outside hallway. No one objected; no one paid much attention.

Cole was counting on this. As he walked out of the room he slipped from a hook on the wall the overcoat which had been hung there shortly before by an American provost sergeant named Carpenter. Moments later, after donning the overcoat, Cole walked out the gates of the Caserne Mortier past the unseeing guard detail, the typewriter still tucked under his arm. A few hundred yards down the street was the Porte des Lilas station of the Paris underground, into which Cole vanished.

There was great consternation at this development, and a manhunt was launched. By one dramatic Fleet Street account, the dragnet "extended over the whole of western Europe, staged by the police of at least three countries, who circulated an urgent message to every capital stating, 'This man is a dangerous traitor.' "

British counterintelligence reissued a search notice, attaching some singularly unalluring mug shots of the traitor taken by authorities at the military prison in Lyon during 1942. The escaper was, according to this notice, "very cunning and plausible." The fugitive Cole would likely "masquerade as British or American officer or other rank or as a civilian. Escaped with papers of Sgt. Carpenter, Provost Company, but will almost certainly obtain other identity documents. May be armed and will probably resist arrest."

The French authorities were also alerted. The Paris Préfecture de Police issued an *avis de recherche* on November 23, warning all police agents that Cole "should be considered very dangerous and will not hesitate, if he is armed, to fire."

◆ ◆ ◆

THE CITY OF PARIS had changed hands since Cole last walked its streets, and its restaurants, hotels, cafés, nightclubs, and 178 licensed brothels now teemed with Allied troops and officers. But Cole quickly saw that this new arrangement, far from working to his disadvantage, offered more possibilities for concealment and illicit gains than anything that had existed in France under German occupation. A seemingly inexhaustible supply of U.S. Army supplies, diverted by the trainload, fed a vast and highly profitable black market. The French press, noting the widespread corruption and violence among occupation troops, referred to the capital city as "Chicago-sur-Seine." Even in a provincial city such as Rouen there were fourteen murders on Christmas Eve 1945. The CID, the Provost Marshal General, and the Judge Advocate General offices were working overtime. For those convicted of capital offenses, death houses were established in Le Mans, Le Havre, and Paris, and did a thriving business.

Cole's former prisonmates at the Caserne Mortier included two U.S. Army privates who, according to a report in the *Stars and Stripes,* had embarked on "a spree of lawlessness that included a murder, a housebreaking and three pistol-point café robberies netting 270 thousand francs in money, jewelry and furs." Still bearing the papers of the American provost sergeant, Cole found it a simple matter to run cons on gullible American and British troops and officers. Arms and ammunition were easily come by in a city filled with soldiers. Cole obtained a weapon for use if he were faced with recapture.

His situation would be precarious so long as he remained in Paris, where his photograph was posted in every commissariat and MP barracks. But travel was still tightly restricted by the Allied forces. So Cole would have to lie low until he had obtained suitable credentials or until the controls on movement had been relaxed. He had often faced such difficulties in the days when he led escapers from one end of France to the other. Now the Americans were in charge, but the essential rules of the game had not changed that much. Cole's first requirement was for shelter; winter was hard upon him and if he stayed in the street he would be picked up before long. As had so often been the case in the past, Cole looked for a sympathetic woman to assist him in his plight. He found Pauline Herveau.

It was actually one of Herveau's three daughters, named Eliane, who brought Cole to her bar in the rue de Grenelle for the first time. He was calling himself Harry, posing as a British soldier awaiting his demobilization and return home. Herveau, 42, was separated from her husband, an industrialist who had given her the money to open the bar, located just off the boulevard Raspail in the *Sixième arrondissement* of Paris. She had taken over and renovated the premises of a *charbonnier*, a neighborhood café and fuel distributor. She called the place Billy's Bar, hoping to draw in some of the thousands of American and British soldiers billeted in hotels in the area.

Monsieur Harry, by his own account an army physician, made a great impression on Herveau. "Charming, very correct, a cultured person, erudite," he spoke French with but a slight accent. Herveau could see immediately that he "wasn't just anybody." She invited friends to come by for drinks in the as-yet unopened bar, telling them, "I know an Englishman who is so intelligent." All listened spellbound as Monsieur Harry spun his tales.

Like many French women, Herveau had a great admiration for the British and the Americans. During the war she had lived in the French countryside of the Loire Valley with her in-laws, and had frequently laid flowers on the wreckage of a downed American bomber. "*Oh la la*," she would say, "If I ever meet an American or an Englishman, that would be my dream." But she later would hasten to add that there was never anything between her and Monsieur Harry. "We weren't that close," she insisted. "We had a drink or two, but that was all." The man came by the bar for a friendly drink in the evening, then went on his way.

The report that had come to the attention of police in the Commissariat Saint-Thomas d'Aquin, near Saint-Germain-des-Près, differed, however. According to local informants, a suspicious individual, possibly an escaped German POW, was hiding out over Billy's Bar. The stranger, said to be on the friendliest of terms with Herveau, only ventured out of his upper-story room at night.

So it was that on the morning of January 8, 1946, police inspectors Raymond Cotty and Edmond Lévy arrived at the bar to make inquiries. Faced with the two police agents, Herveau acknowledged that a man was in her upstairs room. Charges that she had sheltered a criminal were later dropped; Herveau insisted that the man had stopped at the bar that morning to say good-bye, explaining that he was leaving for Brussels. Pleading a headache, Monsieur Harry had asked if he could repose himself in her spare room until it was time to go to the station. While Lévy checked the barman's papers, Cotty followed Herveau up the stairs.

On the fourth floor landing she opened the door of the room and, by one account, announced to its occupant: "*Cheri*, it's the police."

Herveau would deny this, later describing her total astonishment upon finding her new acquaintance standing in the doorway of the room brandishing a pistol.

"Monsieur Harry!" she exclaimed. "What are you doing?" Then she was shoved aside and Cole opened fire.

He had been preparing for this contingency for weeks. Most likely he had readied his weapon as soon as he heard the footsteps coming up the stairs, followed by the knock on the door and Herveau's warning. But Cole, firing at almost point blank range, proved an exceedingly bad shot.

The traitor, cornered in the small upper-story room, had gotten the jump on Cotty and hit him with two bullets. But these only grazed the detective, a Resistance veteran. Cotty returned the fire with deadly accuracy.

Without uttering a word, Cole toppled over backwards onto the bed, a bullet through his heart.

The Cockney's luck had finally run out, and justice, more or less, had been done. No one mourned as his corpse was placed in a wooden coffin and transported to a refrigerated drawer at the Institut medico-legal. The reaction of Peter Hope, who knew the traitor as well as anyone, was typical: "Cole was the worst villain I ever met and deserved all he got."

◆ ◆ ◆

THE DEATH of Harold Cole created a minor sensation in the Parisian press, as it became known that a British traitor had been killed in a shootout with the French police.

"A British Deserter—Former Member of the Gestapo—Receives the Police with Gunfire," announced a front-page headline in the *Parisien Libéré* of January 10. "They Riposte and Kill Him on the Spot."

"A Soldier in Four Armies," declared the evening paper *France-Soir*. "He Betrayed Them One after Another."

The correspondent of the *Daily Mail*, embellished the story with a romantic touch, reporting that Cole had heard of inquiries being made about his presence over the bar, but dismissed them in a cavalier gesture. "Someone is after me, but I shall be gone soon," he reportedly said. "I take the train in a few hours for Belgium."

"Then turning to Mme Herveux [*sic*] he said: 'Come along, chérie, and have some champagne.'

"That delay to have a final drink and farewell celebration led to his capture," wrote the *Mail*'s man in Paris, asserting that Cole's death was the consequence of his chivalrous hesitation to shoot while Herveau was in his line of fire.

Following up the story on January 12, the *Parisien Libéré* stated that "at the time of his arrest, Harold Cole carried a dose of cyanide inside a ring, but the police did not permit this sinister character to have the death of his choice."

Albert Guerisse identified Cole's body some days later in the Paris police morgue. On February 2 Cole was buried in the Cemetery of Thiais, outside Paris. A French bureaucrat in the Paris Bureau des

Cimetières noted later in response to an inquiry that, in keeping with the regulations concerning temporary or charity burials, eventually "the site was reclaimed, and the remains of the deceased were transferred to the ossuary."

Thus the traitor's mortal remains were mingled with those of the common humanity; no stone or marker exists to remind the world that Harold Cole ever existed.

◆ ◆ ◆

THAT WAS VERY MUCH the way British Intelligence preferred to see Cole and his case laid to rest. Far too many awkward questions would have to be answered if his case were to come to trial. Even if he were to have been tried *in camera,* information would likely have come out, particularly in France where the press could not be bound by the legal restrictions applicable in Fleet Street. It really was better that the Cole affair should end with the shootout over Billy's Bar.

In retrospect, however, the entire handling of Cole's case would seem peculiar. Why did he remain so long in Paris when other British traitors were almost immediately brought back to England and swiftly put on trial? Observers had commented on the lapse of time between William Joyce's arrest on May 25 and his return to England by airplane on June 16, 1945. Part of this time was spent under treatment for his bullet wounds. During this hiatus, one Captain William James Scardon of the British Intelligence Corps also interrogated him. Scardon was just beginning a career of confounding traitors of every stripe, including Philby. But then Joyce was held in Brussels from June 10 to 16, a delay thought to have been deliberate, for legal reasons. The Parliament was debating the Treason Act of 1945, streamlining the antiquated procedures called for in treason trials. The act was passed into law on June 15, one day before Joyce's arrival in England.

There was no such complication in Cole's case. By the time he was arrested and had undergone his preliminary interrogation, the new legislation was promulgated. There was, admittedly, the French desire to judge Cole—understandable, given that the majority of his victims had been French Resistance members. But the French government of the time had other preoccupations. And the balance of power at that time, even on French soil, was such that the tenuously installed government in Paris was not likely to overrule the wishes of its Anglo-Saxon partners in the victorious Alliance. If there was a prolonged debate over the disposition of prisoner Cole, this was only because it suited British purposes.

Even the Americans involved in the investigation of Hanft's death remarked a certain reticence on the part of the British officials with whom they dealt—although it was difficult to say whether this was more than the usual English reserve. "The whole way of treating this guy seemed a little strange," according to CID Agent Smith, who was not involved directly in 1945, but would take up the case in depth in 1952. Over the Cole case, he recalls, there seemed to hover the question of "whether or not they were using him in some way."

This ambiguity as to Cole's real status was also remarked by certain of his former Resistance colleagues who had occasion to deal with British intelligence officials. Soon after the 1944 liberation of the north of France, Henri Duprez traveled to London and obtained a meeting with some official within British Intelligence. He wanted to see that those of his network who had given their lives were properly recognized, and sought reimbursement for the receipts signed by Cole, which amounted to many thousands of francs.

Duprez also wanted some answers concerning Cole. But when he asserted that the Cockney was a traitor, the British official with whom he was dealing suddenly became "glacial." This, Duprez was told, was an unacceptable allegation, which he would have to retract before his financial outlay could be reimbursed. He told the official that was out of the question and left the office.

Alfred Lanselle, who returned to Saint-Omer after surviving the Dachau concentration camp, had an even stranger experience. He had not gone looking for answers about Cole, being too much occupied with collecting the shattered pieces of his own life. Four of his five children had been killed in an Allied bombing raid on the Saint-Omer train yards in 1943, leaving his wife distraught and his remaining son disturbed.

In the autumn of 1945, he received a telephone call from the local prefecture, informing him that some British intelligence officers would be around to see him on business related to the International Military Tribunal that opened in Nuremberg that November. However, it was not Nazi war crimes they wanted to discuss, Lanselle relates, but Harold Cole. Their interest, moreover, was not so much to find out what Cole had done, but to issue an astonishing warning. "Don't come to England to kill Harold Cole," one of them told the French businessman. "You won't get away with it."

There was not much to put one's hand on. But over the years stories circulated among the survivors of Cole's former network, fed by snatches of rumors passed down the line from former comrades risen to employment in the French military. Van de Kerckhove and Duprez came to believe that Cole had in some way been linked to the entourage of the Duke of Windsor, the abdicated King Edward VIII. He was a courier, a go-between in an obscure plot to negotiate a separate peace with England. There was nothing to support this idea. But it reflected the confusion which the Cockney had sown in the north, as well as the high esteem in which he was held before his fall.

Lanselle had a different theory about Cole, which in some respects was just as far-fetched, but which nonetheless dovetailed with some of what may be deduced legitimately about Cole's true role in the north. "I believe," he would later state, "that Paul became a double agent for his country, that he received an order from the Intelligence Service to become a double agent."

This did not exclude that Cole abused his position by swindling his French sponsors in the north, and sowed havoc by playing both ends against the middle. But it did explain many things about Cole's erratic behavior while serving as an agent for the Garrow organization, and shed some light on his subsequent value to the Sicherheitsdienst. And if it were true, then another theory advanced by Lanselle would not seem quite so unbelievable: that the January 1946 shooting of Cole in Paris was nothing less than an elaborate montage.

"Harold Cole was not killed," stated Lanselle. "It was staged by the Intelligence Service to get him out of the way, to bury the case. They shot someone who resembled Harold Cole, but it was not Harold Cole who was killed." He continued, "According to all my contacts, people who have gotten in touch with me, I am certain that Harold Cole is living in England. Maybe not now. He may be dead. But he was living in England in 1946, 1947, 1948."

What to make of this? In the absence of evidence and confirmatory witnesses, the version given in the French and British press must stand—that Cole and no one else was shot down in that room over Billy's Bar. But the circumstances of Cole's escape, and his death, may provoke reflection if examined closely. From the time of his arrest until one day before his escape from the Caserne Mortier, not a word about Cole had appeared in the British press. Then on November 17, 1945, a small item appeared in the *Daily Mail*.

"An Englishman whose identity British intelligence authorities are keeping secret has, it is learned tonight, been arrested on grave charges following his illegal activities in France under German occupation," reported the *Mail* in a dispatch datelined Luneberg, Germany, where Haw-Haw had first been questioned after his arrest. "He is accused of having worked in the interrogation department of the Gestapo headquarters and directed and/or personally taken part in torturing French resistance men and patriots engaged in smuggling British soldiers and airmen out of the country.'" The *Mail* added: "It is said that when arrested the Englishman was wearing American uniform and was posing as a Captain of the U.S. Army Counter Intelligence Corps."

British officials had told the *Mail*'s correspondent that "only after he has been tried by the French shall we issue a statement to the

British press." That version of the situation might have passed for the truth, except that the military spokesman specified that Cole was "now in the custody of French officials." This was an outright lie.

Was it merely coincidental that Cole should escape just two days after information concerning this singular case had been made public? Moreover, given the close-mouthed official position on Cole prior to his death, it was curious that British Intelligence should, upon his death, provide a detailed briefing to journalists on both sides of the Channel, going so far as to release photographs of the man whose existence, some months before, had barely been acknowledged. Was this a cover story intended to preclude any other version of the Cole story from gaining currency in France or England? Disinformation meant to defuse a case likely to embarrass intelligence officials who had used Cole in some manner that would not bear the light of day? Lacking documentary proof of this we can only re-examine the evidence in what may well have been the case of a turncoat who was at once something more and something less than a mere traitor.

Or was the truth much simpler than that? Was Cole just a small-time grifter who got in over his head? That was how Roland Lepers, among others, saw it. "Cole was a weak man who liked to make money the easy way," Lepers explained. "He saw a beautiful way of re-establishing himself and having a good life in joining the organization. But of course he could not possibly not make the same mistake he always made, which was to take advantage of a good deal. Then when he got arrested by the Germans, he wanted to save his skin, and he would do anything to save his skin, and he was blackmailed into doing what he did. It was that simple."

But even Lepers would have some lingering doubts. After the war was over he had put the question to Jimmy Langley. "It is certain that he was a deserter," Lepers asked. "So why was he protected?" Langley was in a position to know. He had been Claude Dansey's personal representative to MI9 and thus had to have been informed about Cole. Langley acknowledged that he and other officials had known of Cole's civilian and military criminal record when they approved his use within the escape line. There was no discussion of any other intelligence brief Cole might have held. The somewhat feeble excuse that Langley gave to Lepers was, "We gave him a second chance."

Perhaps many of the questions surrounding Cole's actions could be answered if the wartime files of the Secret Intelligence Service were trundled into the daylight. But even then there would probably remain many dark corners. Given the extent to which the Cockney deceived the Allies and their enemy as well, Cole himself was probably the only one to hold all the pieces to the puzzle. Which takes us back to Cole's own enigmatic character, made up of all pieces, which took him so far to achieve, in the end, little more than disgrace.

Brilliant in his own twisted way, Cole for a time had distinction within his grasp, which is the small tragedy inside the larger one. But of course he could not rise above his limitations. He shared this trait with other British traitors. The trajectory of their downward path was determined by the nature of their weaknesses. Rebecca West, reflecting on the phenomenon of British wartime treason, seemed to identify this basic infirmity correctly in her 1946 work, which, strangely enough, never mentions Cole.

Most of Britain's traitors were, she writes, "strange and disturbing figures, and their trials were full of dream-like incongruities, evoking laughter even while they dismayed by recalling something which it would be preferable to forget and which cannot be completely remembered. For people do not become traitors unless they are unable to fit into the society into which they were born, and the cause of that incapacity in their case is a disturbing society which catches those around them off their guard, and therefore provokes them in their turn to strange behavior. Hence their lives become a series of fantastic events."

Acknowledgments

MANY PEOPLE gave generously of their time and personal recollections of Cole. Chief among these was Count Albert-Marie Edmond Guerisse of Brussels. He submitted graciously to our many questions and was a principal source of information not only on Cole but on the escape line which he commanded between 1941 and 1943 under the nom de guerre of Patrick O'Leary. Other escape line members and their families helped reconstruct the story: Raphaël Ayello, Paula Spriewald Blanchain, Anne-Marie Chedeville, Léone Delsol, Madeleine Marie Deram, Philippe Duclercq, Marguerite Duprez-Beylemans, Henri Duprez, Simone de Fligué, Jacques Holweck, Jeanne Huyge, Ghislaine de Fligué Kerjeau, Simone Micheline Kenny, Alfred Lanselle, Roland Lepers, Robert Leycuras, Jean de la Olla, Gaston Peltret, André Postel-Vinay, Elisa Salingue, François Trancart, Maurice Van de Kerckhove, Jeannine and Jean Voglimacci.

My acknowledgment of debt to other valuable sources on Cole, the escape line and other aspects: Baroness Airey of Abingdon, Camille Allart, Richard Christmann, Air Marshall Sir Denis Crowley-Milling, Jacques Delarue, Mrs. Hugh Stuart Fullerton, Pauline

Herveau, Wing Commander F. W. Higginson, David Holmes, Sir Charles Peter Hope, Else and Winfried Kneussle, P. E. Laughton-Bramley, Edmond Lévy, Jane Beebe Lillyman, Martin Moran, Colonel Paul Paillole, Marguerite Royer, Robert Sheppard, H. Rex Smith, Cornelius Verloop, Air Commodore Archibald Winskill. My thanks also to those former officers of the 117th Cavalry Reconnaissance Squadron and other U.S. Army units who helped me set the context for Cole's postwar career, especially: Santi L. Carnevali, Homer Clinch, Robert Robbins, Harold J. Samsel, James R. Shenk, Richard B. Snyder, Henry E. Windmoeller, Mario J. Zecca. Thanks also to Jean Bennett of the Auburn (N.Y.) *Citizen*, and to Oscar Andre and Winona Eaton of Clarksburg, West Virginia, for their kind assistance, as well as to Rosemarie Hurd of the Saulgau, West Germany, town hall.

I also thank those who went out of their way to help our investigation, advising us and sharing their personal expertise: Professor M. R. D. Foot on British operations in occupied France; Helen and Aidan Long, who shared their findings on the Garrow Organization in Marseilles; Elisabeth Harrison of the RAF Escaping Society, who helped us contact former escapers. Thanks also to Kay Ramsay of the Church of Scotland; Daniel Bénédite and Jean Gemahling on Marseilles in 1940 to 1941; Etienne Dejonghe and Jean-Paul Thuillier on Lille during the German occupation; Roger Morange on the Vichy intelligence services; Thomas M. J. Riordan on the Fourth Division, Royal Engineers; William Scardon and Fred Narborough.

Various journalists generously shared their files and personal contacts. Much thanks to Anthony Read, David Fisher, and Tom Tullett in London, as well as Dominick Flessati of BBC Television, and to Frans Dekkers in Holland and Roger Faligot in France.

Documents on Cole came from a number of sources. I especially wish to thank those in the Modern Military Headquarters and Modern Military Field branches of the U.S. National Archives who helped me uncover material in their holdings: Rich Boylan, Ben Cooper, Elaine Everly, Terry Hammett, Bill Lewis, Henry Mayer, Will

Mahoney, Fred Pernell, David Pfeiffer, Edward Reese, Amy Schmidt, John Taylor, Victoria Washington and Robert Wolfe. Thanks also to the staff of the Diplomatic branch. At the U.S. Army Crime Records Center, Robert A. Brisentine, Jr. and Wilbur Hardy helped me tap into a rich vein of material on Cole's postwar activities. Intelligence material was obtained from the U.S. Army Intelligence and Security Command at Fort George C. Meade, Maryland, with the help of Thomas F. Conley and Marsha Galbreath. Materials were also received from the Albert F. Simpson Historical Research Center, Maxwell AFB, Alabama. I wish to thank Richard Piellisch for his kind hospitality and help in research in Washington, D.C.; Sharon Reed for her research contribution in London; and Kevin Dougherty for his work in Montreal.

In Great Britain, the following were of assistance: the Imperial War Museum, where Terry Charman was particularly helpful in locating references to Cole; the Public Records Office in Kew, London; the British Library; the Air Historical Branch, Ministry of Defence; the Public Information Office, Scotland Yard; the Army Research Center, London; the Daily Mirror Records office; the Hackney Archives Department; the Rose Lipman Library, Hackney; and the Greater London Record Office. In Australia, many thanks to Laura Preston of the Commonwealth Government Archives in Collinswood, and to Joy Wheatley of the Australian Archives in Belconnen. In France and elsewhere on the Continent: the Archives Nationales and Bibliotèque Nationale, Paris; the Institut d'Histoire du Temps Present; the Centre de Recherches et d'Etudes Historiques de la Seconde Guerre Mondiale, Brussels, with great thanks to Frans Selleslagh; the Rijksinstituut voor Oorlogsdocumentatie, Amsterdam, with special thanks to Dr. David Barnouw; the Berlin Document Center and its most helpful director, Daniel P. Simon; the Paris Préfecture de Police; and the Direction Générale de la Gendarmerie Nationale, Division des Affaires Pénales Militaires.

Notes

1 "He Spoke Atrocious French"

Episode in Aix-les-Bains: P. E. Laughton-Bramley, correspondence.

"The worst traitor of the war": Adamson, p. 140.

"At least fifty": Even official figures vary widely. An Allied intelligence card file entry on Cole dated May 15, 1944, held in the U.S. National Archives, Record Group 331, AFHQ, G-2, Reel 450-E, "Index of Nazi, Fascist, and Suspect Persons (Chiefly in Italy)," places the figure at fifty-one. Neave, *Saturday*, p. 307, sets the figure higher, at "more than 150." A 1945 *avis de recherche* issued by the French Police Judiciaire states that he handed over "approximately 150 Frenchmen, of whom fifty-five disappeared."

"He exerted 'a great hold' ": Barclay, p. 155.

"At once an engaging rascal": Sir Charles Peter Hope, correspondence.

"The crime most abhorred": West, p. 185.

"Ranks before murder": Sparrow, p. 12.

"Hideous novelty": West, p. 3.

"The most interesting and dangerous": Neave, *Saturday*, p. 307.

"Not very proud of that": Lepers interview.

2 *"Was That Your Game in Civvy Street?"*

Cole recruitment: Martin Moran, correspondence.

Serial number 1877989: Cole card files, other documents.

Family background: Established by Nigel Willmott and William Sargent from birth, death and marriage certificates, electoral registers, parish and school admission records, and other documents located in the General Register Office, the Greater London Record Office and History Library, the Hackney Archives Department, and the Islington Central Reference Library and Vestry House Museum, Walthamstow; Thomas Sansom, interview.

"Ruinous broken pavements": Besant, p. 21.

"Half the criminals in the world": Ted Harrison, son of a Hoxton sweeper, as quoted in Weightman, p. 144.

"Get the best he could": Hope, interview.

Prison dates: Several sources provide these same dates, evidently given in official briefings: *Echo du Soir* (Lyon), October 15, 1945, p. 1; *Le Parisien Libéré*, January 10, 1946, p. 1.

Booking, February 1939: Reproduced here and dated 1945; when first printed in French and British newspapers it bore the 1939 date.

"Constantly used such expressions": Neave, *Saturday*, p. 307.

Cole advancement: Moran; D. Holmes, correspondence.

Convoy incident: Ibid.

"Was that your game": Ibid.

Embarkment: Riordan, p. 8.

BEF contingent: Ellis, pp. 19–21.

"France's treasure house": Michelin, p. 3.

History of Lille: Mabille de Ponchville, Pierrard, passim.

"Twenty years later": *Le Grand Echo du Nord de la France*, October 12, 1939.

Rowdy soldiers: "Francais et Britanniques dans la Drôle de Guerre," Ed. CNRS, Paris, 1979, p. 31.

"Soldiers of the northern provinces": Spears, p. 69.

Station in Loison-sous-Lens: Holmes, Moran, op. cit.

Deram view of Cole: Deram, interview.

Truck incident: Moran, op. cit.

3 *"His Scheme Never Failed"*

Richard Godfrey identity: Author's deduction. This pseudonym appears on numerous Allied intelligence card files, but nowhere else in Cole's wartime career. One card, of British origin, states that Godfrey was Cole's "real name" although no other evidence supports this. Most likely he used this composite name during his prewar military service.

Cole cashiered: "Police allemande à Lyon pendant la guerre et ses auxiliaires français," semiofficial French account of Cole interrogation in Lyon, 1942; in Rhone dossier, Archives Nationales. Cole's earlier service also confirmed by Hope.

"Seemed to have great faith": Holmes, op. cit.

Sentry duty: Moran, Holmes, op. cit.

"Standing at their post": Holmes, op. cit.

"What kind of a bastard he was": Moran, op. cit.

Cole incrimination: Holmes, op. cit.

Cole escapes: Moran, op. cit.

Theft of checkbook: File card on microfilm; obtained from U.S. Army Intelligence and Security Command, Fort George G. Meade, Maryland.

"His story was amazing": Holmes, op. cit.

Battle of France: Horne, Ellis, Riordan, passim.

Cole-Moran confrontation: Moran, op. cit..

Moran at Dunkirk: Ibid.

"When Jerry came tearing into Lille": Holmes, op. cit.

Cole back in Loison: Deram, op. cit.

4 *"Collect the English and Send Them Home!"*

Case of the four: Michelin, pp. 16–18.

Edith Cavell: Ryder, passim.

"Bordered on terror": Archives Nationales, Ref. 72AJ 169, Dossier Nord A, V-5, "Le Nord et le Pas de Calais pendant le premier année d'occupation, by Etienne Dejonghe, p. 11.

Hegener background: Berlin Document Center, Hegener file.

Verloop background: Correspondence with Dr. David Barnouw, Rijksinstituut Voor Oorlogsdocumentatie, Amsterdam; Archives Nationales, Ref. 72AJ 169, Dossier Nord A, I-2, A II-10; Report of May 8, 1952, Ministerie van Innenlandse Zaken, Netherlands.

"Could expect no mercy": Cited by Foot and Langley, *MI9*, p. 20.

"Our duty was simple": Dumez, pp. 29–32.

Hegedos on convoys: Archives Nationales, Ref. 72 AJ 170, Dossier Nord B, I-19.

"Romantic months": Neave, *Saturday*, p. 18.

"Bewildered figures": Ibid.

"In the confident belief": Foot and Langley, p. 64.

Escape stories: Evans, op. cit.

Better idea how to proceed: Neave cites the escape account *Within Four Walls*, by Colonel Henry Cartwright: "As a small boy I had read it with romantic pleasure, and it played a great part in forming my philosophy of escape." *Saturday*, p. 40.

Second-hand bookstores: Foot and Langley, p. 55.

Huyge activity: Jeanne Huyge, interview.

They "rushed off": Ibid.

"Each was as drunk as the other": Maurice Van de Kerckhove, interview.

Pétain letter: Archives Nationales, Ref. 72AJ 169, Dossier Nord A V1.

Demonstration at grave: Report No. 7, Part II, (13 August 1940) "Pro-English Demonstrations"; Records of German Field Commands—Rear Areas, Occupied Territories, and Others. (National Archives and Records Service, GSA, Washington); Roll 102; Item 17817/5; Image 0259-0260. Provided by Centre de Recherches et d'Etudes Historiques de la Seconde Guerre Mondiale, Brussels.

"People . . . reached agreement": Archives Nationales, Ref. 72AJ 170, Dossier Nord B, I-1.

5 *"This Man Isn't Simple at All"*

Meeting with Duprez: Duprez, *Même combat*, pp. 77–78.

"Absolutely certain": Duprez, interview.

"The prototype of an Englishman": Ibid.

"Our one great enemy": Duprez, interview.

"The strong feeling": Duprez, Ibid.

Cole and Deram in La Madeleine: Deram, interview.

François Duprez background: Marguerite Duprez, interview.

"As if he were a deaf-mute": Ibid.

"Something of a simpleton": Jeannine Voglimacci, interview.

6 *"He Was Smarter Than That"*

"Anything English was God": Roland Lepers, interview.
"Imposing when he spoke": Voglimacci, interview.
"Unsavory": Van de Kerckhove, interview.
"Instinctual distrust": Duprez, interview.
"He knew how to show modesty": Lepers, interview.
Lepers background: Lepers, interview.
"Oh Jeannine": Voglimacci, interview.
Phillips escape: Ibid.
Battle of Britain: Deighton, pp. 217–23.
Lanselle background: Alfred Lanselle, interview.
Burbure network: Elisa Salingue, interview.
"Monsieur Paul": Ibid.
New suit: Voglimacci, interview.
Peugeot 302 sedan: Lepers, interview.
Printer Jean Chevalier: Duprez, *Même combat*, pp. 32–33.
Christmas dinner: Marguerite Duprez, interview.
55 avenue Bernadette: Deram, interview.
Convoy January 6: Ibid.
Cold wave: *Echo du Nord*, January 6, 1941, p. 1.
Headlines: Ibid.
Voyage south: Lepers, interview.
Murchie description: Lepers, interview; Jean Gemahling, interview.
Meeting with Garrow: Lepers, interview.

7 *"A Great Devil of a Scotsman"*

"Reconciled dour determination": Brome, p. 35.
Garrow background: Foot and Langley, Darling, Brome, Caskie, passim.
"You Have Asked for Death": Foot and Langley, p. 66.
British consulates closed: National Archives, 740.00114 EW 1939/1012.
Dodds and Dean: National Archives, Diplomatic Branch, 125.5833/316: "List of Officers and Employees of American Consulate, Marseilles (Nov. 1940).
"A good deal of criticism": Ibid.
"A small neat place.": Neave, *Exits*, p. 125.
Caskie background: Caskie, passim.

Marseilles description: Fry, p. 21.

"France had fallen": Caskie, p. 21.

"The poor dregs of humanity": Fullerton, National Archives, Diplomatic Branch, 740.00114 EW 1939/910.

"Footsore and bleary-eyed": Caskie, p. 26.

"An hour spent in the club": Langley, p. 101.

"Louis amazed me": Neave, *Saturday*, p. 134.

"A great devil of a Scotsman": Nouveau, p. 96.

"Still had whiskey": Ibid.

Nouveau financing: Nouveau, pp. 97–107.

Rodocanachis background: Long, Chap. 1.

"All the old fraudulent and ingenious systems": Ibid, p. 37.

Neighborhood of ill repute: Nouveau, p. 124.

"Immense straw hat": Ibid.

"Tipperary": Nouveau, p. 109.

8 *"The Antithesis of the Scarlet Pimpernel"*

Carpentier background: Duprez, *Même combat*, pp. 25–31; Anne-Marie Chedeville, interview; "L'Eglise à Abbeville," June 1983, p. 2; Documentation provided by Philippe Duclercq of Abbeville.

"An instant dislike": Wake, pp. 49–50.

"He was always on the defensive": Caskie, p. 64.

"Only by kicking": Nouveau, p. 125.

Stove incident: Voglimacci, interview.

Breakdown incident: Marguerite Duprez, interview.

Tandem bicycle: Voglimacci, interview.

"Improvisationist": Jean Voglimacci, interview.

"Nothing but good": Higginson, interview.

"Petrified and perspiring": Ibid.

Highly favorable reports: Langley, cited by Neave, *Saturday*, p. 83.

Darling background: Darling, *Secret*, pp. 9–30; Foot, *MI9*, p. 44.

"The antithesis of the Scarlet Pimpernel": Darling, *Secret*, pp. 31–32.

9 *"Rumor, Suspicion, and Intrigue"*

Development of Garrow organization: Brome, Nouveau, Darling, Foot et al., passim.

"Rumor, Suspicion, and Intrigue": National Archives, 704.00114 EW 1939/910.

"British secret service agents": Ibid.

"In great anxiety": National Archives, 740.00114 EW 1939/1012.

"Admitted with some embarrassment": Ibid.

"Make suitable inquiries": Ibid.

"Show them in one by one": Daniel Benedite, interview.

"The police must be aware": National Archives, 740.00114 EW 1939/1012.

"Discussion of the scandal": Ibid.

"It is quite normal": Ibid.

"No evidence": Ibid.

"Whether or not Dean was involved": Ibid.

"The object of renewed suspicion": National Archives, 740.00114 EW 1939/1286.

10   *"We Thought He Had a Mission"*

"Indescribable brutes": Caskie, p. 25–26.

La Daurade and Vincillione: Fullerton, National Archives, 740.00114 EW 1939/1012; André Bénédite, Jean Gemahling, interview; Guerisse, interview.

Eight thousand francs per man: Fry, p. 165.

Fullerton informed: Guerisse, interview.

James Smith: Statement by James Smith to British Intelligence, 1945.

"Elaborate love life": Darling, *Secret*, p. 32.

"A wide boy": Ibid., p. 54.

Cole circle in Marseilles: Archives Nationales, Dossier Rhone, "Police allemande à Lyon pendant la guerre et ses auxiliaires français." pp. 16–36. Notes from 1942 interrogations of Cole and others by the Direction de la Surveillance du Territoire (DST).

Royer, Peltret backgrounds: Marguerite Royer, Gaston Peltret, interviews.

"When Cole arrived": Royer, op cit.

Peltret assignment, arrest: Peltret, op cit.

Cole introduced Dupuis to Seagrim: Archives Nationales, Ref. 72AJ 169, Dossier Nord A, I-2, "Reseau F-2."

Marie-Louise Gallet: Statement by Maurice Dechaumont, Archives Nationales, Ref. 72AJ 169, Dossier Nord A, I-10.

Carpentier intelligence: Letter transcribed in Nouveau, pp. 444–48.

Duprez collection of documents: Duprez, *Même combat*, p. 78.

"Documents . . . never reached Marseilles": Carpentier letter in Nouveau, pp. 447–48.

11 *"Escapers Don't Win Wars"*

"Metropolitan young gentlemen": Hugh Trevor-Roper, cited in Andrew, p. 461.

"Crooks and fantasists": Read and Fisher, p. 143.

"A complete shambles": West, *MI6*, p. 196.

"None . . . was prepared": Cookridge, p. 10.

Intelligence 1940 to 1941: West, Andrew, Cookridge, Read and Fisher, others.

View of MI9: Foot and Langley; Read and Fisher.

"An utter shit": Quoted by Read and Fisher, p. 12.

"The only real professional": Ibid.

"What Dansey wanted done": Foot and Langley, p. 43.

Z Organization: Read and Fisher, passim.

Crockatt background: Foot and Langley, pp. 33–44.

"Natural grace of bearing": Ibid., p. 34.

"A sort of John Buchan hero": Susan Broomhall, interview.

"Escapers don't win wars": Read and Fisher, p. 255.

"Determined to prevent evaders": Foot and Langley, p. 42.

"Set Europe ablaze": Cookridge, p. 1.

"Dansey could have broken Crockatt": Foot and Langley, p. 43.

"Petrified": Cited by Read and Fisher, p. 264.

"Theoretically you will be on loan": Langley, p. 133.

"A sideshow": Read and Fisher, p. 269.

A "brilliant" job: Garrow, cited by Guerisse, interview.

"Strong personalities": Read and Fisher, p. 268.

12 *"This Chap Was Running a Racket"*

Guerisse-Cole encounter: Guerisse, interview.

"Effervescent": Higginson, interview.

"O'Leary always dominates": Neave, *Saturday*, p. 314.

Guerisse background: Guerisse, interviews; *Who's Who* (Britain) 1983; *Veritor*, Vol. 3, No. 1, pp. 10–13.

"Drink too much": National Archives, 740.00114 EW 1939/1296.

"All the conditions": Guerisse, op. cit..

"Brilliant agent": Ibid.

Guerisse escape: Guerisse, op. cit; Brome, pp. 25–33.

"We were expecting you": Guerisse, op. cit.

Cole and Postel-Vinay: André Postel-Vinay, interview.

Cole and Winskill: Archie Winskill, interview.

13   *"He Just Didn't Give a Damn"*

Bomber raid: Crowley-Milling, interview.

"Running battle in": Ibid.

IFF: Deighton, pp. 60, 118.

MI9 advice: Foot and Langley, Chaps. IV, V, passim.

Escape-evasion statistics: Ibid., pp. 310–11.

Whitney Straight: Neave, *Saturday*, p. 89.

Tom Slack: MI9 report provided to MIS-X, available on microfilm from Albert F. Simpson Historical Research Center, Maxwell AFB, Alabama. Roll 1852, Series 142.76214.

"Twenty-five miles, jolly nearly": Crowley-Milling, op. cit.

Crowley-Milling trip: Ibid.

"A man who liked women": Lepers, interview.

"Affairs everywhere": Van de Kerckhove, interview.

"Like the edge of a knife": Huyge, interview.

Scene in studio: Huyge, Voglimacci, interviews.

Escape of Tobin and Edgar: James Tobin, interview; Young, pp. 39–52.

"Good food, fine wine": Young, p. 60.

Warenghem background: Young, passim; DST report 1944.

"Very much attached": Guerisse, interview.

14   *"He Was Being Closely Watched"*

Smith arrest: Smith statement to British intelligence, 1945.

De Fligué background: Simone Alix De Fligué, interview; DST report.

Holweck background: Jacques Holweck, interview; DST report.

Bernaer background: DST report.

"Established contact with Commandant d'Honicthun": DST report.

"Flattered": Young, p. 62.

Cole boyhood tale: Young, p. 63.

"Started wondering": Lepers, interview.

"Half a man": Caskie (original edition), p. 91.

"He was spending far more money": Guerisse, *Veritor*, Vol. 3, No. 1, pp. 10–13.

"I'm starting to lose confidence": Marguerite Duprez, interview.

"A passable amount of champagne": Voglimacci, interview.

"An air of mystery": Lepers, interview.

"Something that didn't square": Lanselle, interview.

Huyge in Toulouse: Huyge, interview.

"Duped many": Duprez, *Même combat*, pp. 50–51.

Garrow letter: Ibid., p. 79–81.

Polish flier: Ibid., p. 81–82; Duprez, interviews.

German police car: Ibid.

Meeting with British Intelligence: Duprez, op. cit, interviews. Catrice seems to have confirmed this in a 1946 statement to the Comité d'histoire de la deuxième guerre mondiale. He says that his group sent word of Cole's actions "to the Deuxième Bureau at the very moment when two of its members were coming to a meeting already set with the Intelligence Service."

15 *"I Decided Cole Needed Killing"*

Dance hall episode: Guerisse, interview.

"I had discovered": Letter from Garrow to Darling of May 4, 1965. In Long, p. 124.

Guerisse to north: Guerisse, op. cit.

"They disappeared": Marguerite Duprez, interview.

Lepers assignment: Lepers, interview.

Verloop and Henriette: Verloop, interview; Michel Rousseau, "Deux réseaux britanniques dans la région du Nord: Le réseau 'Garrow-Pat O'Leary' et le réseau 'Farmer,'" *Revue d'histoire de la deuxième guerre mondiale*, No. 135 (1984), pp. 87–108.

"Everywhere there were women": Verloop, op. cit.

"Norwegians, Americans": Ibid.

Lille Abwehrstelle: Archives Nationales, Ref. 72AJ 169, Dossier Nord

A, III-12: "L'Abwehr III-F de Lille, 1940–44"; Verloop deposition, Dossier Nord A, II-10.

"The most superb collection": Ibid.

Verloop aliases: Archives Nationales, Dossier Nord A, I-2.

"Everyone has a weakness": Verloop, interview.

16 *"Everyone Seemed to Look Up to Him"*

Newspaper articles: *Echo du Nord,* October 22, 1941, p. 1.

"Hitler and Goering": Neave, *Saturday,* p. 303.

Verloop arrests: Rousseau, op. cit.

George Barclay evasion: Barclay, pp. 141–74.

17 *"He Is Terribly Dangerous"*

"Having the right sympathies": Guerisse, interview.

Garrow in Fort Saint-Nicolas: Garrow, op. cit.

Confrontation with Cole: Guerisse, op. cit.

"He is terribly dangerous": Ibid.

Dowding to north: Ibid.

Carpentier letter: Young, p. 69.

"A bit of a row": Ibid., p. 71.

Cole arrest: Deram, Verloop, interviews.

"That's not hers": Deram, op. cit.

18 *"A Monster of Cowardice and Weakness"*

"He started to tell us everything": Verloop, interview.

Search of Duprez house: Marguerite Duprez-Beylemans, interview.

Death of François Duprez: Ibid; Letter to Marguerite Duprez from Maurice Jones, former prisoner at Sonnenburg, dated July 10, 1945.

"An immediate hecatomb": Hegedos, Archives Nationales, op. cit.

Arrests of Didry, Lanselle: Alfred Lanselle, interview.

"Paul has escaped": Deram, interview.

"I'm not going anywhere": Guerisse, interview.

"We don't have any papers": Anne-Marie Chedeville, interview.

Dowding at Carpentier home: Brome, pp. 57–58; Nouveau, p. 155. Carpentier's prison letters, excerpted in Nouveau's appendix, don't refer to

Dowding's presence, but Nouveau conjectures this omission was deliberate in case the missive was intercepted.

"Ignobly betrayed": Carpentier letter from prison dated March 3, 1942, excerpted in Nouveau, pp. 444–48.

Arrests in Burbure: Elisa Salingue, interview and correspondence.

Dechaumont arrest: Dechaumont, op. cit.

"Jeer and ridicule": Carpentier, op. cit.

Execution of Carpentier, others: Fossier, p. 359.

19 *"Meet My New Boss"*

"I want you to explain": Young, p. 103.

Warenghem at de Fligué's: Simone de Fligué, interview.

Arrest of de Fligué, Holweck: Young, pp. 104–6; Lyon DST report.

Cole meets Bernaer: DST report.

Bernaer held money: *Rapport au chef de l'état français*, secretariat d'état à la guerre, September 29, 1942.

Warenghem movements: Young, pp. 71–74.

"Had an accident": Ibid., p. 73.

Cole's version: Ibid., p. 75.

"In a state of collapse": Lyon DST report.

Postel-Vinay arrest: Postel-Vinay, interview.

Cole, Warenghem escape: Young, pp. 76–79.

"Faites gaffe!": Verloop, interview.

20 *"Who Are You, Really?"*

Guerisse to north: Guerisse, interview.

"Who are you?": Voglimacci, interview.

"Where has Mason gone?": Guerisse, op. cit.

Letters from Carpentier: Voglimacci, op. cit.

Carpentier in Loos: Voglimacci, op. cit.; Dupres, *Même combat*, pp. 24–31.

Carpentier and Voglimacci: Voglimacci, op. cit.

Letter from Cole: Ibid.

Cole in Paris: Young, pp. 79–85.

21 *"I Swear I'll Cure Him"*

"For God's sake": Higginson, interview.

"I sent a detailed letter": Darling, *Secret*, pp. 34–35.

"The power of life and death": Read and Fisher, p. 11.

"Kill him": Ibid., p. 266.

"Kill them.": Ibid., p. 284.

"Cole was not only an embezzler": Darling, *Secret*, p. 54.

"If God is just": Darling, *Secret*, letter reproduced preceding p. 65.

"The evidence was there": Guerisse, interview.

Discussions in Gibraltar: Ibid.

Nouveau in Geneva: Nouveau, pp. 164–82.

Whittinghill background: *Who's Who; Biographic Register of the Department of State*, October 1, 1945, p. 310.

"It had taken over a year": Darling, *Secret*, p. 58.

22 *"His True Identity Was Established"*

Cole and Warenghem: Young, pp. 82–93.

Witnesses: Certificate of religious marriage, dated April 10, 1942.

"A real charmer": Young, p. 93.

Warenghem missions: Ibid, pp. 107–12.

"Please forgive me": Ibid, pp. 126–31.

Visit to Whittinghill: Guerisse, interview.

41 thousand francs: *Rapport au chef de l'état français,* p. 1.

Guerisse trip: Guerisse, op. cit.

BMA, Travaux Ruraux: Stead, pp. 36–61; Cluseau, Capitaine, "L'Arrestation du Deuxième Bureau"; *Revue d'histoire de la deuxième guerre mondiale*, No. 29, January 1958, pp. 32–48.

"Search its prisons": Steadman, p. 43.

Triffe background: Robert Sheppard, interview.

Warenghem in jail: Ibid.

"Successively claimed": Lyon DST report.

"The names of Frenchmen": *Rapport au chef de l'état français,* p. 4.

Plan to betray Warenghem: Young, pp. 114–15.

Sheppard and Triffe: Sheppard, op. cit.

Cole-Warenghem meeting: Young, pp. 117–19.

"Good acting, wasn't it?": Ibid, p. 122.

"Unstable and an adventuress: Lyon DST report.

"Cynicism and refinement": *Rapport au chef de l'état français,* p. 5.

Cole condemned to death: *"Jugement rendu par le tribunal militaire permanent de la 14ème division militaire,"* No. 6814, July 21, 1942.

"Listened without emotion": Ibid.

23 *"He Was Backing a Losing Cause"*

Warenghem out of prison: Young, pp. 125–35.

Guerisse certainty: Guerisse, interview.

Birth of Alain Warenghem: Birth certificate, Marseilles.

Child's ill health: Young, op. cit.

Death of Alain Warenghem: Death certificate, Marseilles.

Sheppard-Cole meeting: Sheppard, interview.

Sheppard escape: Ibid.

Garrow escape: Guerisse, interviews; Brome, pp. 144–52.

Escape line flourishing: Guerisse, op. cit.; Brome, passim.

Le Neveu: Brome, pp. 168–201.

"A certificate of courage": Nouveau, p. 389.

Guerisse deportation: Brome, passim: Guerisse, op. cit.

Sentence commuted: Annotations, *Jugement.*

Montron, Compiegne: Entry, MIS-X Section, Decimal File, "383 Conduct of War w/Relation to Persons (Atrocities, etc.)," U.S. National Archives; Annual Index to Foreign Office General Correspondence, 1944.

"Posing as a guide": Fuller, *Double*, p. 74.

"A runner": Hope, op. cit.

Warenghem to England: *Sunday Mirror*, February 12, 1956.

Sicherheitsdienst ascendancy: Foot, *SOE*, p. 116; Cookridge, p. 132c.

"Dredged its way": Cookridge, p. 132.

Kieffer background: Kieffer SS file, Berlin Document Center; Foot, *SOE*, p. 119.

Kieffer/Sicherheitsdienst: Technically, Kieffer's Amt IVE was part of the Gestapo, or Geheime Staatspolizei, the entire Amt IV of the Reichssicherheitshauptamt, or RSHA. But as Foot points out (*SOE*, p. 118): "Arguments about the distinctions and resemblances between the Gestapo and the SD (Sicherheitsdienst) are as valueless as the old disputes about how many angels can dance on the point of a pin. The practical point is that they worked, from an allied agent's point of view, as one." Furthermore,

Major Kieffer wore an SD flash on the forearm of his uniform, according to a Belgian informant present in the SD offices on the avenue Foch during 1943. (U.S. National Archives, Record Group 165, G-2 Regional File 1933–44, France, Box 983, Item 6960.

"A modest and calm man": Delarue, p. 521.

Cole at avenue Foch: Fuller, *Double*, p. 74.

"Hundreds of trucks": Galtier-Boissière, *Journal*, in Pryce-Jones, p. 198.

Retreat into Belgium: Darling, *Secret*, pp. 195–96.

"A losing cause": Report of Investigation, U.S. Army Criminal Investigation Division, File No. 6th-CID-3001, (1953), p. 5. (N.B. Successive reports in the U.S. Army investigation relating to Cole, issued in 1945, 1953, and 1954, bore different file references. For simplicity I will refer to the overall file as 6th-CID-3001, giving the year where relevant.

24 *"The Widest Latitude to Operate"*

Cole at war's end: Cole statement, June 17, 1945, from 6th-CID-3001.

VI Corps progress: National Archives, Record Group 94, Box No. 3600: 206-0.3/HQ, VI Corps, After Action Report, 1-31 May 1945.

"Unending reports": National Archives, Record Group 331, Box 162, Entry 242-A: 6th Army Group 314.7, Final Report G-2 Section HQ 12th Army Group 1945, p. 23.

"Completely slashed": G-3 Final Report, HQ 6th Army Group, 1 July 1945 U.S. National Archives, Record Group 94, Box 1743, Folder 99/06-3.

Nearly 79 thousand prisoners: Ibid.

117th Cavalry Reconnaissance Squadron: U.S. National Archives, Record Group 94, World War II Operations Reports, Cavs-117-0.7, Box No. 18304; Cavs-117-0.3, Box 18286; Cavs-117-HQ-0.1, Box 18308, History - Hq & Service Troop - 117th Cav. Rcn. Sqd. (Mecz), 1 April 1944 - 31 Oct. 1945; Interviews with Harold J. Samsel, James Shenk, Mario J. Zecca, Robert Robbins et al.

"Two thousand fully armed Germans": Robbins, interview.

Snowfalls May 1, 2: U.S. National Archives, Record Group 94, Box 18308, "History - Troop B - 117th Cavalry Rcn Squadron (Mecz).

Mason identity: Cole, CID, op. cit.

"Bulgarians": Robbins, op. cit.

Moore background: Oscar Andre, correspondence; National Archives,

Diplomatic Branch, Nos. 851.247/25, 857.247/81, 857.247/82; Samsel, Shenk, Zecca, interviews.

"A little bit different": Robbins, op. cit.

"An amazing character": Zecca, op. cit.

Colonel Don W. Dixon: Cole, CID, op. cit; VI Corps documents.

Costello, Martin, 206 CIC: Cole did not specify which CIC unit handled his case, but the 206th was then attached to VI Corps Headquarters.

Uniform, revolver, money: Cole, CID, op. cit.

Kieffer plans, execution: Hope, interview; Foot, *SOE*, p. 305.

Douglas Chandler: National Archives, Record Group 94, Box No. 3600, 206-0.3: HQ VI Corps - After Action Report, 1–31 May 1945.

Meets LePage: Cole, CID, op. cit.

Model V170 Mercedes: Anton Kneussle statement, CID, op. cit.

Cole proposal: Fernand LePage statement, CID, op. cit.

To Heimertingen: Cole, CID, op. cit.

Rubber stamps: Ibid.

"The above officer": Ibid.

"A forgotten corner": H. Rex Smith, interview.

Displaced persons in French Zone: Hillel, p. 97.

Third Battalion, Ninth Zouaves Regiment: Jacques Dureng de Maisonneuve statement, CID, op. cit.

"Working as much for the English": Camille Allart, interview.

"Commanding presence": Ibid.

"The widest latitude to operate": Summary (1953), CID, op. cit.

Cole, Dureng to jail: Dureng, CID, op. cit.

Cole offer to Dureng: Ibid.

25   *"The March of Prisoners Began"*

Cole description: Anton Kneussle statement, CID, op. cit.

"Ardent look": Maria Hanft statement, CID, op. cit.

"Mutually valuable information": Pierre Laze statement, CID, op. cit.

"A trifle strange": Ibid.

"Always coming in person": Adolphe Kieffer statement, CID, op. cit.

Allart uniform: Allart, interview.

"Put them in his pocket": Ibid.

"In the event of dispersal": Cole, CID, op. cit.

Dureng background: Dureng, CID, op. cit; Roger Trarieux, Dr. Yves Aigueberse, interviews.

Hanft background: Hanft statement, CID, op. cit; Dureng, CID, op. cit.

Confiscated items: Ibid.

"Other Allied officers": Dureng, CID, op. cit.

"Somebody bring me a carbine": Franz Widenmann statement, CID, op. cit.

LePage threats: Anton Kneussle, CID, op. cit.

"Extremely brutal gestures": Ibid.

"The march of prisoners": Ibid.

Between forty and fifty: Ibid.

"A most violent nature": Else Kneussle statement, CID, op. cit.

"Nefarious interrogations": Summary (1953), CID, op. cit.

Krug interrogation: Eugen Krug statement, CID, op. cit.

"How do you do?": Frank L. Lillyman statement, CID, op. cit.

"Do you know how to box?": Anton Kneussle, CID, op. cit.

"Mason would start": Dureng, CID, op. cit.

"Threw up his hands": William King Richardson statement, CID, op. cit.

26 *"I Decided to Bump Him Off"*

In *The New York Times*: New York Times, June 8, 1944.

Lillyman background: Jane Beebe Lillyman, interview.

Lillyman assignment: Lillyman, Richardson, CID, op. cit.

"Bloody": Lillyman interrogation (1954), CID, op. cit..

"Quite a bit of thought": Lillyman, CID, op. cit.

"Anything that struck his fancy": Ibid.

"Mason backhanded her": Lillyman, CID, op. cit.

"Pounded about the body": Ibid.

Overstepped his OSS brief: The 1945 summary of 6-CI-3001 states that "Neither of above officers (Lillyman and Richardson) were authorized to conduct security investigations."

"Chasing war criminals": Jane Beebe Lillyman, op. cit.

"Military embarrassment": Lillyman, CID, op. cit.

Surreptitiously inspected credentials: Ibid.

"Dubious about Captain Mason": Edward O. Smith statement, CID, op. cit.

"Full authority": Ibid.

"In the pipeline": Richardson, CID, op. cit.

"Practically never left": Dureng, CID, op. cit.

"Took the initiative": Ibid.

"Prowess": Louis J. Desantis statement, CID, op. cit.

"Prisoners whipped": Adolphe Kiefer statement, CID, op. cit.

"Looking for thrills": H. Rex Smith, interview.

"Atrocities, arrests": Summary, 6-CI-3001 (1953).

"Cry out and even howl": Anton Kneussle, CID, op. cit.

Gunshots: Ibid.

"A big Nazi pig": Else Kneussle, CID, op. cit.

Blood-soaked clothing: Maria Hanft statement, CID, op. cit.

"Constant fear": Summary, 6-CI-3001 (1953).

"Nothing more to learn": Dureng, CID, op. cit.

Murder sequence: Dureng, Lillyman, Allart, Cole statements, CID, op. cit.; Allart, interview.

Hanfts' last meeting: Allart, CID, op. cit.

"Degenerated": Dureng, CID, op. cit.

"Proceed with the execution": Allart, CID, op. cit.

"Proposing to bump him off": Lillyman, CID, op. cit.

"Poor little bastard": Lillyman interrogation, 1954.

27 *"You're Cole, Aren't You?"*

"One of those at the top": Hope, interview.

"Arch-traitor": *The Daily Mail*, January 10, 1946.

"A thug": J. A. Cole, p. 243.

Hope background: *Who's Who*; Hope statement, CID, op. cit; West, *MI5*, p. 171.

Spooner background: Adamson, passim.

"Pushed out into the field": Hope, op. cit.

Description, aliases: Index card, microfilm copy held by U.S. Army Security and Intelligence Command.

Joyce arrest: J. A. Cole, pp. 238–49.

"Cherie": Neave, *Saturday*, p. 310.

Eager to share this news: Sylvia Guerisse, interview. Other versions would have that the woman brought the letter to controvert the allegations against

Cole. But Mrs. Guerisse, with whom I spoke of this once before her death in 1984, said the woman was uninformed of the charges.

"From Mason's own lips": François Finas statement, CID, op. cit.

"Conflicts . . . settled": Dureng, CID, op. cit.

General Nicholls: Ibid.

Guests at dinner: Ibid.

"Ill at ease": Anton Kneussle, CID, op. cit.

Smith misgivings: Edward O. Smith, CID, op. cit.

Visit to airstrip: Desantis statement, CID, op. cit.

"Considerable astonishment": Hope, op. cit.

Cole interrogation: Ibid.

"My true sentiments": Cole, CID, op. cit.

28   "The King's Enemies"

Investigation launched: 6th-CID-3001 (1945) p. 3.

Hanft body found: Clemens Haas, Rosa Hirsch, Maria Diebold statements, CID, op. cit.

Graveside episode: Adolphe Kiefer statement, CID, op. cit.

Recriminations: Ibid.

"Three eye witnesses": 6th-CID-3001 (1945), p. 1. Mulcahy's recommendations were deleted from the 1945 report before it was released to the author.

Lillyman at Pennsylvania Hotel: Jane Beebe Lillyman, interview: *New York Times*, November 15, 16, 24, 1945 *Life*, December 3, 1945.

"Hot scrap iron": *New York Times*, November 15, 1945.

"Thoroughly re-investigate": 6th-CID-3001 (1953).

Smith conclusion: Ibid.

Non lieu: 6th-CID-3001 (1954), p. 2.

Lillyman re-interrogation: CID, op. cit.

Lepers identification: Lepers, interview.

Cole transfer: Hope, interview.

Cooper: *Times*, December 4, 5, 8, 1945; R. West, pp. 151–156. 4, 5, 8 December 1945.

Schurch: *Times*, September 18, 1945; R. West, p. 148; Entry in National Archives, Record Group 332, MIS-X Section, Decimal File, "383 Conduct of War W/Relation to Persons (Atrocities, etc.)."

Baillie-Stewart: *Times*, November 3, 1945; R. West, pp. 228–41.

Joyce: J. A. Cole, R. West, passim.

Amery: *Times*, July 30, September 9, October 18, November 29, December 20, 1945; R. West, pp. 211–27.

"Far too much sense": R. West, p. 144.

"Daily grew more drunken": Ibid, p. 155.

"Dropping down the ladder": Cited in R. West, p. 144.

29 *"A Fantastic Chain of Events"*

"Wanted him like mad": Hope, interview.

"Lay there": Brome, p. 257.

Cole escape: Adamson, p. 152.

Dragnet: *Daily Mail*, January 10, 1946.

Description: File card, microfilm copy held by U.S. Army Security and Intelligence Command, Fort George C. Meade, Maryland.

Avis de recherche: Copy provided by Edmond Lévy.

178 licensed brothels: *Stars and Stripes*, European Edition, January 11, 1946.

"Chicago-sur-Seine": H. Rex Smith, interview.

"Spree of lawlessness": *Stars and Stripes*, European Edition, November 19, 1945.

"Monsieur Harry": Pauline Herveau, interview.

Shootout: Edmond Lévy, correspondence and interview; *Le Parisien Libéré*, January 10, 12, 1946; *France-Soir*, January 11, 1946; *Paris-Presse*, January 10, 1946.

"Have some champagne": *Daily Mail*, op. cit.

Guerisse identification: Guerisse, interview.

Burial: Certificat d'Inhumation, Ville de Paris, Cimetière Parisien de Thiais, May 15, 1985; Letter of July 24, 1985 from Guy Defarge, Chief, Bureau des Cimetières, Ville de Paris.

"Whole way of treating this guy": H. Rex Smith, interview.

Duprez account: Henri Duprez, interview.

Lanselle theory: Lanselle, interview.

News item: *Daily Mail*, November 17, 1945.

"A weak man": Lepers, interview.

"Greatness went": R. West, p. 228.

Selective Bibliography

For simplification, all relevant periodical and documentary references are contained in the notes.

Adamson, Iain, *The Great Detective; A Life of Deputy Commander Reginald Spooner of Scotland Yard*. London: Frederick Muller Limited, 1966.

Andrew, Christopher, *Secret Service; The Making of the British Intelligence Community*. London: William Heinemann Ltd., 1985.

Barclay, George, *Fighter Pilot: A Self Portrait*. London: William Kimber, 1976.

Bénédite, Daniel, *La Filière Marseillaise*. Paris: Éditions Clancier Guénaud, 1984.

Besant, Walter, *Shoreditch and the East End*. London: Adam and Charles Black, 1908.

Bishop, Edward, *The Battle of Britain*. London: George Allen and Unwin Ltd., 1960.

Braddon, Russell, *Nancy Wake: The Thrilling True Story of a Great War Heroine*. London: Pan Books Ltd., 1958.

Brome, Vincent, *The Way Back: The Story of Lieut. Commander Pat O'Leary*. London, Cassell & Co. Ltd., 1958.

Brown, Anthony Cave, *Bodyguard of Lies*. New York: Bantam, 1976.

Cardigan, The Earl of, *I Walked Alone*. London: Routledge & Kegan Paul Ltd., 1950.

Caskie, Donald, *The Tartan Pimpernel*. Basingstoke, Hants: Marshall Morgan & Scott, 1984.

————, *The Tartan Pimpernel*. London: Oldbourne Book Co., 1957.

Cobban, Alfred, *A History of Modern France*. London: Penguin, 1982.

Cole, J. A., *Lord Haw-Haw & William Joyce*. New York: Farrar, Strauss, Giroux, 1964.

Collier, Richard, *1940: The World in Flames*. Harmondsworth: Penguin Books, 1980.

Cookridge, E. H., *Inside SOE*. London: Arthur Barker Ltd., 1966.

————, *Set Europe Ablaze*. New York: Thomas Y. Crowell Company, 1967.

Crockatt, Norman, *MI9 War Diary*. Unpublished, 1946; Copy held by Public Records Office, Kew.

Darling, Donald, *Secret Sunday*. London: William Kimber, 1975.

————, *Sunday at Large*. London, William Kimber, 1977.

Debergh, Francois and Jean Piquet, *Carrefour des Invasions*. Paris: Editions France-Empire, 1966.

Deighton, Len, *Fighter: The True Story of the Battle of Britain*. London: Triad/Granada, 1979.

Delarue, Jacques, *Histoire de la Gestapo*. Paris: Fayard, 1962.

Devlin, Gerard M., *Paratrooper!* New York: St. Martin's Press, 1979.

Dumez, Natalis, *Le Mensonge Reculera*. Lille: Imprimerie F. Planquart, 1946.

Duprez, Henri, *1940–1945 Même combat dans l'ombre et la lumière; Épisodes de la résistance dans le nord de la France*. Paris: La Pensée Universelle, 1979.

Ellis, Major L. F., *The War in France and Flanders, 1939–1940*. London: H. M. Stationery Office, 1953.

Evans, A. J., *The Escaping Club*. Harmondsworth: Penguin, 1939.

Farago, Ladislas, *The Game of the Foxes*. New York: David McKay Company, 1971.

Foot, M. R. D., *SOE in France*. London: H. M. Stationery Office, 1966.

———— and J. M. Langley, *MI9: Escape and Evasion 1939–1945*. London: The Bodley Head, 1979.

Fossier, Jean-Marie, *Zone Interdite, Nord-Pas de Calais*. Paris: Editions Sociales, 1977.

Fry, Varian, *Surrender on Demand*. New York: Random House, 1945.

Fuller, Jean Overton, *Double Agent*. London: Pan Books Ltd., 1961.

————, *The German Penetration of SOE*. London: William Kimber, 1975.

————, *Madeleine*. London: Victor Gollancz, Ltd., 1952.

————, *The Starr Affair*. London: Victor Gollancz, Ltd., 1954.

Gaillard, Lucien, *Marseille sous l'occupation*. Rennes: Ouest-France, 1982.

Garby-Czerniawski, Roman, *The Big Network*. London: George Ronald, 1961.

Garder, Michel, *La Guerre Secrète des Services Spéciaux Français (1933–1945)*. Paris: Plon, 1967.

Giskes, Hermann, *London Calling North Pole*. London: William Kimber, 1953.

Gleeson, James, *They Feared No Evil*. London: White Lion, 1976.

Gulbenkian, Nubar, *Pantaraxia*. London: Hutchinson, 1965.

Hillel, Marc, *L'Occupation française en Allemagne, 1945–1949*. Paris: Balland, 1983.

Hinsley, F. H., *British Intelligence in the Second World War*. London: H. M. Stationery Office, 1979.

Horne, Alistair, *To Lose a Battle; France 1940*. Harmondsworth: Penguin, 1982.

Huguen, Roger, *Par les Nuits les Plus Longues; Réseaux d'Evasion d'Aviateurs en Bretagne*. Saint-Brieuc: Les Presses Bretonnes, 1976.

Karslake, Basil, *1940: The Last Act*. London: Leo Cooper, 1979.

Krausnick, Helmut and Martin Broszat, *Anatomy of the SS State*. London: Granada Publishing Ltd., 1970.

Landry, Gérard, *Lille-Roubaix-Tourcoing sous l'occupation*. Rennes: Ouest-France, 1982.

Lane, John, *Escapers All*. London: The Bodley Head, 1932.

Langley, J. M., *Fight Another Day*. London: Collins Ltd., 1974.

Long, Helen, *Safe Houses Are Dangerous*. London: William Kinber, 1985.

Mabille de Poncheville, A., *Lille-en-Flandre*. Paris: La Renaissance du Livre, 1936.

Marshall, Bruce, *The White Rabbit*. London: Pan Books, Ltd., 1954.

Michelin & Cie, *Lille, Before and During the War*. Clermont-Ferrand: Michelin & Cie, 1919.

Moorehead, Alan, *The Traitors*. London: Hamish Hamilton, 1952.

Neave, Airey, *Saturday at MI9*. London: Hodder & Stoughton, 1969.

————, *They Have Their Exits*. London: Hodder & Stoughton, 1953.

Nicholas, Elizabeth, *Death Be Not Proud*. White Lion, 1958.

Nouveau, Louis, *Des capitaines par milliers*. Paris: Calmann-Lévy, 1958.

Pierrard, Pierre, *Histoire de Lille*. Paris: Mazarine, 1982.

————, *Lille; dix siecles d'histoire*. La Madeleine: Editions Actica, 1972.

Pierrard, Pierre, *Lille et les Lillois*. Paris: Bloud et Gay, 1967.

Pryce-Jones, David, *Paris in the Third Reich*. New York: Holt, Rinehart and Winston, 1981.

Read, Anthony and David Fisher, *Colonel Z, The Secret Life of a Master of Spies*. London: Hodder & Stoughton, 1984.

Rebatet, Lucien, *Les Mémoires d'un Fasciste*. Paris: Pauvert, 1976.

Remy, Col, *La Résistance Dans La Nord*. Genève: Editions Famot, 1974.

Riordan, Thomas M. J., *A History of the 7th Field Company RE, 1939–1946*. Strensoll, York: T. M. J. Riordan, 1984.

Ryder, Rowland, *Edith Cavell*. London: Hamish Hamilton, 1975.

Sayer, Ian and Douglas Botting, *Nazi Gold*. London: Panther Books, 1984.

Singer, Kurt, *Spies and Traitors of World War II*. New York: Prentice-Hall, 1945.

Sparrow, Gerald, *The Great Traitors*. London: John Long, 1965.

Spears, Major-General Sir Edward, *Assignment to Catastrophe, Vol. I; Prelude to Dunkirk July 1939–May 1940*. New York: A. A. Wyn, Inc., 1954.

Stead, Philip John, *Second Bureau*. London: Evans Brothers Limited, 1959.

Wake, Nancy, *The White House*. Melbourne: Macmillan, 1985.

Weightman, Gavin, *The Making of Modern London, 1815–1914*. London, Fidgwick & Jackson, 1984.

West, Nigel, *MI5*. London: Bodley Head, 1981.

————, *MI6*. London: Panther, 1985.

West, Rebecca, *The Meaning of Treason*. New York: The Viking Press, 1947.

Wheeler-Bennett, John, *Munich: Prologue to Tragedy*. New York: Viking Press, 1964.

Williams, Eric, *Great Escape Stories*. Harmondsworth: Penguin, 1958.

Young, Gordon, *In Trust & Treason*. London: Edward Hulton, 1959.

Index

Abwehr (German
  counterintelligence): in Lille, 32,
  131–33; and HC, 148–59, 165, 172,
  198–99; mentioned, 123, 200. See
  also GFP; Verloop, Cornelius
  Johannes Antonius
Allart, Camille, 215, 220, 231–33,
  244–47
Amery, John, 235, 252–53
Amy (priest), 181
Anderson, David, 136
Ayello, Raphaël, 85, 149–50

Baillie-Stewart, Norman, 250–51
Baldwin, Stanley, 2
Barbie, Klaus, 189, 193
Barclay, George, 136–40, 156
Battle of Britain, 47
Battle of France, 48
BEF. See British Expeditionary
  Force

Bernaer, Édouard, 118, 160–62
Berthier, Roger, 192
Biche, Jean, 184, 191
Billy's Bar (Paris), 257–58, 260, 263
Blavoux, André, 245
Blunt, Anthony, 6
BMA (Bureau of Anti-National
  Intrigues), 185
Bouchez, Octave, 136
Breuvert, Claudine (alias of Jeanne
  Huyge), 122
British and American Seamen's
  Mission. See Seamen's Mission
British Expeditionary Force: and
  HC, 6, 25–27, 88; as refugees in
  France, 30–37, 42, 79, 94, 108, 132;
  mentioned, 56
British Free Corps, 7, 235, 252–53
British Intelligence, 6. See also
  British Security Service; Secret
  Intelligence Service; MI9

British Museum, 35
British Security Service (MI5), 5, 235
British Union of Fascists, 250
Brown, John Henry Owen, 250
Buck (Sergeant), 28
Bufton, Harry, 138–39, 156
Burbure (France), 49
Bureau, Isabelle, 181, 182–83
Bureau of Anti-National Intrigues (BMA), 185

Canaris, Wilhelm Franz, 200
Carpenter (Sergeant), 255
Carpentier, Julia, 154
Carpentier, Pierre: as escape agent, 64–65, 68, 85–86, 102, 108, 116, 130; distrusts HC, 145–46, 172, 174–75; arrest of, 154–58, 167–69, 182
Cartier, Joseph (alias of Guerisse), 96, 100, 130, 167, 197
"Case of the Four" (Lille), 31
Caskie, Donald, 58–60, 66, 73–75, 77, 78, 113, 120
Catrice, Jean, 37, 124–25
Cavell, Edith, 31–32
Chandler, Douglas ("Paul Revere"), 209
Charlier, Leon, 135
Chevalier, Jean, 50, 123
Chevauchée (Captain), 212
Chôpe du Pont Neuf (Paris), 119, 139, 161, 162, 165, 170, 199
Churchill, Winston, 92
CIC (Counter Intelligence Corps— U.S. Army), 207–8, 210, 212, 228, 263
Cinquième Bureau (French Army intelligence), 101, 185, 186
Citadelle (Lille), 24, 27–28, 31
Codrington, John, 175, 178–79

Cole, Albert (HC's father), 10–12
Cole, Alice Ann Godfrey. See Godfrey, Alice Ann
Cole, Harold (HC): character, 4–6, 13, 41, 66–67, 220–24; military experience, 9–10, 14–21; criminal record, 10; youth, 10–14; aliases, 20, 37, 49, 184, 198, 205, 236; arrests and escapes, 23–28, 184–85, 248–49, 254–56; as head of La Madeleine escape network, 45–54, 141–45; as womanizer, 50, 81, 111–12; as British secret agent, 80, 84–87, 93–95, 205; and German intelligence, 145–59; marriage, 180–82; as Allied intelligence officer in Saulgau, 205–41; death, 257–59; rumors about his continued existence, 260–65. See also Aliases he used; Secret Intelligence Service
Cole, Paul (alias of HC): 37, 63, 71, 85, 97, 124–25, 177–78, 238
Colson, Captain (alias of HC), 37, 131, 136, 146, 236
Commissaire de la Surveillance du Territoire. See DST
Cooper, Thomas Haller, 250
Cooper Smith, Sylvia, 237–38
Costello, Harry, 207
Cotty, Raymond, 258
Counter Intelligence Corps. See CIC
Courlander, Roy Nicolas, 252–53
Courquin (priest), 121
Cresswell, Michael, 175
Crockatt, Norman R., 91–92
Crowley-Milling, Denis, 105, 107–10

Daily Mail, 259, 263–64
Damerment, Georges, 168, 201

Damerment, Madeleine, 156, 167, 169, 201
Dansey, Claude Edward Marjoribanks, 90–96, 173–74, 179, 264
Darling, Donald: and HC, 70–72, 81, 94, 95, 129, 173–75, 179, 237–38; mentioned, 92
Darnand, Joseph, 249
Daurade, La (Marseilles restaurant), 78–79
Dean, Arthur, 57, 75–77
Dean, August, 157
Dechaumont, Maurice ("X-10"), 85, 150, 157
de Cortes, Fabien, 198
de Fligué, Vladimir, 117–18, 159–62
de Gaulle, Charles, 46, 81, 170
Delarue, Jacques, 247
Delobel, Franck (alias of HC), 184
Delobel, Paul (alias of HC), 37, 39, 41, 118, 236
Delsol, Jean-Baptiste, 199
Deram, Joseph (alias of HC), 41–42, 184, 236
Deram, Madeleine Marie: as escape agent, 18, 28–29, 41–42, 44, 51, 137–38; and the Germans, 146–47, 154; mentioned, 67
Deram, Marcel, 29, 42, 51, 138
Desantis, Louis J., 240
d'Harcourt, Pierre, 101
d'Honicthun (Commandant), 118
Didry, Desiré, 107, 121, 153–54, 158
Dijon, Gaston, 58
Direction de la Surveillance du Territoire (DST), 122, 141, 184–89, 191, 193, 238
Dixon, Don W., 207–10
Dodds, Hugh, 57, 74–77

Dowding, Bruce, 113, 142–46, 152, 154–56, 158, 167–68, 182
DST (Direction de la Surveillance du Territoire), 122, 141, 184–89, 191, 193, 238
Dubois, Drotais, 49, 156, 158
Dufour, Maurice, 129–30
Duhayon, Marcel, 147, 158
Dumez, Natalis, 33
Duprez, François: as escape agent, 42–44, 47, 50, 68, 137; distrusts HC, 120, 130; HC's lies about, 97; confronts HC, 140, 146; arrest and death of, 151–53, 167, 169, 172
Duprez, Henri: as escape agent, 38–42, 45 46, 50, 86, 123–25, 261–62
Duprez, Marguerite, 44, 152–53, 166–67, 172
Dupuis, Eugène, 84
Durand, Armand, 135
Durand, Eugène, 119, 161, 199
Dureng de Maisonneuve, Jacques, 212–17, 219, 221–22, 225, 227–28, 230–33, 239, 243–47

Echo. See Grand Echo du Nord de la France
Edgar, Thomas, 112–13
Edward VIII (King of England). See Windsor, Duke and Duchess of
Eighteenth Field Park Company. See Royal Engineers
Enigma code (German), 89
Entreprise Générale de Travaux Ruraux (TR), 186
Escape networks: HC's involvement with, 5, 7, 35–51, 56–57, 65; in World War I, 31–32, 34–35; mentioned, 79, 136. See also Garrow organization; MI9

Escapers: treatment of, by Germans, 33
Escaper's Log, An, 35
Escapes of Captain O'Brien, The, 35
Escaping Club, The, 35

Farrell, Victor, 93, 176, 178, 198
Fawkes, Guy, 6, 11
Fergusson (crewman), 99
Fillerin, Norbert, 107, 196
Finas, François, 238
Fiocca, Henri, 194
Fiocca, Nancy Wake, 65–66, 194
Fitch (Captain), 56
France-Soir, 259
Fraser (Frenchwoman), 154
Free French, 89, 98
French Resistance: and HC, 6, 80, 85, 124–25; mentioned, 33, 37, 198, 199, 261, 263
Fullerton, Hugh S., 73–77, 79
"*Funkspiel,*" 200–201

Gabrielle (one of HC's mistresses), 84
Galant, M. and Mme., 45
Gallet, Marie-Louise, 85, 157
Gandicki (SS man), 204
Garrow, Ian: works with HC as escape agent, 53–66, 70–72, 80, 93–94, 179; and Guerisse's suspicions, 96–97, 99–102, 104, 114, 123–24, 127–29; arrest of, 117, 141–42, 185; escape of, 194–96; mentioned, 73–74, 90, 161, 182
Garrow organization: HC joins, 54, 63, 71, 263; work of, 58–63, 79, 82–83, 86, 87, 121, 176; HC embezzles from, 103; distrusts HC, 130, 145, 146; HC betrays, to

Germans, 151, 163; mentioned, 107, 111, 113, 116, 135, 165. *See also* Escape networks; Organization Pat
Gaubert, Marguerite, 211, 219, 221, 222
Geheime Feldpolizei. *See* GFP
Geheime Politsche Polizei, 31
GFP (Geheime Feldpolizei): and escapers and escape agents, 33, 131–33, 135, 136, 139; and HC, 147–48, 150, 153–54, 156, 157, 159, 160. *See also* Abwehr
Ghorice, Maurice, 137
Godart (Mademoiselle), 136
Godfrey, Alice Ann (HC's mother), 10–12
Godfrey, Annie (HC's grandmother), 18
Godfrey, Richard (alias of HC), 20, 236
Goering, Hermann, 136
Goetz, Josef, 200, 203
Gort, Lord, 175
Grand Echo du Nord de la France (Lille newspaper), 17, 51, 135
Guerisse, Albert-Marie Edmond: distrusts HC, 96–101, 103, 114–15, 120, 127–31; confronts HC, 140–45; fears HC's involvement with Germans, 147, 166–69, 172–75, 178–79, 183–85; helps Garrow escape, 194–95; sets up Organization Pat, 195–96; arrested, 196–97; hears of HC, 237–38; identifies HC's body, 259; mentioned, 163, 182, 188, 192. *See also* Cartier, Joseph; O'Leary, Patrick Albert
Gut Krumbach farm, 218–21, 228, 229, 239–41

Haas, Clemens, 244
Haden-Guest, Anthony, 62
Haden-Guest, Elizabeth, 62
Hanft, Georg: HC's pursuit of, 213, 215–18, 220–21, 223, 229–33, 238, 243–44, 247
Hanft, Maria, 217, 218, 227, 230, 231
Hanft, Waltraud, 218
Hansen, Wilhelm (alias of William Joyce), 236
Hauk (SS man), 204–5, 207–8
Haw Haw, Lord. *See* Joyce, William
Hegedos, Antoine, 33–34
Hegener, Karl, 32–33, 133, 165
Henoch, Victor, 85
Henriette (Verloop's mistress), 131
Herveau, Eliane, 257
Herveau, Pauline, 257–59
Higginson, F. W. ("Taffy"), 68–70, 98, 172–73
Hilaire (François Duprez's driver), 152–53
Himmler, Heinrich, 200
Hitler, Adolph, 136
H.M.S. Fidelity, 99, 100
Holmes (Sergeant), 18, 21, 24–25, 28
Holweck, Fernand, 118, 160–62
Hong Kong Defence Force, 18
Hope, Peter, 235, 237–38, 240–43, 248–49, 254, 259
Huyge, Jeanne, 35–36, 45, 49, 111, 122–23, 149

Interallié, 85
Ironside, Edmund, 19

Jacquet, Eugene, 31
Jacquet, Geneviève, 31
"Johnny Belinda" (song), 108

Jousset, George Robert, 210–11, 217, 219, 221
Joyce, William ("Lord Haw Haw"), 6–7, 234, 236, 250–52, 260, 263

Kieffer, Hans, 200–205, 207–9, 215
King, Mr., 177–78
King's African Rifles, 10, 20
Kipling, Rudyard, 253
Kirman, Agnes, 118, 160
Kneussle, Anton, 218–20, 222, 229–30, 239–41
Kneussle, Else, 222, 229–30
Kneussle, Wolfgang, 230
Krug, Eugen, 220–23
Krug, Mrs. Eugen, 223

Langley, Jimmy, 56–57, 59–60, 90, 92–93, 178–79, 195, 264–65
Lanselle, Alfred, 47–48, 121, 150, 154, 261–63
Laughton-Bramley, Philip E., 2–3
Laval, Pierre, 37, 249
Laze, Pierre, 214–15, 239, 240
Lebrun, Albert, 17
Le Gale, Aline (alias of Suzanne Warenghem), 199
"Légionnaire, Le." *See* Le Neveu, Roger
Le Neveu, Roger, 196–98
LePage, Fernand Auguste, 209–11, 217–19, 221, 230
Lepers, Roland: his work with HC, 46, 47, 50–55, 64, 79, 81, 107, 114; HC threatens, 109; distrusts HC, 119–21, 123, 130, 139–40; observes HC's betrayal, 153; identifies HC, 248–49; on HC, 264; mentioned, 7, 111, 156, 167, 170–71, 201
Lévy, Edmond, 258

Lille (France): and the BEF, 16–17, 30–34, 37, 47–49, 56, 80, 94; and the Germans, 32–33, 135; and escape network, 44, 107, 114; intelligence gathered in, 85; mentioned, 43, 53, 55, 84, 97, 130
Lillyman, Frank, 221–22, 225–29, 231–33, 239–40, 244–48
Lillyman, Jane, 246
Lillyman, Susan, 246
Loison-sous-Lens (France), 18, 28
Lotte (one of HC's mistresses), 237–38

McAuliffe, Anthony C., 226
Madeleine-les-Lille, La (France): and the BEF, 19, 21, 24, 25, 30; and HC's escape network, 29, 37–39, 41–44, 53–54, 64, 68, 107, 129, 137, 166, 225; mentioned, 49, 168
Mapplebeck (Lieutenant), 31
Marquette-lez-Lille (France), 30
Marseilles (France), 56–63, 78–83, 94, 114. See also Garrow organization; Petit Poucet, Le; Seamen's Mission
Martin, Paul, 208–9
Mason, Robert (alias of HC), 205, 208–9, 211, 214, 218–22, 224, 226–29, 233, 238–39
Mason, Robert Thomas (HC's half-brother), 12, 13
Mason, Robert Thomas (HC's stepfather), 12, 205
Masson, Jean (alias of HC?), 198
Menzies, Stewart, 90–91
Metropolitan Police (London), 4
MI5. See British Security Service
MI6. See Secret Intelligence Service
MI9 (escape branch of British

Intelligence): and HC, 7, 56–57, 70–72, 106–7, 135, 237, 264–65; SIS uses, 86, 87, 89–95, 179; mentioned, 35
Milburn (Captain), 3
Miller, John R., 243
MIS-X (U.S. escape program), 106
Modave, André, 136
Monsieur Harry (alias of HC), 257–58
Monsieur Paul (alias of HC), 49
Monteagle, Lord, 11
Moore, Clarence, 206–7
Moore, Lloyd, 206
Moore, Mabelle Swift, 206
Moran, Martin, 9–10, 14–16, 18–23, 26–27
Muggeridge, Malcolm, 90
Mulcahy, William L., 243, 246
Murchie, Mr., 53, 61, 74, 87
Murphy, Captain. See Murchie, Mr.

Neave, Airey, 7, 58, 60, 98, 136
Nicholls, Leslie, 239
Niehoff (General), 32
Nouveau, Louis, 60–62, 66, 176–78, 196–97

Office of Strategic Services (OSS), 226, 227
Official Secrets Act (Gt. Brit.), 8
O'Leary, Patrick Albert (alias of Guerisse), 96, 98, 141, 174–75, 178, 197, 237
117th Cavalry (U.S. Army), 205–7
Organization Pat, 191, 196
OSS (Office of Strategic Services), 226, 227

Pachy (escape agent), 136
Paris: and HC, 114–20
Parisien Libéré, 259
Pelletier, Roger, 112
Peltret, Gaston, 81–84
Penny (Private), 21
Pétain, Philippe, 36–37, 211
Petit Poucet, Le (Marseilles café), 58, 65, 102
Philby, Kim, 8, 260
Phillips, J. W., 47
Porzic, Antoine Geoffrey Rodellec de. *See* Rodellec de Porzic
Postel-Vinay, André, 101–2, 142, 163–65
Praxinos, Mario, 142–44, 176

Quien, Georges Gaston ("Lamp Post"), 31–32

RAF pilots: as refugees, 47, 49, 53, 68–70, 79, 105–10, 135–40
"Revere, Paul," 209
Richardson, William King, 221–22, 226, 228, 239
Ringeval, Eugène, 136
Road to En-Dor, The, 35
Rodellec de Porzic, Antoine Geoffrey, 75–76
Rodocanachi, Fanny, 62, 100, 110, 141, 142, 144
Rodocanachi, Georges, 60–63, 96, 106, 121, 129, 140, 142, 184, 192
Rogers (crewman), 99–100
Rommel, Erwin, 43, 81–82
Rose (driver), 22–23
Roubaix (France), 30, 45, 50, 150
Rousseaux, Marcel, 49, 156–57

Royal Engineers: HC joins, 9–10, 249. *See also* British Expeditionary Force
Royer, Marguerite, 81, 84
Royer, Maurice, 81

Saint George's Legion. *See* British Free Corps
Saint-Hippolyte-du-Fort (Nîmes), 63, 75, 99–100, 129
Salingue, Elisa, 49, 138, 156–57
Salingue, Fernand, 49, 138, 156–57
Salvation Army, 12
Samiez, "Widow," 33, 56
Samsel, Harold, 206
Sansom, Thomas, 11, 12, 13
Saulgau, 211–17, 221, 222, 227, 228, 230, 238
Savinos (escape agent), 144
Sawyer (Major), 74, 87
Scardon, William James, 260
Schurch, Theodore John William, 250
Scotland Yard: and HC, 4, 41, 72, 235
SD. *See* Sicherheitsdienst
Seagrim (Colonel), 84–85
Seamen's Mission, 58–60, 65, 73–77, 112–13. *See also* Caskie, Donald
Secret Intelligence Service (MI6): and HC, 7–8, 37, 71, 86–89, 93–94, 189; protects HC, 125–26, 172–79, 263–65; and HC's work with German intelligence, 150, 263–64
Shenk, James, 207
Sheppard, Robert, 186–88, 192–93
Sicherheitsdienst (SD): and HC, 150, 200–201, 205, 215, 224, 233, 263;

Sicherheitsdienst (SD) (*cont.*)
mentioned, 174, 221
Simpson, Mrs. Wallis Warfield.
See Windsor, Duke and
Duchess of
SIS. *See* Secret Intelligence Service
Slack, Tom, 106–7
Smith, Edward O., 213, 228–29, 239
Smith, H. Rex, 247–48, 261
Smith, James, 80–81, 85, 116–17,
123
SOE. *See* Special Operations
Executive
"Sonny Boy" (alias of HC), 12, 235,
237–38
Spears, Edward, 17
Special Operations Executive (SOE),
92, 186, 192, 201
Spooner, Reginald, 7, 235, 238, 243
Stork (soldier), 204
Straight, Whitney, 106

Taylor, Maxwell B., 225
Tisserand, Madame, 46–47
Tobin, James, 112–13
Tourcoing (France), 30
TR. *See* Entreprise Generale de
Travaux Ruraux
Treason: and HC, 6–8, 265
Treason Act of 1351 (Gt. Brit.), 252
Treason Act of 1945 (Gt. Brit.), 260
Treveille, Fernand, 157
Trevor-Roper, Hugh, 90
Triffe, Louis, 186–88, 192–93
Twilight over England (Joyce), 251
206th Counter Intelligence Corps.
See CIC

U.S. Consulates: in unoccupied
France, 57, 59. *See also* Fullerton,
Hugh S.

U.S. Dept. of State, 57, 59
U.S. VI Corps, 204–7, 210, 228, 239
"Ultra," 89

Vambergue (escape agent), 157
Van Camelbecke, Maurice, 124–25,
150
Van de Kerckhove, Maurice, 36–37,
45, 111, 262
Vanhout, Leopold. *See* Verloop,
Cornelius Johannes Antonius
Verbeke (escape agent), 136
Verbroeck, Charles, 154–55
Verloop, Cornelius Johannes
Antonius, 33, 131–34, 136, 139,
146, 148, 150–51, 165
Vincillione, Charles, 79, 183
Voglimacci, Jean, 46–57, 67
Voglimacci, Jeannine: her memories
of HC, 44–47, 67–68, 120; as
escape agent, 49–51, 111, 122, 124,
166–69, 172; not betrayed by HC,
151
Voglimacci, Marc, 46
Voix du Nord, La (French Resistance
newspaper), 33
Voix du Nord Resistance movement.
See French Resistance
Votier, Suzanne, 211, 219, 221, 222,
230

Wain, Wing Commander (alias of
HC), 2–4, 41
Warenghem, Alain Patrick, 192
Warenghem, Georges, 113
Warenghem, Jeanne, 114, 170,
181–83
Warenghem, Suzanne: becomes
involved with HC, 111–15,
117–19, 128, 145–46, 159–63, 165,
170–71; marriage, arrest and

pregnancy, 180–89, 191–93;
 arrives in England, 199;
 mentioned, 139
Wattrelos (France), 30, 35
West, Rebecca, 6, 253, 265
Whittinghill, David, 176, 183–85
Widenmann, Franz, 217–19, 220
Winckler, Philippe. *See*
 Verloop, Cornelius Johannes
 Antonius

Windsor, Duke and Duchess of, 57,
 253, 262
Winskill, Archie, 102–4

Yenn (radio operator), 221–22, 226,
 227
Young, Gordon, 113–14, 119, 170,
 181–82, 188

"Z Organization," 90–91, 93

BELGIUM

Dunkirk

Calais

Saint Omer

FRANCE

Roubaix

Lille

Loos

La Madeleine

Burbure

Bethune

Marles

Loison-sous-Lens

0   20 Miles
0   20 Km

Forbidden Zone

ENGLAND

Colchester

LONDON

SEE
INSET
AT LEFT

Bristol

Avonmouth

Boulogne-sur-Mer

Lille

Abbeville

Amiens

ENGLISH CHANNEL

Chauny

Compiègne

Le Havre

PARIS

Sei

ATLANTIC
OCEAN

OCCUPIED   ZONE

Saint Nazaire

Tours

Bléré

Saint-Martin-le-Beau

Loche

Cher

Châteauroux

Allier

Clermont-
Ferrand

Vic

FRANCE

UNOCCUPIED

Saint-Hippolyt
du-For

Toulouse

PYRENEES   MTS.

Perpignan

Can
Plag

Burgos

Barcelona

MADRID

LISBON

PORTUGAL

SPAIN

MEDITERRANEAN

Ship or
flying boat
to London

Gibraltar

© 1987 A.Karl/J. Kemp